Patients Beyond Borders

Everybody's Guide to Affordable, World-Class Medical Tourism

Josef Woodman

HEALTHY TRAVEL MEDIA

www.patientsbeyondborders.com

PATIENTS BEYOND BORDERS:
Everybody's Guide to Affordable, World-Class Medical Tourism

Copyright © 2007 by Josef Woodman

ISBN 10: 0-9791079-0-3
ISBN 13: 978-0-9791079-0-0

Cover art and page design: Anne Winslow
Developmental Editing: Yvette Bozzini
Copy Editing and Proofreading: Faith Brynie
Medical Terminology Review: Renee Euchner, RN;
American Medical Writers Association
Index: Cindy Fleming-Wood
Typesetting and Production: Copperline Book Services
Printing: Catawba Publishing, LLC

Printed in the United States of America

Healthy Travel Media
P.O. Box 17057
Chapel Hill NC 27516
919 370 7380
info@healthtraveler.net
www.patientsbeyondborders.com

12/09

Patients Beyond Borders

To Angelmine

Limits of Liability and Disclaimer of Warranty
Please Read Carefully

ACKNOWLEDGMENTS

NEARLY THREE YEARS and the collaboration of hundreds of patients, practitioners, providers and institutions went into the creation of this book.

I would like to thank literary agent Peter Beren, whose tireless energy and encouragement breathed early life into the manuscript. Gerald and Kathleen Hill contributed greatly to the early research.

I have so much gratitude to the dozens of gracious professionals at Apollo Hospitals in Delhi and Chennai, who helped me gain an early understanding of the important health considerations behind any medical journey. Special thanks to Anil Maini, Sunita Reddy, and the consummate surgeon Vijay Bose. Also to Doug and Anne Stoda, whose courageous medical trip helped me to locate the true voice and audience for this book.

Thanks to Bob Taber of Duke Medical Center and Jason Yap of the Singapore Tourism Board for their many insights into the burgeoning Asian healthcare arena. And to Sharon Kleefield of Harvard Medical International, whose insights into quality assurance forced a thorough medical terminology review of the book.

Health travel planners and concierges, already pre-disposed toward empathy and assistance, offered so much potentially competitive information, which greatly enhanced the offerings in Part Two. Special thanks to Jag and Dipa Jethwa of Taj Medical Group, Julie Munro of Cosmetic Surgery Travel, Suresh Pondurai of Malaysian Healthcare Networks, Rich Feldman of Medical Tourism of Costa Rica, Rudy Rupak of PlanetHospital, Pat Marsek of MedRetreat and Stephanie Sulger of Medical Tours International, for indulging my relentless queries.

A heartfelt note of appreciation to the three editors who crafted the bones of a manuscript into a readable and accessible work. Thanks, Bozzini, for your early vision; and Renee Euchner for your tireless enthusiasm for medical nuance, and to Faith Brynie, who relentlessly re-hammered and polished the pages, and did them proud.

Josef Woodman

Contents

PART TWO: THE MOST-TRAVELED HEALTH DESTINATIONS

PART THREE: RESOURCES AND REFERENCES

Introduction

Beginnings

The seeds of this book were sown nearly five years ago, when my father, age 72 at the time, traveled to Mexico for extensive dental work. I well remember my first reaction upon hearing his plans: a mixture of bewilderment and fear, then resignation, knowing that despite my protestations, he was going anyway.

In spite of my concerns — some of them quite real — I'm pleased to report a happy ending. Dad and his wife Alinda selected a US-trained dentist in Puerto Vallarta and paid around $11,000 — including two weeks noodling around the Pacific Coast. They returned tanned and smiling, Dad with new pearly whites and Alinda with an impromptu skin resurfacing. The same procedure would have cost them $24,000 in the United States.

After his treatment, when I told the story of my father's trip, most friends responded with the same shock and disbelief that I had felt initially. Then, when I explained the quality of care and the savings, more often than not, those same folks followed me out the door, asking for Dad's email address. I even had an airport customs agent abandon his post and follow me to the boarding gate, seeking additional information for his son, who he had just learned required heart surgery.

Late in 2005, I contracted an infected root canal and found myself following my father's example. My research led me abroad for extraction and implant work. While pleasantly surprised at the quality of the care, the prices, and the all-around good experience of the trip, I nonetheless made a number of mistakes and created unnecessary difficulties and discomforts for myself. Had I done some simple things differently, my trip would have been more successful and more economical.

In seeking additional data on medical travel, I found no reliable source of information. Everybody had something to sell or a political axe to grind. Books, magazine articles, and newspaper reports seemed more like tourists' brochures than health-travel references. Thus the idea for *Patients Beyond Borders* was born: a well-researched guide, written in plain English, which would offer an impartial look at contemporary medical travel, while helping prospective patients ask the right questions and make informed choices.

As we contemplate our options in an over-burdened US health-care environment, nearly all of us will eventually find ourselves seeking alternatives to costly treatments — either for ourselves or for our loved ones. Americans are in the midst of a global shift in healthcare service: in a few short years, big government investment, corporate partnerships, and increased media attention have spawned a new industry — medical tourism — bringing with it a host of encouraging new choices, ranging from dental care and cosmetic surgery to some of the more costly procedures, such as hip replacement and heart surgery. Those patients who take the time to become informed about our changing healthcare world will be pleasantly surprised by a smorgasbord of affordable, high-quality, American-accredited medical options abroad. Those who do not may find themselves grappling with an ungainly, prohibitively expensive healthcare system, and a rising absence of choice.

There is no single type of health traveler. In researching and writing *Patients Beyond Borders,* I've talked with wealthy women from Beverly Hills who, despite their affluence, prefer the quality of treatment and attention they receive in Brazil or South Africa to medical care California-style. I've met a hard-working couple from Wisconsin who, facing the prospect of refinancing their home to get a $65,000 hip operation here in the US, headed to India instead. I interviewed a Vietnam vet who became weary of long waits and red tape. He said bon voyage to this country's ever-deteriorating healthcare system, and headed overseas for treatment.

From these patients' experiences, and many more like them, you'll learn when and how health travel abroad might meet your medical and financial needs. And you'll become a more informed healthcare consumer — both here and abroad.

You Deserve an Impartial Perspective

This new phenomenon of medical tourism — or international health travel — has received a good deal of wide-eyed attention of late. While one newspaper or blog giddily touts the fun 'n sun travel side of treatment abroad, another issues dire Code Blue warnings about filthy hospitals, shady treatment practices, and procedures gone bad. As with most things in life, the truth lies somewhere in between.

In short, I've found the term medical tourism is something of a misnomer, often leading patients to emphasize the recreational more than the procedural in their quest for medical care abroad. Unlike much of the hype that surrounds contemporary health travel, *Patients Beyond Borders* focuses more on your health than on your travel preferences. Thus, throughout this book, you won't see many references to the terms "medical tourism" or "health tourism." In the same way business travelers don't normally consider themselves tourists, you'll begin to think more in terms of medical travel and health travel.

"At least 28 countries on four continents cater to the international health traveler, with more than a million patients visiting hospitals and clinics each year in countries other than their own."

My research, including countless interviews, has convinced me: with diligence, perseverance, and good information, patients considering traveling abroad for treatment indeed have legitimate, safe choices, not to mention an opportunity to save thousands of dollars over the same treatment here in the US. Hundreds of patients who have returned from successful treatment overseas provide overwhelmingly positive feedback. They persuaded me to write this impartial, scrutinizing guide to becoming an informed international patient. I designed it to help readers reach their own conclusions about whether and when to seek treatment abroad.

> If the notion of complex medical procedures in far-flung lands seems intimidating, don't feel alone.

What Exactly *Is* Medical Tourism?

Last year, more than 150,000 Americans, Canadians, and Europeans packed their bags and headed overseas for nearly every imaginable type of medical treatment: tummy tucks in Brazil, heart valve replacement procedures in Thailand, hip resurfacing surgeries in India, addiction recovery in Antigua, fertility diagnosis and treatments in South Africa, thalassotherapy in Hungary, or restorative oral dentistry in Mexico.

Currently, at least 28 countries on four continents cater to the international health traveler, with more than a million patients visiting hospitals and clinics each year in countries other than their own. The roster of treatments is as varied as the travelers.

If the notion of complex medical procedures in far-flung lands seems intimidating, don't feel alone. That's why we wrote this book, drawing from the varied experiences of hundreds of patients who, for dozens of reasons, have beaten a well-worn path to successful treatments abroad.

Why Go Abroad for Medical Care?

Cost Savings. Most people like to get the most for their dollar. The single biggest reason Americans travel to other countries for medical treatment is the opportunity to save money. Depending upon the country and type of treatment, uninsured and underinsured patients, as well as those seeking elective care, can realize 15 – 85 percent savings over the cost of treatment in the US. Or, as one successful health traveler put it, "I took out my credit card instead of a second mortgage on my home."

As baby boomers become senior boomers, costs of healthcare and prescriptions are devouring nearly 30 percent of retirement and pre-retirement incomes. With the word getting out about top-quality treatments at deep discounts overseas, informed patients are finding creative alternatives abroad.

✦ Margaret S., a patient from Santa Ana, California, was quoted $6,600 for a tooth extraction, two implants, and two crowns. One of the 120 million Americans without dental insurance, Margaret had heard of less expensive dental care abroad. Through a friend, she learned about Escazu, Costa Rica, known for its excellent dental and cosmetic surgery clinics. Margaret got the same treatment in Costa Rica for $2,600. Her dentist was a US-trained oral surgeon who used state-of-the-art instrumentation and top-quality materials. Add in airfare, lodging, meals, and other travel costs, and this savvy global patient still came out way ahead.

> "I took out my credit card instead of a second mortgage on my home."

✈ Doug S., a small business owner from Wisconsin, journeyed with his wife, Anne, to Chennai, India, for a double hip resurfacing procedure that would have cost more than $55,000 in the US. The total bill, including travel for him and his wife, lodging, meals, and two-week recuperation in a five-star beach hotel was $14,000. "We were treated like royalty," said Doug, "and I'm riding a bicycle for the first time in six years. We could not have afforded this operation in the US."

> "We were treated like royalty, and I'm riding a bicycle for the first time in six years. We could not have afforded this operation in the US."

Big Surgeries: Comparative Costs in Asia and Southeast Asia

Procedure	US Cost	India	Thailand	Singapore	Malaysia
Heart Bypass	$130,000+	$10,000	$11,000	$18,500	$9,000
Heart Valve Replacement	$160,000	$ 9,000	$10,000	$12,500	$ 9,000
Angioplasty	$ 57,000	$11,000	$13,000	$13,000	$11,000
Hip Replacement	$ 43,000	$ 9,000	$12,000	$12,000	$10,000
Hysterectomy	$ 20,000	$ 3,000	$ 4,500	$ 6,000	$ 3,000
Knee Replacement	$ 40,000	$ 8,500	$10,000	$13,000	$ 8,000
Spinal Fusion	$ 62,000	$ 5,500	$ 7,000	$ 9,000	$ 6,000

The above costs are for surgery, including hospital stay. Airfare and lodging costs are governed by individual preferences. To compute a ballpark estimate of total costs, add $5,000 for you and a companion, figuring coach airfare and hotel rooms averaging $150 per night.

For example, a hip replacement in Bangkok, Thailand, would cost about $17,000, for an estimated savings of $26,000 over treatment in the US.

Dentistry: Comparative Costs in Popular Destinations

Procedure	US Cost	Mexico	Costa Rica	South Africa	Thailand
Implants	$2,400	$1,500	$1,650	$2,000	$1,600
Crowns	$ 800	$ 375	$ 400	$ 800	$ 270
Porcelain Veneers	$ 800	$ 120	$ 160	$ 300	$ 240
Dentures (Upper & Lower)	$1,600	$1,000	$1,100	$1,700	$ 900
Inlays & Onlays	$ 420	$ 220	$ 240	$ 320	$ 300
Surgical Extractions	$ 260	$ 120	$ 120	$ 250	$ 120
Root Canals	$ 750	$ 260	$ 280	$ 400	$ 110

The estimates above are for treatments alone. Airfare, hospital stay (if any) and lodging vary considerably.

Savings on dentistry become more dramatic when "big mouth work" is required, involving several teeth or full restorations. Savings of $15,000 or more are common.

Better quality care. Veteran health travelers know that facilities, instrumentation, and customer service in treatment centers abroad often equal or exceed those found in the US. In fact, governments of countries like India and Thailand have poured billions of dollars into improving their healthcare systems, which are now aggressively catering to the international health traveler. VIP waiting lounges, deluxe hospital suites, and staffed recuperation resorts are common amenities, along with free transportation to and from airports, low-cost meal plans for companions, and discounted hotels affiliated with the hospital.

Moreover, physicians and staff in treatment centers abroad are often far more accessible than their US counterparts. "My surgeon gave me his cell phone number, and I spoke directly with him at least a dozen times during my stay," said David P., who traveled to Bangkok for a heart valve replacement procedure.

Governments of countries like India and Thailand have poured billions of dollars into improving their healthcare systems, which are now aggressively catering to the international health traveler.

Excluded treatments. Even the most robust health insurance plans exclude a variety of conditions and treatments. You, the policyholder, must pay these expenses out-of-pocket. Although health insurance policies vary according to the underwriter and individual, your plan probably excludes a variety of treatments, such as cosmetic surgeries, dental care, vision treatments, reproductive/infertility procedures, certain non-emergency cardiovascular and orthopedic surgeries, weight loss and substance abuse rehabilitation programs, and prosthetics — to name only a few. In addition, many policies place restrictions on prescrip-

"My surgeon gave me his cell phone number, and I spoke directly with him at least a dozen times during my stay."

tions (some quite expensive), post-operative care, congenital disorders, and pre-existing conditions.

Rich or cash-challenged, young or not-so-young, heavily or only lightly insured — folks who get sick or desire a treatment (even one recommended by their physician) often find their insurance won't cover it. Confronting increasingly expensive choices at home, nearly 40 percent of American health travelers hit the road for elective treatments. In countries such as Costa Rica, Singapore, Dubai, and Thailand, this trend has spawned entire industries, offering excellent treatment and ancillary facilities at costs far lower than US prices.

Specialty treatments. Some procedures and prescriptions are simply not allowed in this country. Either Congress or the FDA has specifically disallowed a certain procedure, or perhaps it's still in the testing and clinical trials stage, or was only recently approved. Such treatments are often offered abroad. One example is an orthopedic procedure known as hip resurfacing, for most patients a far superior, longer-lasting, and less expensive alternative to the traditional hip replacement still practiced in the US. While this procedure has been performed for more than a decade throughout Europe and Asia, it was only recently approved in the US and the procedure's availability here remains spotty and unproven. Hundreds of forward-thinking Americans, many having suffered years of chronic pain, have found relief in India, where hip resurfacing techniques, materials, and instrumentation have been perfected, and the procedure is routine.

Shorter waiting periods. For decades, thousands of Canadian and British subscribers to universal, "free" healthcare plans have endured waits as long as two years for established procedures. "Some of us die before we get to the operating table," commented one exasperated patient, who journeyed to India for an open-heart procedure.

Here in the US, long waits are a growing problem, particularly among war veterans covered under the Veterans Administration Act, where long queues are becoming far too common. Some patients figure it's better to pay out-of-pocket to get out of pain or to halt a deteriorating condition than to suffer the anxiety and frustration of waiting for a far-future appointment and other medical uncertainties.

The lure of the new and different. Although traveling abroad for medical care can often be challenging, many patients welcome the chance to blaze a trail, and they find the creature comforts often offered abroad a welcome relief from the sterile, impersonal hospital environments so often encountered in US treatment centers. For others, simply being in a new and interesting culture lends distraction to an otherwise worrisome, tedious process. And getting away from the myriad obligations of home and professional life can yield healthful effects at a stressful time.

What's more, travel — and particularly international travel — can be a life-changing experience. You might be humbled by the limousine ride from Indira Gandhi International Airport to a hotel in central New Delhi, struck by the simple, elegant graciousness of professionals and ordinary people in a foreign land, or wowed by the sheer beauty of the mountain range outside a dental office window. As one veteran medical traveler put it, "I brought back far more from this trip than a new set of teeth."

Who Should Read *Patients Beyond Borders*

You'll benefit from reading this book if

✦ you're one of 84 million uninsured or underinsured individuals who wish to explore less expensive options for a treatment often covered by health insurance.

✦ you're one of 120 million Americans without a dental plan who wish to take advantage of the full range of affordable dental procedures in other countries.

✦ you wish to pursue an elective treatment (such as cosmetic surgery, in vitro fertilization, or homeopathy) not normally covered by health insurance policies.

✦ you're exploring one of many treatments either not offered or not approved in the US.

✦ you feel a friend or family member might benefit from learning more about health travel, yet that person might lack the confidence or focus to launch an inquiry.

✦ you plan to join a family member or friend for treatment abroad (see Chapter Seven, "For Companions").

What *Patients Beyond Borders* Will (and Won't) Do for You

Patients Beyond Borders isn't a guide to medical diagnosis and treatment, nor does it provide medical advice on specific treatments or caregiver referrals. Your condition, diagnosis, treatment options, and travel preferences are unique, and only you—in consultation with your physician and loved ones—can determine the best course of action.

Should you decide to investigate traveling abroad for treatment, we *do* provide you with all the resources and tools necessary to become an informed medical traveler, so that you'll have the best possible travel experience and treatment your money can buy.

> Your condition, diagnosis, treatment options, and travel preferences are unique, and only you— in consultation with your physician and loved ones—can determine the best course of action.

Our job is to

+ help you become a knowledgeable, confident health traveler;
+ assist you in planning and budgeting your trip and treatment;
+ provide you up-to-date information about the most popular, widely used treatment centers;
+ make your in-country visit as comfortable and hassle-free as possible;

✦ recommend good lodging and travel leisure options;

✦ provide tips, tricks, and advice for a successful medical travel experience — before, during, and after treatment.

Your job is to

✦ consult with your US doctor(s) to ensure you've reached a satisfactory diagnosis and recommended course of treatment;

✦ decide, based on your research and the material featured in this book, whether you wish to travel abroad for treatment; and if so,

✦ select a travel destination, treatment center, and physician based on the information you find in this book and elsewhere.

It's a truism: Every journey begins with the first step. Health travel is no exception; yet once you've taken that first step toward learning more, you'll find your friends, family, this book, and a trusty Internet connection will speed you on your way.

How to Use This Book

Before you dive into Part Two, "The Most-Traveled Health Destinations," you'll want to carefully read Part One, "How to Become a Savvy, Informed Medical Traveler." It provides you the basic resources and tools you'll need to do your research and make an informed decision.

Chapter One, "What Am I Getting Into? Some Quick Answers for Health Travelers," addresses the questions and concerns most often voiced by patients and their loved ones considering a medical journey abroad.

Chapter Two, "Planning Your Health Journey," helps you create your trip step-by-step. The chapter provides data and advice culled from interviews with hundreds of patients and treatment centers. You'll learn how to cut through the chaff quickly to find the right clinics, determine physician accreditation, narrow your destination choices, choose the right companion, and more.

Chapter Three, "Budgeting Your Treatment and Trip," walks you through the financial basics of a medical trip and gives you the tools you need to prepare an estimated budget. Our *"Patients Beyond Borders* Budget Planner" helps you determine specific cost-savings and avoid financial surprises.

Chapter Four, "Choosing and Working with a Health Travel Planner," shows you how to avoid hassles and save money by finding and engaging the right health travel agent.

Chapter Five, "While You're There," provides valuable information on what to expect from your treatment center and physician, plus general tips for dealing with local cultures, language barriers, and more. A section on communicating while on the road will help you use cell phones and computers to communicate with physicians in-country, as well as loved ones back home.

Chapter Six, "Home Again, Home Again," helps you get settled in post-treatment, offering practical advice on working with your hometown doctor, shaking off the "post-treatment blues," coping with discomforts and complications, and getting back on your feet.

Chapter Seven, "For Companions," is written especially for those caring family members or friends who accompany patients on health journeys.

Chapter Eight, "Dos and Don'ts for the Smart Health Traveler," helps you avoid common speed bumps and potholes on the health travel road.

Part Two, "The Most-Traveled Health Destinations," features 22 destinations in 14 countries, with up-to-date information on hospitals and clinics, specialties, accreditation, recovery centers and recuperation resorts, transportation, communication, and more. You'll use the information in this section to get a good idea about where to travel for your particular procedure and about what to expect for the costs of common treatments.

Part Three: "Resources and References," provides additional medical travel information and helpful links, plus a glossary of commonly used medical terms.

As you work your way through decision-making and subsequent planning, remember that you're following in the footsteps of tens of thousands of health travelers who have made the journey before you. The overwhelming majority have returned home successfully treated, with money to spare in their savings accounts.

Still, the process — particularly in the early planning — can be daunting, frustrating, even a little scary. That's normal, and every health traveler we interviewed experienced "the Big Fear" at one time or another. Healthcare abroad is not for everyone, and part of being a smart consumer is evaluating all the impartial data available before making an informed decision. If you accomplished that in reading *Patients Beyond Borders*, we've achieved our mission.

Let's get started.

PART ONE

How to Become a Savvy, Informed, Medical Traveler

What Am I Getting Into? Some Quick Answers for Health Travelers

Is Healthcare Overseas Safe?

Interestingly, the friends and family members of patients considering healthcare abroad ask this question more often than do the patients themselves. In fact, at least one friend or family member is virtually guaranteed to balk at the thought of your heading overseas for treatment. Most of these concerns are unfounded. They usually arise either from a lack of knowledge or from cultural myopia.

Although no medical procedure is 100 percent risk free anywhere in the world, the best hospitals and clinics abroad maintain health and procedural standards equal to, or higher than, those you'll encounter here in the United States. In fact, many hospitals abroad are accredited by the same US agency (the Joint Commission on Accreditation of Healthcare Organizations)

> Many hospitals abroad are accredited by the same US agency that certifies hospitals here.

that certifies hospitals here. (For more information on hospital accreditation and safety standards, see Chapter Two, "Planning Your Health Journey.")

It's not hard to find overseas physicians, dentists, and surgeons who received their medical training and degrees at first-rate medical schools in the United States, Great Britain, Canada, Switzerland, or Germany. All the countries listed in *Patients Beyond Borders* enforce strict governmental and private standards for healthcare, hospital, and clinic certification.

Finally, many hospitals—particularly the larger institutions in Asia and Southeast Asia—boast lower morbidity rates than in the United States, particularly when it comes to complex cardiac and orthopedic surgeries, where success rates higher than 98.5 percent are the norm.

If Healthcare in Other Countries Is So Good, How Can It Be So Cheap?

This question is best answered by another question: why is US healthcare so expensive? High facilities costs, unpaid hospital bills totaling billions of dollars, high-priced medical education, costly research, and excessive malpractice litigation all add up to exorbitant prices for healthcare in the US.

In addition, US physicians who perform elective and specialty procedures—such as cosmetic surgeries, in vitro fertilization, and certain hip, spine and cardiac procedures—command astronomical fees from patients willing and able to pay, leaving those of more modest means in the lurch, and seeking alternatives.

Healthcare in other countries is also less costly because standards of living are more modest, doctors and staff command lower wages, government-subsidized healthcare keeps private healthcare costs down, and malpractice attorneys are, if not docile, at least considerably more restrained.

How Much Can I Save?

Your savings will depend on your treatment, the destination you select, and your travel and lifestyle preferences. Patients who travel to India for complex heart bypass surgeries will probably save more than $50,000 over the retail price in the US. People traveling to Costa Rica for reconstructive dentistry or extensive breast and abdominal cosmetic surgery can save $10,000 or more.

A good rule of thumb is "the $6,000 Rule": if your US specialist quotes you a price of $6,000 or more for a treatment, chances are good that one or more foreign countries can offer you the same procedure and quality for less, even including your travel and lodging ex-

> If your US specialist quotes you a price of $6,000 or more for a treatment, chances are good that one or more foreign countries can offer you the same procedure and quality for less, even including your travel and lodging expenses.

penses. If your quote is less than $6,000, you're probably better off having your treatment at home.

Is It Safe to Travel Overseas?

For many, a medical trip is their first journey abroad. That can be a scary prospect. Post-9/11 news is fear inducing enough to make any novice international traveler think twice about packing a suitcase. Yet it's easy to forget that most other countries enjoy far lower crime rates than ours. In fact, many citizens outside the United States are afraid to travel to this country because of the well-publicized rates of violent crime here.

Your own behavior will determine much of your experience abroad. If you follow the common sense rules of courtesy and observe cultural norms, you should be safe in any country featured in this book. Outcomes prove that's true. Hundreds of thousands of international health travelers return home safe and sound each year.

Health travelers can be further reassured because, from the moment of arrival in another country until embarking on a homebound plane, most are under the constant care of a hospital, health travel broker, tour agency, or other third-party agent. Most health travelers are met at their airport arrival gate and whisked to an American-style hospital or hotel. From that point, they're usually either under someone's care in a treatment center, in a restaurant, or in a cozy hotel room.

What Medical Treatments Are Available Abroad?

Although nearly every kind of treatment is possible abroad, most Westerners head overseas for orthopedics (hip replacement, knee replacement, spinal work); cardiovascular surgery (bypass surgery, valve replacement, heart transplants); cancer diagnosis and treatment; dental care (usually more extensive cosmetic or restorative surgery); or cosmetic surgery. In addition, US patients seek specialty treatments such as fertility and in vitro fertilization procedures, weight loss (such as bariatric surgeries), and procedures not yet allowed in this country, such as stem cell therapies. In Part Two, you'll discover a range of treatment specialties and super-specialties that run the full medical gamut.

What all those treatments have in common is great expense. The huge savings to be garnered abroad can outweigh the challenges of traveling overseas for treatment.

How Do I Know Where to Travel for Treatment?

Most countries are known for a particular category of treatment, and your diagnosis will distill your list of choices down to a handful of destinations. If you're seeking cosmetic surgery, Brazil, Costa Rica, and South Africa rank among the most popular destinations. Dentistry will have you exploring Mexico, Costa Rica, or Hungary. The more expensive, invasive surgeries, such as open-heart surgery or a knee replacement, make a longer trip to India, Thailand, Singapore, or Malaysia well worth the cost, time, and distance of travel.

To get a preliminary idea of where you're likely to be heading, refer to the "Treatment and Country Finder" at the beginning of Part Two. Use Chapters Two and Three (on planning and budgeting your trip), along with your own travel and lifestyle preferences, to pinpoint your country of choice.

 Action item: **Consult the "Treatment and Country Finder" in Part Two to find out where you can save the most on the treatment you want.**

Can Someone Come Along with Me? I Don't Like Traveling Alone.

That's good, because we don't recommend you travel alone. We've found that most health travelers fare better with a companion in tow — a spouse, family member, or friend. Companions don't greatly increase the overall costs of a trip, and they can actually save you time and money in the end, because they are looking out for your interests every step of the way.

Even if you cannot travel with a companion, or prefer not to, you'll not be going it alone in-country. If staying in a hospital, the quality of care and attention you'll receive in the better centers is truly remarkable, with low nurse-to-patient ratios and a host of staffers, orderlies, physician's assistants, and dieticians in and out of your room with great frequency. You'll make fast friends during your stay.

If you're not planning to travel with a companion, we strongly recommend you engage the services of a health travel planning agency. A good agent is with you almost daily, particularly at the more stressful junctures, such as arrival in-country, medical consultations, and immediately before and after a surgical procedure. For more information on agents, see Chapter Four, "Choosing and Working with a Health Travel Agent."

For more information on traveling with family or friends, see Chapter Seven, "For Companions."

What If They Don't Speak English?

Every country catering to international health travel travelers offers a host of English-speaking physicians, staff, and third-party agencies. If English is your native tongue and you're uncomfortable speaking another language, then insist on English. If a hospital or clinic can't furnish English-speaking doctors, don't be embarrassed. Politely thank them and move on. Your continued research will lead you to professionals who can converse in your native tongue.

How Realistic Is the "Vacation" Part of the Trip?

That depends on the type of treatment you're seeking, how much time you have, and how comfortable you feel combining leisure travel with the medical side of your trip. Most patients who take a vacation as part of a health travel journey are either planning to travel anyway or have allocated a good deal of additional time for recreation as well as recovery (there's a big difference, which we cover in Chapter Five, "While You're There").

Throughout this book, we encourage patients to focus more on their treatment and recovery than on tourism, even for the less invasive procedures. Web sites and health travel brochures peppered with zealous promotion ("Enjoy Fabulous Rainforest Vacation While Recovering from Your Tummy Tuck!") ignore the realities of health travel. Long flights, post-treatment recovery, and just plain being alone in a faraway place can be overwhelming, even for the most optimistic health traveler.

> We encourage patients to focus more on their treatment and recovery than on tourism.

Think of your medical journey more as a business trip than a leisure junket. Consider socking away some of your savings for a separate vacation you and a loved one can take after the primary challenge of managing your immediate health need is behind you. Then, by all means, break out the champagne on a far-flung exotic hideaway and celebrate your health and good fortune.

What If Complications Arise after I Return Home?

Depending on your treatment, your physician will usually strongly advise you to stay in-country for at least a few days post-treatment. Your doctor will want to make sure that your treatment went well, your prescriptions are working as they should, you're settling into any recommended physical therapies, and required follow-ups are going according to plan. Thus, by the time you board the plane home, your risk of complications will be greatly reduced.

In the unlikely event that you develop complications after returning home, you'll need to decide whether to make a return trip or to continue your treatment at home. Some procedures, such as dental work, are guaranteed; so it may well be financially worthwhile, albeit inconvenient, to return. If you choose not to, most overseas dentists and surgeons are happy to talk with your hometown physician to discuss complications and recommend further action.

Prior to traveling abroad for treatment, be sure to let your local doctor(s) know your plans. It's better to alert them beforehand than to surprise them after the fact.

For more information on complications and other post-treatment considerations, see Chapter Six, "Home Again, Home Again."

Can I Sue?

While all countries listed in *Patients Beyond Borders* have established channels of legal recourse, the intricacies of working with foreign statutes, legal systems, and counsel make such action impractical except in the most egregious cases.

For better or worse, most countries outside the US do not share our attitude toward personal and institutional liability, and the US is well known as Earth's most litigious nation. A full discussion of the reasons lies outside the scope of this book. That said, here's a good rule of thumb: if legal recourse is a primary concern in making your health travel decision, you probably shouldn't head abroad for medical treatment.

Can I Finance My Treatment?

Increasingly, established hospitals abroad, and some health travel agents, offer financing plans in the form of loans or delayed payment. Ask your agent or clinic for details.

Most hospitals, clinics, and health travel brokers accept credit cards, but many charge an additional fee to cover their processing costs. Ask beforehand.

Nearly all hotels, restaurants, retailers, and businesses abroad happily accept major cards. Automatic teller machines are common in most cities and towns, and it's fun to watch your cash come out in an unfamiliar currency.

CHAPTER TWO

Planning your Health Travel Journey

First Things First—Seek Guidance

As you've probably learned from previous trips, an expert guide can teach you things and take you places you would not have otherwise discovered. Consider Part One of *Patients Beyond Borders* your "health travel planning companion," a trusty sidekick who helps ease the burdens of your journey. You'll progress more safely and easily if you draw upon the collective wisdom of those who have traveled successfully before you.

Although each journey varies according to the traveler's preferences and pocketbook, good planning is essential to the success of any trip. That goes double for the medical traveler. In this chapter you'll learn how to become an informed global patient. If you decide that a medical trip is right for you, we'll help you gain confidence about finding the right destination, selecting the best clinic and physician, and working with others to help ensure your success.

 Action Item: Research several physicians, clinics, or hospitals that offer the treatment you need. Don't snap up the first option you find.

Trust Yourself

Most likely, you're considering health travel because you want an elective treatment (such as cosmetic, dental, reproductive, or other) or because you've been diagnosed with a condition that requires surgical intervention, such as orthopedic or cardiovascular surgery. Whatever the reason, a condition you want or need treated — usually coupled with a desire or need to realize substantial cost savings (and for some of you, a sense of adventure or trying something new) — is what brought you to this point.

Other factors may be influencing your decision. It's no secret that contemporary economic and medical trends in the United States have spawned overworked practitioners, crowded hospitals, and vast variations in the quality of care available for all but the wealthiest citizens. Your dad's or grandmother's friendly, chatty, all-knowing family doctor has become a medical oddity, supplanted by a bevy of busy assistants, hurried consultations, arms-length testing, hasty diagnoses, and increasingly faulty treatment. The fact that, as *USA Today* put it, "as many as 98,000 American's die each year because of medical errors" made headlines everywhere recently. As a result, the traditional trusting patients of yesteryear, who unquestioningly put their lives in the hands of the medical system, are a rapidly disappearing breed.

Today, patients are urged to educate themselves, take a proactive stance, and ask questions. Our medical system is based on market principles. This makes you a consumer of healthcare. As a consumer, you should remember: "buyer beware" in all your choices.

If you're holding this book in your hand right now, chances are you've left the old world of unquestioning blind faith and have appropriately adapted to modern medical times, evolving into a curious, assertive, informed patient. Congratulations! Your prognosis for becoming a successful health traveler is vastly improved.

Knowledge is power, and the more thought you put into weighing your options, the more confidence you'll gain in reaching the decision that's best for you and your loved ones. Even if you skim the rest of *Patients Beyond Borders*, read this chapter carefully and thoroughly. At the end of it, you'll have answered enough questions to know whether, when, and where to travel for your medical care.

Plan Ahead

OK. You're beginning to recover from the heart-stopping quote your medical specialist laid on you two weeks ago. You've talked with friends and family about heading abroad for treatment. They're skeptical but reluctantly willing to trust your judgment. Truth be told, you're still a tad skeptical yourself, but you're also willing to consider medical travel as an option.

Long before you pack your bags, you have a lot to do and a logical progression of events to work through. The first item of business is to plan — ahead — as far in advance as you can. Three months prior to treatment is good. Six months ahead of time is great. One month is not so good. Avoid it if at all possible. Here's why:

✦ **The best overseas physicians are also the busiest.** That's a fact everywhere. Just as here in the US, doctors, surgeons and specialists abroad work 24/7, and their schedules are often established a month or more in advance. If you want the most qualified doctor and the best care your global patient money can buy, give the doctors and treatment centers you select plenty of time to work you into their calendars.

✦ **The lowest international airfares go to those who book early.** As veteran international travelers know, out-of-country fares rise savagely as the departure date draws closer. Most punishing of all are last-minute fares, reserved for family tragedies, rich jetsetters, and busy corporate executives. Booking at least 60 days prior to treatment allows you to avoid the unhappy spiral of rising air travel costs.

If you're planning to redeem frequent flyer miles, try to book at least 90 days in advance — even if you're not 100 percent certain of your treatment date. At this writing, most airlines don't charge

> Plan ahead — as far in advance as you can. Three months prior to treatment is good. Six months ahead of time is great. One month is not so good.

for schedule changes on frequent flyer fares, and you're better off reserving a date — then changing it later — than being stuck without any reservation at all.

Similarly, for paid fares, it's usually better to reserve your trip as far in advance as you can, giving your best guess at a schedule. Then, budget in the $100 penalty in the event you need to change your flight itinerary.

✦ **Peak seasons can snarl the best-laid plans.** International tourism is again on the rise. If you want or need to travel during the busy tourist season for a given region, start planning your global health trip four-to-six months in advance.

✦ **Preparation is a big part of planning.** When you paint your living room wall, you know that preparation is half the effort. By the time you pick up the paintbrush, you're halfway done. The same is true with health travel. Before you can book that flight or reserve your hotel room, you must first confirm your treatment appointment. Before you do that, you'll need to decide which country you want to visit, which physician(s) suit your needs, and much more.

While such planning is not rocket science, an organized approach in the preparation stages will save you time and money in the end. That's what we provide in the following pages.

Set Your Mind to It

As you plan, your mindset is as important as any set of skills. So cultivate and practice the following:

An open mind. Our twenty-first-century world is increasingly becoming a global village, with American cultural influences leading the charge. Still, contrasts abound: different time zones (they're sleeping while we're working); different accents (English can take on many forms, some of them barely comprehensible); different clothes (burkas? turbans? exotic neckwear?); different table manners (don't eat with your left hand?).

Those with a strictly US-centric cultural bias may have trouble absorbing and accommodating such diversity. You need an open mind to accept that other points of view and ways of life are not only valid, but in some respects perhaps more refined than ours. After all, our culture is adolescent compared to thousands of years of Indian or European civilization.

Patience. As you embark on your health journey, you'll find that patience is indeed a virtue, particularly in the planning stages.

For starts, the pace abroad is generally slower — and more cordial — than in the US. While here you might expect your inquiry returned within three hours, you may not hear back from a hospital in Bangkok for three days. Be patient. Call or email a second time. If you don't get an answer in a week, move on. There are plenty of hospitals and clinics in the world willing and able to work with you. Finding the right one is a systematic process, sometimes involving false starts.

And what about that receptionist in Mumbai who always wants to know how your family is doing? Well, it's customary in many cultures to talk for a few moments about your personal life, beginning with inquiring about family and loved ones. Take a deep breath and chat it up. You'll be glad you did when you're working with an in-country doctor who's willing to spend an hour with you as part of the clinic's normal routine.

Persistence. When planning any international trip, you'll encounter a host of tasks, contingencies, and sometimes setbacks. Health travel is no exception. When your phone calls and emails are not returned as quickly as you would like, remember that delays don't necessarily arise from a lack of professionalism. The pace of business in a foreign country can often be slower than Americans anticipate.

So, be flexible and persistent in your planning. If Plan A isn't working, move to Plan B. You'll sometimes find yourself at Plan D, only to discover that Plan B worked out after all, although not on your expected timetable.

Generally, the early planning stages require the most perseverance. Once you're in-country, you'll be pleased to see other people sweating the details.

> If you're willing to go with the flow of another culture, you'll soon learn to appreciate the expanded world perspective that you gain from a slower pace and more flexible approach.

Email and Internet Searching

Although you needn't be a computer whiz, you'll gain a huge advantage from an Internet connection for two important reasons:

Communication. As annoying and inefficient as telephones have become as a daily part of our lives, they are exponentially more so when trying to conduct business from afar. Email, on the other hand, knows no time zones, lowers the language barrier, and provides an efficient information trail for contacts, recommendations, and myriad other details you'd otherwise be obliged to somehow remember.

Email is vital for making initial inquiries, following up on research, confirming and reconfirming appointments, booking airline and hotel reservations, and keeping records of your transactions with physicians and staff. You needn't be a great journalist or business correspondent; if you can correspond successfully with your kids in Duluth or your Aunt May in Oklahoma, you'll do fine.

Research. What a world we live in, where the world's knowledge is now truly at our fingertips! The rise of the Web and the refinement of search engines such as Google, Yahoo, and others have allowed anyone with an Internet connection to gain reliable research results quickly and easily.

Primary to successful health travel planning is a basic ability to gather and sort information. The Internet offers some big keys to the research kingdom. Indeed, ten years ago, medical travel as we know it would have been possible only for those with professional leverage or inside information. Today, the power of knowledge is available to us all.

For some of us, however, these new Internet tools are as bewildering as they are powerful. If you don't like doing the required digging, or if you are not confident about your research skills, perhaps a family member or friend is willing to help. Make your fact-finding a shared project — perhaps working with a younger member of your circle who can show off his or her computer prowess. Although *Patients Beyond Borders* provides sufficient guidelines to help get anyone started in finding the right fit for particular treatment needs, the specifics of where to go and which doctor to engage are up to the individual. Making such decision requires doing your homework, and the Internet is a great homework tool.

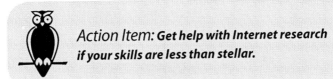

Action Item: *Get help with Internet research if your skills are less than stellar.*

Chutzpah!

During the planning stages, make sure you maintain the will to keep moving forward, the courage to do things a little differently, and the confidence that you're making the right choices. Along your health journey you're likely to encounter US physicians who aren't happy that you're heading overseas for treatment, friends and relatives who think you're nuts (even if they didn't previously), and days of genuine self-doubt. But stick with it. Don't let other people talk you out of your quest because of their ignorance, anxiety, or competitive zeal. If you do your homework and follow the guidelines in this book, you'll make the right decisions.

THE TWELVE-FOLD PATH TO ENLIGHTENED HEALTH TRAVEL PLANNING

The following is culled from hundreds of interviews with patients and treatment center staff members around the world. Follow the steps and advice outlined here and you'll streamline your planning, organize your trip well, select the best physician(s), communicate effectively with staff and agents, save money, and prepare to pack your bags with confidence.

1 Doctors often recommend a range of choices for a given condition; then leave it up to you and your family to settle upon a course of action, based on their recommendations. After all, the buck stops with your body, especially these days, and no one else besides you can make those important health-related judgment calls. Most physicians respect that, and that's why they usually stop short of advising you what specific course of treatment to take. That's wise, because your body is your own, and no one except you can or should make such vital decisions. Most physicians respect their patient's autonomy. That's why they usually stop short of advising you on a specific course of treatment.

If you have doubts about your diagnosis or feel dissatisfaction with your relationship with your physician or specialist, don't be timid about seeking a second — or even third — opinion. At the very least, a second opinion expands your knowledge base about your condition. The more you and your hometown health team learn about — and discuss — your condition, diagnosis, and treatment options, the more precisely and confidently you'll communicate with your overseas practitioners.

Action item: **Request copies of all local consultations and recommendations in writing, along with cost estimates for treatment. Then begin a file for all paperwork related to your treatment and travel.**

As you sort through your treatment options and consider courses of action, you'll want to learn as much as you can about your condition. You'll get better care from your overseas practitioners if you are a knowledgeable and responsive patient.

It works both ways: your experiences and challenges as an informed medical traveler will sharpen your skills on the home front, better equipping you and your loved ones to survive and flourish in the increasingly complex morass that has become our contemporary healthcare system.

Becoming Informed Here and Abroad

Toward becoming the best possible patient — both at home and abroad — we highly recommend you buy, beg, or borrow and read — cover to cover — *You: The Smart Patient: An Insider's Guide for Getting the Best Treatment* by Michael F. Roizen and Mehmet C. Oz. These two physicians have written a witty, often irreverent, and highly useful guide to becoming an informed patient, whether in your doctor's office or dentist's chair, on the surgeon's table, or in an emergency room. This 400-page consumer bible is packed with information on patients' rights, surgical precautions, second and third opinions, health insurance plans, health records, and precautionary advice that falls outside the scope of *Patients Beyond Borders*.

Step 2: Narrow Your Destinations

2 Once you've resolved what treatment you're seeking, refer to the *Patients Beyond Borders* "Treatment and Country Finder" found at the beginning of Part Two. This handy reference will help you locate the destinations cited throughout the book that offer the care you're seeking. In addition, you may also want to consult the Web or other trusted sources you may know.

Your searches will likely produce a dozen or so places that offer, for example, excellent dental care. Great! Choice is good. You will now want to narrow your search based on your circumstance and personal preferences. For example, if you have a choice in travel times, you may prefer a cooler climate in Eastern Europe over the coastal humid heat of Cape Town, South Africa. Or perhaps you speak a little Spanish and are more comfortable conversing with Costa Ricans than Croatians. For sheer travel convenience, a patient living in California or Oregon may prefer Mexico as a destination for dental treatment, while Costa Rica makes more sense to a Florida or Georgia resident.

The point is to narrow your options based on your travel preferences, geography, budget, time requirements, and other variables. Part Two, "The Most-Traveled Health Destinations," provides a wealth of information on the most widely visited regions and treatment centers.

To help you narrow your options, ask yourself these questions:

✦ When do I want — or need — to travel?

✦ If I'm taking a companion, when can he or she travel?

✦ How much do I mind a ten-hour flight? An 18-hour flight?

✦ Do I have a preference for a hotter or cooler climate?

✦ If I'm planning on leisure activities while abroad, what types most interest me? Hiking? Museum-hopping? Shopping? Beaches? Night Life?

✦ How much cultural diversity can I tolerate?

For Big Surgeries, Think Big

If you're heading abroad for a liposuction or tooth whitening, you can skip this. However, if you're going under the knife for major surgery, including

- open heart surgery of all kinds

- any type of transplant

- invasive cancer treatment

- orthopedic surgery (including knee or hip replacement)

- spinal surgery of any kind,

you want to be certain you're getting the best. Your life is at stake. For big surgeries, you should head to the big hospitals that have performed large numbers of *exactly* your kind of procedure, with the accreditation numbers and success ratios to prove it. A JCI-accredited hospital — such as Apollo in Chennai or Bumrungrad in Bangkok — carries the necessary staff, medical talent, administrative infrastructure, expensive instrumentation, and institutional follow-up needed to pull off a complex larger surgery. They make it look easy. They've done thousands of jobs like yours. It's almost routine. You want that. (Note: for more information on JCI, the Joint Commission International, see "The "What and Why of JCI" below).

Be sure to ask about success and morbidity rates *for your particular procedure*; find out how they compare with those in the US. Finally, ask your surgeon how many *surgeries of exactly your procedure* he or she has performed in the past two years. While there are no set standards, fewer than ten is not so good. More than 50 is much better.

Step 3: Engage a Great Health Travel Agent

3 Good news: if you don't want to do all the planning, research, and booking work yourself, you don't have to. The medical travel industry has recently given rise to the specialty services of the health travel planner. A qualified agent is usually a specialist in a given region or treatment, with the best doctors, accommodations, and in-country contacts at their fingertips.

Once you've settled on your health travel destination, it pays to seek out the services of that locale's best health travel agent. Agents usually pay for themselves and are well worth the relatively modest additional fees they typically charge.

The better health travel agents do all the work of a traditional travel agent and more, including some or all of the following:

✦ **Match you with the appropriate clinic and physician(s).** By far the most important service a health travel agent provides is that of matchmaker. The best agents have years of experience with treatment centers, physicians, and staffs, and are in a position to find the best fit among a variety of choices, in addition to weeding out bad apples. Because the agency's success depends on references from satisfied customers, top agents work hard to make the physician-patient relationship a good match from the start.

✦ *Arrange and confirm appointments.* Once you've selected or approved a physician, the agent can handle the details of making appointments for consultations, tests, and treatment. Agents know all the assistants and aides; they can push the right buttons to fast track your arrangements.

✦ **Expedite the transfer of your medical information.** Your agent can work with you and your physicians at home and abroad to relay medical data, including history, x-rays, test results, recommendations, and other documentation. Agents can help you get data into the right format for emailing or help you determine the best way to ship documents.

✦ **Book air travel.** Agents sometimes have arrangements with airlines for good deals on airfares, and booking international flights is usually a standard part of an agent's service offering.

✦ **Obtain visas.** For a relatively modest fee, a health travel agent can help you avoid the hassles of purchasing a visa (if required), updating your passport, procuring tourist cards, and hounding the appropriate embassy for service.

✦ **Reserve lodging and other accommodations.** These folks can work with your budget and lifestyle preferences to put you in touch with hotels closest to your treatment center; they'll often book reservations and arrange amenities such as private nursing care. Many agents have forged partnerships with hotels for discounted rates.

✦ **Arrange in-country transportation.** Most agencies either provide transportation from the airport to your hotel or treatment center, or they work directly with the hotel or hospital to arrange transport. If transport is required between your hotel and treatment center, they'll also help with arrangements.

✦ **Help manage post-treatment procedures.** Agents can be hugely helpful at the point of discharge from your treatment center, ensuring that your exit paperwork and other documentation are in order.

✦ **Help with recovery and recuperation.** Little publicized and often overlooked are the recovery resorts, surgical retreats, and recuperation hotels that can make a week or two of post-treatment more bearable — sometimes even enjoyable. Agents know all about facilities in their area and work in close partnership with the better ones. The international travel services coordinator at your hospital can also help on this front.

✦ **Help with leisure activity planning.** If you and your companion are up for a pre- or post-treatment trip, most agents offer assistance with side trips, car rentals, hotels, restaurants, and other travel amenities.

For more information on health travel agents in your preferred destinations, see Chapter Four, "Choosing and Working with a Health Travel Agent." For information on specific agents, see the "Health Travel Agent" sections in Part Two.

Step 4: Choose a Reliable, Fun Companion

4 This is such an important component of successful health travel that we've dedicated an entire chapter to it, Chapter Seven, "For Companions."

Folks who journey to far-flung places for medical treatment fare much better with a companion than if they go solo. Whether a mate or friend or family member, the right companion can provide great help and support before, during, and after treatment. Together, you and your companion may also add in some fun and adventure when your health permits.

Most health travelers choose either a good friend or spouse as companion. If you have the luxury of choice, make sure you're not packing a lot of emotional baggage for the trip. The successful medical journey requires large and prolonged doses of support. In an ideal world, you should get on fabulously with your capable, reliable, organized, and fun companion.

If you've already found a willing and able companion, you are blessed. Be sure to involve him or her in the early planning stages. That's the best way to cement the relationship and to learn at the outset if you'll be compatible. Ask your companion to accompany you to the doctor, help with second opinions, and make initial international inquiries. You'll begin to work as a team. If you don't feel comfortable at the early stages, find a cordial, diplomatic way to part company.

And always remember to be as supportive and complimentary of your companion as you can possibly be. Your companion is a treasure. Cherish the relationship.

How can you choose the right companion? Three words: Capable. Organized. Fun.

Above all, travel with an individual you can count on in any number of circumstances. From taking notes in your doctor's office to talking your way past a snarly customs agent to fetching a post-surgery prescription, you'll be immeasurably aided and comforted having someone beside you who will take the job seriously and stay with the program.

> **The successful medical journey requires large and prolonged doses of support. In an ideal world, you should get on fabulously with your capable, reliable, organized, and fun companion.**

Good organizational skills are essential. No job description is complete without that requirement, and the same holds true for your companion. He or she will remind you to bug the travel agency for your passport renewal application, help you organize and email your medical documentation, keep track of your in-country appointments, monitor your post-treatment prescription regimen, encourage you to follow your doctor's orders, and assist with myriad other tasks that call for sustained bouts of left-brain activity.

Step 5: Find Dr. Right

5 For most folks considering a medical trip abroad, this step is the most challenging — and perhaps the most emotionally charged. Yet if you follow a few basics and caveats, you'll find the process far less mysterious and daunting. Remember, the final choice in selecting a physician — like the decision whether to travel at all — remains always in your hands.

Here are some tips to aid you in your search:

✦ **Insist on English.** While this advice may sound provincial and harshly xenophobic, if English is your only tongue, then insist that the parties you're working with speak only English. Your health is too important to risk important information getting lost in translation.

Don't settle for poor English. Do your best to listen and understand, but if you find yourself constantly asking people to repeat themselves, don't blame yourself. Hospitals, clinics, and agents who cater to an international clientele will have English-speaking staff. If not, then apologize graciously for your lack of language skills, and move on.

✦ **Seek Dr. Right, not Dr. Personality.** OK, if a practitioner candidate is downright rude to you, then move on, but otherwise, give your physician some "personality latitude," at least initially. Focus on skill sets, credentials, and accreditations, not charm.

Even in this country, many of the finest medical practitioners are technicians. While they may love what they do and be quite good at their chosen specialty, their personal presentation skills may be lacking. This is doubly true where language and culture create additional social awkwardness.

Use your judgment and give the charm factor — or lack of it — the benefit of the doubt. If credentials and other criteria check out, and if you're otherwise comfortable with your choice, then charm and personality can probably take a back seat.

✦ **Expect good service.** Although patience is often required when corresponding with international healthcare providers, rudeness should never be excused, and no culture condones it. If anything, you're likely to encounter greater courtesy and graciousness abroad than here. If parties on the other end appear rude or indifferent, move on.

In corresponding with hospitals and clinics overseas, you will often find yourself directly in contact with your physician or surgeon. The good news is that you're engaged in a real dialogue with the professional who will be treating you. The downside is that he or she is probably very busy. Expect delays — sometimes two or three days — between email exchanges. If longer, then politely, but firmly, request a response.

Ten "Must-Ask" Questions for Your Physician Candidate

Make the following initial inquiries, either of your health travel agent or the physician(s) you're interviewing. Note that for some of these questions, there's no right or wrong answer. Your initial round of inquiry will help establish a dialogue. If the doctor is evasive, hurried, or frequently interrupted, or if you can't understand his or her English, then either dig deeper or move on.

1. *What are your credentials? Where did you receive your medical degree? Where was your internship? What types of continuing education workshops have you attended recently?* The right international physician either has credentials posted on the Web or will be happy to email you a complete CV.

2. *How many patients do you see each month?* Hopefully, more than 50 and less than 500. The physician who says, "I don't know," should make you suspicious. Doctors should be in touch with their customer base and have such information readily available.

3. *To what associations do you belong?* Any worthwhile physician or surgeon is a member of at least one medical association. Particularly in areas where formal accreditation is weak, your practitioner should be keeping good company with others in the field. For example, if you're seeking cosmetic surgery in Mexico, your surgeon should be a member of the Mexican Association of Plastic, Reconstructive, and Aesthetic Surgery. It's also a plus to see physicians who are members of, or affiliated with, American medical or dental associations.

4. *How many patients have you treated who have had my condition?* There's safety in numbers, and you'll want to know them. Find out how many general procedures your hospital has performed. Ask how many of *your specific treatments for your specific condition* your doctor has personally conducted. While numbers vary according to procedure, five cases are not good. Fifty or 200 are much better.

5. *What are the fees for your initial consultation?* Answers will vary, and you should compare prices with other physicians you interview. Some consultations are free; some are deducted from the bill, should you choose to be treated with that physician; some are a straight nonrefundable fee. In any event, it pays to have this information in advance.

6. *May I call you on your cell phone before, during, and after treatment?* Direct and personal access to your doctor is foreign to the American experience. Yet most international physicians stay in close, direct contact with their patients, and cell phones are their tools of choice. When physicians aren't treating patients, you'll find cells or headsets glued to their ears.

7. *What medical and personal health records do you need to assess my condition and treatment needs?* Most physicians require at least the basics: recent notes and recommendations from consultations with your local physician or specialists, x-rays directly related to your condition, perhaps patient histories, and other health records. Be wary of the physician who requires no personal paperwork.

8. *Do you practice alone or with others in a clinic or hospital?* "Safety in numbers" is a good bet on this front. Look for a physician who practices among a group of certified professionals with a broad range of related skills. For example, your initial consultation might reveal that you need a dental implant instead of bridgework, and it just so happens that Dr. Guerrero down the hall is one of the country's leading implantologists. Or, on a return visit, your regular doctor is on vacation, but Dr. Cho who's available in the clinic can access your history and records, check your progress, and help you determine your next steps.

For surgery:

9. *Who's holding the knife during my procedure? Do you do the surgery yourself, or do you have assistants do the surgery?* This is one area where delegation isn't desirable. You want specific assurances that all the trouble you went through to find the right surgeon isn't wasted because the procedure is actually being performed by your practitioner's able protégé.

10. *Are you the physician who oversees my entire treatment, including pre-surgery, surgery, prescriptions, physical therapy recommendations, and post-surgery checkups?* For larger surgical procedures, you want the designated team captain. While that's usually the surgeon, check to make sure.

Step 6: Get to Know your Hospital or Clinic

6 At this point, you've probably chosen a date and destination for your treatment, settled on one or two physicians you like, and perhaps you or your health travel planner have even scheduled a consultation. Excellent! You've made great headway, and most of the heavy lifting is behind you.

Before you start booking air travel and accommodations or planning the more relaxing parts of the trip, you'll be wise to stop and do some sleuthing, beginning with your treatment center. Although detail-driven, this investigation is not as daunting as it sounds, and most of your research involves simple fact-checking. Here's what to do and how:

✦ **Check hospital accreditation.** If you're looking into a treatment that requires hospital care, check to see whether the center is JCI-accredited. (See "The What and Why of JCI" below.) While JCI accreditation is not essential, it's an important new benchmark and the only official American seal of approval. Learning that your treatment center is JCI-approved lends a comfort to the process, and the remainder of your searching and checking need not be as rigorous. That said, many excellent hospitals abroad, while not JCI-approved, have received local accreditation at the same levels as American-approved treatment centers.

✦ **Check for affiliations and partnerships.** Did you know that many of the best overseas hospitals enjoy close partnerships with universities and US medical centers? For example,

Gleneagles Hospital in Singapore has a working partnership and information exchange program with Johns Hopkins Hospital in Baltimore. Similarly, Malaysia's Pantai Medical Center has forged working partnerships with Duke University Medical Center and the Cleveland Clinic.

✛ **Learn about success rates.** Although smaller clinics don't offer such information, the larger and more established hospitals freely publish their "success rates," or "morbidity rates." These are usually calculated as a ratio of successful operations achieved to overall number of operations performed.

For larger surgeries (such as cardiovascular and orthopedic), success rates of 98+ percent are on par with those found in the US. For the more common surgeries, you should further investigate any rates under 98 percent.

✛ **Learn about number of surgeries.** Most large hospitals will happily furnish information on numbers of surgeries performed. Generally, the more the better, for there's safety in numbers on this front. For example, the Manipal Heart Hospital in Bangalore, India, has performed more than 14,000 cardiac surgeries in the past five years, with a success rate of 98.8 percent. You will rest easier on your outbound flight knowing that your destination hospital has performed large numbers of procedures with high success rates.

Many of the best overseas hospitals enjoy close partnerships with US medical centers and universities, such as Harvard, Duke, and Johns Hopkins.

The What and Why of JCI

When you walk into a hospital or clinic in the US, chances are good it's "accredited," meaning that it's in compliance with standards and "good practices" set by an independent accreditation agency. In the US, by far the largest and most respected accreditation agency is JCAHO, the Joint Commission on Accreditation of Healthcare Organizations. The commission casts a wide net of approval for hospitals, clinics, home health care, ambulatory services, and a host of other healthcare facilities and services throughout this country.

Responding to a global demand for accreditation standards, JCAHO launched its international affiliate accreditation agency in 1999, the Joint Commission International. In order to be accredited, an international healthcare provider must meet the same set of rigorous standards set forth in the US by JCAHO.

At this writing, nearly 100 hospitals outside the US have been JCI-approved, with more coming on board each month. This is good news for the medical traveler, who can walk with greater confidence into a JCI-accredited site, knowing that standards are high and that staff, procedures, instrumentation, and administrative infrastructure are monitored regularly.

Please note that many very fine hospitals and clinics throughout the world are not yet JCI-accredited, and it's sometimes tougher for some of these organizations to receive approval for highly specialized or experimental treatments. However, if you're considering one of these hospitals, you'll want to ask some tough questions about accreditation and standards.

A general rule of thumb for global patients, particularly if you're planning on major surgery, is to first seek out JCI-approved sites. Then, when you've settled on a JCI-approved hospital, don't stop there. Scrutinize rigorously your physician's or surgeon's educational background, certification, and affiliations.

JCI's Web site carries far more information than you'll ever want to explore on accreditation standards and procedures. To view JCI's current roster of JCI-accredited hospitals abroad, go to www.joint-commissioninternational.com. In the left column, click "JCI Accredited Organizations."

A note about ISO: When researching hospitals and clinics abroad, you'll often come across the phrase "ISO-accredited." Based in Geneva, Switzerland, the International Organization for Standardization is a 157-country network of national standards institutes that approves and accredits a wide range of product and service sectors worldwide, including hospitals and clinics. ISO mostly oversees facilities and administration, *not healthcare procedures, practices, and methods.* Thus, while ISO accreditation is good to see, it's of limited value in terms of your treatment.

Step 7: Follow up with Credentials

Once you've located one or two competent physicians, be sure to obtain their resumes. Many physicians post such data on the Web. If yours don't, then request that your doctors or your health travel agent send you full background information, including education, degrees, areas of specialty, number of years in practice, number of patients served, and association memberships.

✦ **Get references, recommendations, and referrals.** If possible, speak with some of the doctor's former patients to get their feedback. Understandably, many former patients wish their privacy respected, and international law protects us all in that regard. Thus, it's often difficult for a physician to put you in direct contact with a former patient.

If you're unable to talk with former patients, ask your physician to provide you with testimonials, newspaper or magazine articles, and letters of recommendation — in short, anything credible that will help assess this individual's expertise. If you're using the services of a health travel agency, ask your representative to check credentials and background of physicians to help you narrow your search.

Specifically, here's what you're looking for:

✦ **Education.** Universities, medical schools attended, degrees held and when awarded. Any special achievement awards or honors.

✦ **Certification.** Exactly what is this physician licensed to practice? If you're having implants done, then you want a certified implantologist's fingers in your mouth.

✦ *Professional history.* How long has he or she been practicing, and where? If a surgeon, how many surgeries have been performed, and what types of procedures? Information on presentations, publications, honors, and awards gained along the career path will help you evaluate a doctor's talent, performance, and commitment to his trade.

✦ *Affiliations.* With what medical and related associations are your physician affiliated? Information about community involvement is useful as well.

✦ *Continuing education.* Mandatory in many countries, continuing education helps a physician stay abreast of new trends in his or her field. Most good physicians travel at least once a year to accredited conferences and workshops. Find out where your doctor goes and how often.

✦ *Patient references and letters of recommendation.* Nearly as useful as professional histories are reference letters or letters of recommendation from patients, colleagues, or other credible sources.

If you've not engaged the services of a health travel agent, ask your physician or medical staff to email you a copy of your doctor's resume or CV. If you want to take your search a step further, contact the universities, associations, and references listed in the resume to verify authenticity.

For more information, see "Ten 'Must-Ask' Questions for Your Physician Candidate" in this chapter.

Step 8: Gather Your Medical Records

8 Once you've established a relationship or scheduled a consultation with one or more overseas physicians, they'll probably ask to see supporting information. Such data usually include the following:

✦ reports or written recommendations made by your local specialist related to your condition

✦ x-rays or imaging reports from your specialist's office or your radiology lab

✦ test results from your specialist's office or third-party laboratories

Depending upon your treatment, some physicians may ask for additional data, including your general medical history, health record, or pathology reports from previous treatments.

Some patients are timid about requesting health information from their doctors. If you're one of those people, it's important for you to know that as of April 2003, any physician, surgeon, specialist, hospital, or laboratory you visit *is required by law* to provide you copies of any and all medical information they've compiled about you. These data include consent forms, consultation records, lab reports, test results, x-rays, immunization history, and any other information compiled as a result of your visits. Although most won't, your doctor or laboratory has the right to charge you a nominal fee for making copies.

These days, more and more medical information is going digital, particularly all-important x-rays and other imaging data. When you request your medical records, ask staff to email you the data in digital form and to provide you with a hard copy as well. If you can obtain only hard-copy documents, then have them scanned. If you're uncomfortable with technology and computers, perhaps your companion or friend or family member can tweak the paperwork into computer files into the form of an electronic file (scanning is not time consuming for those who know how to do it). A full-service copy shop or office supply center can convert hard-copy paperwork to digital files for a nominal fee, and you'll save real money over international courier rates if you transmit via email. Overseas physicians generally prefer digital records, particularly x-rays, which are easier to study and manipulate.

Any physician, surgeon, specialist, hospital, or laboratory you visit *is required by law* to provide you copies of any and all medical information they've compiled about you.

Step 9: Plan Your Recuperation and Recovery

9 For patients abroad, the days or weeks you spend post-treatment can be particularly difficult. Perhaps you've been on the road vacationing prior to treatment, and you're ready to head home. Or seemingly urgent work challenges are piling up back at the office. Or you're just feeling far away and becoming homesick.

Any surgeon, dentist, or other medical specialist can tell you that if complications are to develop, they're most likely to occur in the first few days following treatment. That's the time when your body is doing everything it can to compensate for the stress and trauma of your treatment. Rest and a healthful lifestyle are essential during recovery, but in these busy, overworked times, many people don't take recuperation as seriously as they should. At the first glimmer of normalcy, we're off and running again.

Do yourself and your loved ones a big favor: follow your doctor's post-treatment orders, allowing your body and spirit time to return to health. It's not that much more time out of your life. For extensive dental work, recovery is usually a matter of a few days. Even the more invasive surgeries have you back to something approaching normalcy within a couple of weeks.

You might be surprised—and encouraged—to learn that many international health travelers enjoy recovery and recuperation accommodations not available in the US. Recovery resorts, surgical retreats, hospital residences, and a host of other options are available in many of the destinations featured in this book. Services offered include

- ✦ *on-site medical staff* to assist with bathing, getting in and out of bed, physical therapy, medication, and more
- ✦ *gyms* and other accommodations for physical therapy and daily exercise
- ✦ *room service* for meals and laundry
- ✦ *Internet access*
- ✦ *liaison with hospital*

Another big plus for recovery accommodations is the company you keep. The guests are people like you who have recently undergone treatment. There's comfort in sharing experiences, and dinner-table conversations with fellow patients can yield a wealth of medical tips and travel advice. If recovery retreats are not offered in your region of choice, ask your health travel planner or hospital for recommendations on hotels or apartments nearby.

Step 10: Create Your Health Travel Vacation

For most health travelers, vacations take a back seat to treatment and recovery. Many simply don't have the time or the motivation to tack a vacation onto an already time-consuming health travel trip. Some patients require more invasive procedures with longer recovery and the planning alone (not to mention the usual discomforts of recuperation) knock a beached-whale Riviera jaunt clean out of the picture.

Medical travelers planning for less demanding treatments, such as light cosmetic surgery or nonsurgical dentistry, should take a brief inventory of their treatment schedule and time requirements. Ask the following questions:

✦ How many appointments does my treatment require?

✦ How long need I remain near my treatment center during my stay?

✦ How long is my expected recuperation period?

Unexpected tests, appointment reshuffles, and travel delays can eat up leisure time. As a rule, the treatment part of your trip will probably be three or four days longer than your appointment schedule indicates.

Whether you can work in a vacation or not, the most important consideration is your health. Focus on your treatment and try not to bite off too much. Remember that you can always take that vacation later, happily spending the money you saved by being treated abroad.

Step 11: Book Air Travel and Accommodations

11 Why isn't this the first step, you may ask. Although it may seem counterintuitive to book your travel and accommodations last, remember that you must first determine where you want to go, select a treatment center and physician, and schedule your consultations or procedure. Only at that point can you begin contacting airlines and hotels; otherwise you're likely to spend needless effort and expense changing itineraries.

You see now why planning ahead is so important to successful medical travel. Some airlines and most hotels carry stiff penalties for changes and cancellations. That's another reason why it pays to begin your initial planning 60-90 days prior to your expected departure date and book your flight *after* you've scheduled your treatment.

When it's time to book air travel and hotels, your health travel agent can provide information on good hotels and recovery accommodations near your treatment center. Some agents have made arrangements with airlines for special discounts, so ask about favored rates before you book.

Be sure also to give your health travel representative a good idea of your budget. You might be surprised to learn that hotel rooms in developing countries can cost as much as the best accommodations in New York. Confirm rates and amenities before pulling out your credit card.

The same holds true for airfares. First-class and business-class fares are usually quite punishing; they're reserved for jetsetters, corporate executives, and frequent flyers. If you don't mind traveling coach or economy class, you'll save a bundle.

If you're making your travel plans on your own, ask your physician to recommend some hotels nearby. Some of the larger hospitals have partnerships with hotels at discounted rates. Such information is often posted on their Web sites.

Just Ask

When it comes to asking for special assistance from the airlines, many travelers believe they must be severely handicapped to request a wheelchair or some other service. And some folks are just shy about asking for help or embarrassed to be wheeled around airport corridors and jetways.

Get over it! If you're heading to India for hip surgery and you've been in chronic pain for three years, there's no shame in requesting a wheelchair, and every airline company we contacted ministers happily to medical travelers. In the same vein, if you're still feeling the effects of surgery on the return trip, it's perfectly reasonable to request wheelchair assistance.

Airlines ask that you or your companion request a wheelchair 48 hours prior to the trip. Then, when you arrive at the airport, check in with the skycap at curbside, where a wheelchair is usually nearby. Remember to tip folks who assist you a few dollars; they'll appreciate the gesture and remember you the next time your paths cross.

Step 12: Triple Check Details and Documents

12 In addition to ensuring that the kids, dog, and other loved ones are looked after in your absence, it's crucial on a medical trip to remember to take everything that you and your companion will need. Unlike forgetting your favorite tie or blouse, leaving important documents behind can create unnecessary hassles on the other side of the world. Make sure you have all your paperwork in order, including travel itinerary, airline tickets or etickets, passports, visa, immunization records, and plenty of cash for airport taxes and other unexpected expenses. Be sure to pack all medical records, consultation notes, agreements, and hard copies of email correspondence. Also remember to take the telephone numbers, fax numbers, and email addresses of all your contacts, at home as well as in-country.

Pack Smart

You've likely heard the cardinal rule of international travel: pack light. Less to carry, less to lose. Don't worry if you leave behind some basic item like shampoo or a comb. Once abroad you can always buy essential items you may have forgotten, and picking up socks or toothpaste is a great excuse for you or your companion to hit the local market.

That said, below are several items you absolutely, positively shouldn't forget:

- Passport
- Visa (if required)
- ATM card or travelers' checks, plus enough cash to handle unexpected expenses
- Prescriptions you're taking
- Hard-to-find over-the-counter drugs you're taking
- Alcohol-based hand-sanitizing gel (for cleaning hands while traveling)
- Your medical records, current x-rays, consultations, and notes
- Phone numbers, postal addresses, and email addresses of people you need or want to contact at home or in-country

Budgeting Your Treatment and Trip

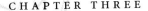

First Things First: Consider Your Treatment and Travel Preferences

As with any other trip, your health travel costs will depend largely upon your tastes, lifestyle preferences, length of stay, side trips, and pocketbook. A patient flying Virgin Airways first class and staying at the Hotel Taj Palace New Delhi can naturally expect fewer savings than one who spends frequent flyer miles and lodges in a nearby — and perfectly satisfactory — guesthouse .

To set reasonable expectations and avoid surprises, you should calculate an estimate of your trip's cost. This chapter offers advice, tips, and milestones that will help you plan.

To derive an estimate of your health travel costs and savings, we suggest you use the *"Patients Beyond Borders* Budget Planner" at the end of this chapter. As you get an idea of each cost, a realistic estimate of your savings will emerge.

Don't feel pressured to fill in every line item in your Budget Planner. At first, focus on the big expenses, such as treatment and airfare, and fill in the remainder as your planning progresses. You probably won't use all the categories. For example, some countries don't require a visa; or you may stay only at a hospital and never visit a hotel. The planner simply lists all the common health travel expenses. As you plan, you can fill in the blanks that apply to you and arrive at a rough estimate of your costs — and your savings!

As you complete the items in your Budget Planner, consider the following:

Passport and Visa

If you don't have a passport and are purchasing one for the first time, budget around $150 for fees, photographs, and shipping. If you're renewing your passport, budget around $100.

Depending on where your travels take you, visa expenses can run from $0 (for those countries that do not require visas) to around $120.

> Air transportation will likely be your biggest non-treatment cost; it pays to shop hard for bargains.

To avoid punishing rush charges and needless pretreatment anxiety, take care of your passport and visa purchases early — passports at least two months in advance of your trip, and visas at least 30 days prior.

Airfare

Unless you're driving to Mexico (automobile travel can sometimes have undesirable post-treatment drawbacks!), air transportation will likely be your biggest non-treatment cost. It pays to shop hard for bargains. If you're OK flying coach, by all means do so; business and first-class international travel is wildly expensive.

If you have a *trusted* travel agency, use it, although with caution. Most have side deals with airlines, and their commissions and fees can cut into your savings.

If you're comfortable using the Internet, take advantage of one of the many discount online travel agencies, such as Orbitz (www.orbitz.com), Expedia (www.expedia.com) Travelocity (www.travelocity.com), or CheapTickets (www.cheaptickets .com). Or, go to individual airlines' Web sites, where you can sometimes snag special Internet fares.

Auction and deep-discount services, such as Priceline (www .priceline.com), take a little more knowledge and patience. Exercise buyer caution with some of the lesser-known "cheap-trip" agencies

Action Item: *Keep your budget current. As your plans change, so will your cost estimate.*

International Entry and Exit Fees

They're usually around $30 US per person, and they may be due upon arrival at your in-country airport, departure, or both. Most countries will not accept credit cards or checks for these fees, only cash. In some countries the fees must be paid in dollars, pounds, or marks. Local currency is not accepted. Some countries do not levy these fees.

Rental Car

When traveling, some people feel they can't manage without a car. It's the American way! Yet international car rentals are expensive, big-city parking is a hassle, and driving in a foreign country can land you in the hospital well ahead of your scheduled stay.

Even the most adventurous health traveler should think twice about driving a car while full of sutures and post-operative medications, especially on the left side of the road.

It's better to use taxis or limousines. They're comparatively inexpensive and, despite the overworked horror stories, cab drivers are generally cooperative when you follow the basics found in any travel guide.

As a medical traveler, your transportation needs — at least immediately pre- and post-treatment — are likely to be limited to hotels and restaurants. The hospital, hotel, or your health travel agent usually provides local transportation free or at modest cost.

If you're planning to head out of town on a post-treatment

vacation, then renting a car is fine. Just be sure that you, your companion, or your agent books the car in advance, as sometimes a conference, festival, or other special event can deplete inventories fast.

Other Transportation

Transportation to and from the airport will probably be handled by the hospital, your health travel agent, or the hotel where you or your companion reside. You should budget for the cost of transportation to and from your US airport, as well as in-country transportation costs. Taxis and buses are usually not expensive; $100 should cover nearly any two-week trip.

Companions

Most health travelers we interviewed were glad that a friend or family member accompanied them. In addition to providing love, support, and a shoulder to cry on during difficult moments, companions can attend to myriad details. Many of those who traveled alone expressed a desire for a companion or assistant during those inevitable, trying travel moments even the healthiest of tourists experience.

You should budget for the additional airfare and meals for your companion and—depending on whether you'll be doubling up—lodging. Items you can usually share include local taxi rides, mobile phone, and computer and Internet services. Items you can't share include passport and visa costs, airfare, airport fees and taxes, rail fares, meals, and entertainment.

Treatment

Treatment costs vary widely, depending upon the procedure, preferred country, room choice, service options, and post-treatment care. In Section Two of this book, each destination features a comparative cost-of-treatment chart, which provides cost estimates for the typical and specialty treatments available at a given destination. While these figures are not hard and fast, they'll give you a good idea of what to expect.

When you are considering a treatment center or physician, request the cost details in writing (email is OK), including the price for basic treatment, plus ancillaries such as anesthesia, room fees, prescriptions, nursing services, and more. Other useful questions include these: Are meals included in my hospital stay? Do you supply a bed for my companion? Is there an Internet connection in the room or lobby?

If you're using a health travel agency, make sure your representative gets specific answers in writing to these important questions, along with a firm cost estimate for treatment and ancillary fees. Then, once you've decided to head abroad, check, double-check, confirm, and reconfirm your hospital's and physician's quotes.

Lodging During Treatment

These costs are straightforward and are largely a function of your tastes and pocketbook. If you're not staying in a hospital or treatment center, search for a hotel or treatment retreat near the hospital. Long cross-town treks can be time-consuming, hot, frenzied, and costly. Your doctor, or the treatment center's staff, can provide you a list of preferred hotels nearby.

You may wish to take advantage of the specialty lodging a region offers. Be sure to ask your agent or treatment center about surgical retreats or recovery lodging facilities recommended by, or affiliated with, the hospital.

Post-treatment Lodging

Unless you're undergoing nothing more than tests or light dental work, it's a good idea to stick around for at least a week post-treatment, instead of jumping on the first plane out of town. Your physician will want to keep an eye on how your recovery is progressing. We highly recommend you take advantage of this important period to gain strength, guard against complications, and adjust to new prescriptions, physical therapies, and lifestyle changes.

Many hospitals offer nearby recuperation resorts or other facilities, which include resident nurses and other staff who can assist you with your post-treatment needs. Many of these facilities are four- or five-star hotels in excellent — sometimes exotic — settings, and your stay there can be the most memorable and relaxing part of your trip. Ask your treatment center or agent about such facilities in your region.

Whether you're recuperating in a recovery resort or hotel, budget around

> Many hospitals offer nearby recuperation resorts or other facilities, which include resident nurses and other staff who can assist you with your post-treatment needs.

$150 per day, including lodging, meals, post-treatment services, and tips.

Meals

If you're staying in a hospital, most of your meals will probably be provided, and the food is often surprisingly good. Many overseas hospitals offer reasonable meal plans for companions. Ask the facility or your agent about costs. Otherwise, budget your dining out according to taste, both for you and for your companion. Any reputable travel guide can give you a good idea of costs in a given country. And, of course, avoid street food and restaurants of questionable repute. You don't want to complicate your medical travels with a rising bout of "Delhi Belly" just prior to treatment.

Tips

Tipping protocols vary according to country; check your travel guide on recommended tipping for taxi drivers, baggage handlers, waiters, and maids. A two-week trip shouldn't set you back more than $75 in tips.

We spoke with many patients who were so happy with the quality of service they received that, upon exit, they left an envelope on the bed with $20-$100 in local currency for nurses, aides, and service personnel. While a tip is entirely up to you, the gesture is generally much appreciated when handled discreetly.

Leisure Travel

Many health travelers plan a vacation for either before or after treatment. While this expense isn't strictly a part of your health travel budget, you may want to add into your health travel budget the costs of vacation-related lodging, transportation, meals, and other expenses.

Don't feel pressured to fill in every line item in your Budget Planner. You probably won't use all the categories. For example, some countries don't require a visa; or you may stay only at a hospital and never visit a hotel. The planner simply lists all the common health travel expenses. As you plan, you can fill in the blanks that apply to you and arrive at a rough estimate of your costs — and your savings.

The $6,000 Health Travel Rule Revisited

While we've mentioned it elsewhere in this book, it's worth stating again: a good monetary barometer of whether your medical trip is financially worthwhile is the *Patients Beyond Borders* "$6,000 Health Travel Rule." If your total quote for treatment (including consultations, procedure, and hospital stay) is $6,000 or more, you'll probably save money traveling abroad for your care. If less than $6,000, you're likely better off having your treatment at home.

This rule varies depending on your financial position and lifestyle preferences. For some, a $500 savings might offset the hassles of travel. Others might be traveling anyway, so savings considerations are fuzzier.

Patients Beyond Borders Budget Planner

Item	Cost	Comment
IN-COUNTRY		
Passport/Visa	$150.00	For passport and visa, non-expedited
Rush charges, if any:		
Treatment Estimate		
Procedure:		
Hospital room, if extra:		Often included in treatment package
Lab work, x-rays, etc:		
Additional consultations:		
Tips/gifts for staff:	$100.00	
Other:		
Other:		
Post-Treatment		
Recuperation lodging:		Hospital room or hotel
Physical therapy:		
Prescriptions:		
Concierge services:		Optional
Other:		
Other:		
Airfare		
You:		
Your companion:		
Other travelers:		
Aiport exit fee:	$25.00	
Other:		
Other:		
In-Country Transportation		
Taxi's, buses, limo's:	$100.00	
Rental car:		
Other:		
Other:		

Patients Beyond Borders Budget Planner (*continued*)

Item	Cost	Comment
Leisure Travel (if any)		
Hotel:		
Food:		
Entertainment/sightseeing:		
Transportation:		
Other:		
Other:		
"While You're Away" Costs		
Petsitter/housesitter:		
Other:		
Other:		
IN-COUNTRY TREATMENT SUBTOTAL		
HOME-TOWN		
Procedure:		
Lab work, x-rays, etc:		
Hospital room, if extra		
Additional consultations:		
Physical therapy:		
Prescriptions:		
Other:		
Other:		
HOME-TOWN SUBTOTAL		
TOTAL SAVINGS:		Subtract "In-Country" Subtotal
		from "Home-Town" Subtotal

Patients Beyond Borders Sample Budget Planner

Item	Cost	Comment
IN-COUNTRY		
Passport/Visa	$150.00	For passport an-expedited
Rush charges, if any:		
Treatment Estimate		
Procedure:	$9,000.00	
Hospital room, if extra:		Often included in treatment package
Lab work, x-rays, etc:	$45.00	
Additional consultations:	$200.00	
Tips/gifts for staff:	$100.00	
Other:		
Other:		
Post-Treatment		
Recuperation lodging:	$1,100.00	Hospital room or hotel
Physical therapy:		
Prescriptions:	$65.00	
Concierge services:	$300.00	Optional
Other:		
Other:		
Airfare		
You:	$880.00	
Your companion:	$880.00	
Other travelers:		
Aiport exit fee:	$25.00	
Other:		
Other:		
In-Country Transportation		
Taxi's, buses, limo's:	$100.00	
Rental car:		
Other:		
Other:		

Patients Beyond Borders Sample Budget Planner (*continued*)

Item	Cost	Comment
Room and Board		
Hotel:	$1,500.00	
Food:	$650.00	
Entertainment/sightseeing:	$500.00	
Other:		
Other:		
"While You're Away" Costs		
Petsitter/housesitter:	$300.00	
Other:		
Other:		
IN-COUNTRY SUBTOTAL	$15,795.00	
HOME-TOWN		
Procedure:	$55,000.00	
Lab work, x-rays, etc:	$375.00	
Hospital room, if extra:	$4,400.00	
Additional consultations:		
Physical therapy:	$400.00	
Prescriptions:	$500.00	
Other:		
Other:		
HOME-TOWN SUBTOTAL	$60,675.00	
TOTAL SAVINGS:	$44,880.00	Subtract "In-Country" Subtotal from "Home-Town" Subtotal

Is Your Medical Trip Tax Deductible?

What do tortillas, taxi rides, and treatments have in common? All these expenses may be tax deductible as part of your health travel. Depending upon your income level and cost of treatment, some or most of your health journey can be itemized as a straight deduction from your adjusted gross income.

In brief, if you're itemizing your deductions, and if IRS-authorized medical treatment and related expenses amount to more than 7.5 percent of your adjusted gross income, you're allowed to deduct the remainder of those expenses, whether they were incurred in Toledo, Ohio or Toledo, Spain.

For example, if your adjusted gross income is $90,000, then any allowed medical expense over $6,750 ($90,000 x 7.5%) becomes a straight deduction. Suppose, for example, that your medical trip cost you a total of $14,000 including treatment, travel, lodging, and, of course, a two-week surgeon-recommended stay in a five-star beachfront recuperation resort. For that trip, you could deduct $7,250 ($14,000 – $6,750) from your adjusted gross income.

Examples of typical tax-deductible items include

- any treatment normally covered by a health insurance plan
- transportation expenses, including air, plane, train, boat or car travel
- lodging and in-treatment meals
- recovery hotels, surgical retreats, and recuperation resorts

Of course, your expenses must be directly related to your treatment, and many specific items are disallowed. (See below to learn more about allowed expenses.)

Be sure to save all your receipts. That's often easier said than done in foreign lands. Hotel and treatment bills are sometimes not computer-generated overseas, and just try getting a receipt from a three-wheel taxi operator in New Delhi. Receipts or not, keep a detailed expense log, noting time, date, purpose, and amount paid. Ask for letters and other documentation from your in-country healthcare provider, particularly any recommendations made for outside lodging, special diets, and other services.

For more information, you can go straight to the source. Go to www.irs.gov, click on "individual," then search for "medical deductions." You can also call the IRS directly at 1-800-829-1040. Believe it or not, most IRS customer service representatives are friendly and competent, and if you are sufficiently persistent, you'll eventually be put in touch with a medical tax specialist. As always with such matters, you should consult your tax advisor with questions or concerns.

Action Item: **Research IRS rules on allowable deductions for healthcare and health travel.**

A Typical Medical Expense and Tax Spreadsheet

When it comes to taxes, we're no experts, nor are we professionally or legally qualified to advise you. That said, readers often ask us how exactly the medical deduction works. Here's our best shot, a theoretical scenario of Robert Thrifty, a patient who traveled to Delhi, India, for hip resurfacing surgery. His allowable expenses went something like this:

- 90-day Visa to India: $140

- Immunization: Yellow fever $72

- Birmingham Hip Resurfacing Treatment: $9,000

- Hospital Room (four days): $350

- In-Hospital Meals: $110

- Recovery Retreat (physician recommended): $1,750

- Physical Therapy (physician mandated): $200

- Prescriptions (physician mandated): $65

- Transportation (airfare): $1,450

- Transportation (other): $200

    Total: **$13,357**

When Robert sat down to complete his tax return, his initial Adjusted Gross Income (AGI) totaled $83,000.

Adjusted Gross Income: $83,000

In order to calculate his medical deduction, Robert first calculated 7.5 percent of his AGI. (Don't ask us how the IRS came to this figure. It's just the one they use.)

$$7.5\% \times \$83,000.00 = \$6,225$$

Then, Bob subtracted his $6,225 medical expense baseline from his actual trip costs.

$$\$13,357 - \$6,225 = \$7,126$$

Finally, Robert calculated his new, improved Adjusted Gross Income of $75,874:

$$\$83,000 - \$7,126 = \$75,874$$

Naturally, if your income were lower or if your allowable health travel expenses were higher, you'd gain even more. But the calculation process is the same in all cases.

If the above is clear as mud, then a good rule of thumb is this: if your Adjusted Gross Income is less than $100,000 and your allowable medical expenses are more than $10,000, then you probably have a tax benefit worth pursuing.

Before you submit your return, consult your tax advisor or the friendly folks at the IRS on this important tax provision.

Choosing and Working with a Health Travel Planner

The New Good Old Days of Hitting the Road

Many of you remember the pre-Internet days of the Friendly Local Travel Agent, when you or your parents picked up the phone and called — or actually visited — the small office of an agency that took care of all your vacation planning needs. If you didn't know where you wanted to travel, your agent helped you find a destination. If you knew where you wanted to go, then your trusty, loyal agent helped you book flights, hotels, and tours, matching accommodations and amenities to your budget and lifestyle preferences. And best of all, the services were usually free — the costs borne by airlines, hotels, and tour companies.

Those days are long gone, the travel agent having, for the most part, lost trade to the Web, which appears to be slowly strangling us with the joys of ubiquitous, dehumanized self-service.

So, you ask, why bother to work with an agent who specializes in medical travel, when Expedia, Travelocity, CheapTrips, and dozens of other reliable Web sites now serve all our travel needs?

As you'll see below, the answer lies in getting the best available healthcare in the best destination. Health travel planners can usually ensure a superior, personalized medical travel experience, and no general travel agent or Internet service will be able to offer that service anytime soon.

What Is a Health Travel Planner?

They answer to many names: brokers, facilitators, planners, expediters. Throughout this book, we use the phrase "health travel planner" or "agent," to mean any agency or representative who specializes in helping a patient find medical treatment abroad. Agents, representatives, and agencies come in all shapes and sizes. Some are departments of larger agencies; others are family-run businesses. Some reside in the country of treatment and specialize only in cosmetic surgery or orthopedics. Others have corporate offices in the US and provide general services for multiple destinations.

As larger numbers of travelers head abroad for medical care, the health travel industry will mature, offering new infrastructure and amenities that only larger corporations can bring. Some countries, like India and Costa Rica, boast a wide choice of excellent planners. Others, such as Hungary and Mexico, offer slimmer pickings and demand greater scrutiny on your part. At the moment, however, most health travel agencies are small, dedicated businesses with lean budgets and small staffs. All have their unique characteristics, along with distinct pros and cons. This chapter will help you match your needs and interests to those who can best meet them.

Why Use a Health Travel Planner?

Convenience. Some health travelers like to take it all on themselves, searching the Web and other sources to check destination opportunities, hospitals' accreditation, physicians' credentials, and patients' references; and to research and arrange air travel, hotel accommodations, airport pickups and drop-offs, sightseeing, and more. Yet, if you're like many working people today, you're too busy to make such arrangements solo, particularly if you're not accustomed to sorting through all the complexities of international travel. Planners help with all that and more, leaving you additional time to make the important decisions and to care for yourself pretreatment.

Experience. While health travel agents are not generally licensed physicians, most have long-standing affiliations with in-country treatment centers and practitioners. They cannot provide you advice on your particular treatment, and many will not recommend one particular physician or surgeon over another. However, all agents featured in *Patients Beyond Borders* maintain a dossier of their preferred hospitals, clinics, physicians, and surgeons, and they can readily provide you with a list of healthcare providers to match your requirements.

From the hundreds of hospitals and thousands of physicians in a given country, reputable agents have selected practitioners that are tops in their respective specialties, often working within the walls of the most prestigious hospitals. After all, the reputation of any agency depends on delivering consistent treatment success and a high level of patient satisfaction. Any agent who doesn't is soon out of business.

> The reputation of any agency depends on delivering consistent treatment success and a high level of patient satisfaction. Any agent who doesn't is soon out of business.

Savings. Most health travel planners have worked hard to negotiate better-than-retail rates with hospitals, clinics, physicians, hotels, and sometimes airlines. They'll also save you money on local transportation by providing airport pickup and drop-off, as well as transport to and from your clinic. Some agents are also hooked into tour companies, so they can provide discounts on in-country vacations and sightseeing as well.

Collaboration. Whether in the planning stages or in-country, the health traveler is more often than not a "stranger in a strange land." Unless you're unusually adventurous or have a PhD in research, it's good to have a planner to help you work through the complexities of your treatment options and to act as an intermediary between you and your local doctor, your in-country practitioner(s), and all the third-parties involved in your trip. Sometimes it's just good to have a shoulder to cry on or a caring but dispassionate third party who's "been there and done that" before and can reassure you that all will turn out well.

A good health travel agent works in collaboration with you, your companion, and your family, working your treatment needs, budget, and lifestyle preferences into one package designed to result in the most healthy, comfortable experience possible.

> Check in with your agent from time to time, and always end your conversation with an understanding of the next steps, and when you can expect to again hear from him or her.

What a Health Travel Planner Does

Although not all agents offer the same services, here's what you can generally expect:

Planning and Budgeting

✦ **Information exchange.** Once you've established a working relationship, your planner will begin sending you information on hospitals and physicians who can meet your treatment needs. Agents can supply data on hospital accreditation, as well as physician's credentials, board affiliations, number of surgeries performed, association memberships, and ongoing training.

✦ **Match you with the appropriate physician(s).** By far the most important service a health travel agent provides is that of matchmaker. The best planners have years of experience with treatment centers, physicians, and staffs. They long ago weeded out the bad apples and are now in a position to find the best options for you among a variety of choices. Because the agency's success depends on references from satisfied customers, top agents work very hard to make the physician-patient relationship a good match from the start.

✦ **Arrange and confirm appointments.** Once you've selected or approved a physician, your planner can easily handle the details of making appointments for consultations, tests, and treatment. Agents also know the assistants and aides who can pull the strings and push the buttons you need.

✦ **Teleconsultation.** Once you've narrowed your search to a few candidates or settled on a physician, most agents will arrange a telephone consultation with your physician, surgeon, or dentist during which you can share information about your condition, review your medical history and needs, and discuss your procedure. You'll be able to get a feel for your practitioner's working style and assess the "chemistry" between you.

✦ **Travel arrangements.** Most planners help arrange the best flight schedules and fares, and some have negotiated discounts with airlines or affiliated tour agencies.

✦ **Obtain visas.** For a relatively modest fee, a health travel agent can help you avoid the hassles of purchasing a visa (if required), updating your passport, procuring tourist cards, and hounding the appropriate embassy for service.

✦ ***Reserve lodging and make living arrangements.*** Agents will work with your budget and lifestyle preferences to put you in touch with several hotels close to your treatment center. They'll often book hotel reservations and make arrangements for local travel. For an additional fee, they can organize "concierge services" such as take-out food from restaurants, tickets for events, dry cleaning and laundry services, and more.

✦ ***Expedite the transfer of your medical information.*** Your planner can work with you and your physicians at home and abroad to relay medical data, including history, x-rays, test results, recommendations, and other documentation. Agents can help you get data into the right format for emailing or help you determine the best way to ship documents.

In-Country

✦ ***Arrange in-country transportation.*** Most agencies either provide transportation from the airport to your hotel or treatment center, or they work directly with the hotel or hospital to arrange transport. If transport is required between your hotel and treatment center, they'll also help with arrangements.

✦ ***Communication.*** An agent can usually arrange for the use of a cell phone for in-country calls. For more information on telephones and Internet, see Chapter Five, "Staying in Touch While on the Road."

✦ ***Consultation.*** Most agents will arrange for you to be accompanied on your first consultation, where you'll be guided through your health assessment, including tests, blood work, scans, and other pretreatment procedures. The agent's representative will help answer any questions about your treatment before confirming the date for your procedure.

✦ **Pre-treatment.** An agent's representative will accompany you on appointments up to the day of surgery.

✦ **Hospital admission.** Upon your arrival, an agent's representative will usually meet you to help with check-in and registration.

✦ **Post-treatment.** Your agent or representative will check on you from time to time and arrange for you to be transported to any recovery hotel or resort you might have booked.

✦ **Hospital discharge.** Prior to your heading home, your agent will usually be available to help assess your fitness for travel, as well as to ensure that all your exit paperwork — including post-treatment instructions, records, notes, scans, prescriptions, and receipts — is in order.

✦ **Help with leisure activity planning.** If you and yours are up for a pre- or post-treatment excursion, planners can often help you with side trips, car rentals, hotels, restaurants, and other travel amenities.

Back Home

✦ **Aftercare and follow-up.** Once you've returned home, most agents are happy to help with any difficulties you might experience, particularly if complications arise. It's helpful to have someone on the other end when you need an x-ray your home doctor requests or you have misplaced your prescription and notes for physical therapy.

Many physicians guarantee their work, particularly in the specialties of dentistry and cosmetic surgery. In the unlikely event that post-treatment complications make a return trip necessary, your planner acts as a liaison to arranging travel, appointments, and follow-up treatment.

Fees, Packages, and Payment

There are probably as many fee and "package" arrangements as there are health travel agents. Most agents offer packages, which include various bundles of services priced according to what is included. Package prices depend most on your specific medical treatment. For example, one agent serving India offers the following as a complete knee replacement package:

Basic Package

✦ Surgery

✦ All directly related medical expenses

✦ Two-day hospital stay

✦ Consultations before and after surgery

✦ Curatives and post-operative services

✦ Support team during your stay

Deluxe Package

✦ Surgery

✦ Seven-day hospital stay

✦ All directly related medical expenses

✦ Consultations before and after surgery

✦ Pre-operative exams and tests

✦ Prescriptions and post-operative services

✦ Lodging in a five-star hotel for one person for seven days, with breakfast

✦ Transport transfers between airport, hotel, and hospital

✦ Cell phone for local and international calls (500 minutes)

✦ Support team during your stay

Action Item: **Some planners offer "all-in-one" package deals, which are fine. However, at tax time, you may need to show Uncle Sam your itemized cost breakdown, including treatment, lodging, meals, transportation, and health travel agent fees. Spreadsheets are universal these days. Ask your planner to give you a detailed expense log.**

Costs and payments are usually handled in one of three ways:

+ **Membership, upfront fee required.** This arrangement requires a patient to pay a nonrefundable membership fee (usually $50 – $300) before any services are rendered. The membership fee is usually folded into the package price should you engage that agent.

+ **Package, advance deposit required.** In this arrangement, an agent provides enough information to get you well along your path — data on specific treatment centers and physicians, advice on medical records and in-country procedures, and perhaps even a telephone consultation with your physician or surgeon. At that point, if you decide to engage the agent, you'll be asked to submit a deposit, perhaps 25 – 50 percent of the price of the entire package. Another payment is due prior to surgery, and the remainder is payable when you leave the hospital.

> If paying with a credit card, be sure to alert your bank or credit card company to any overseas transactions, so their fraud department doesn't shut you down just when you most need your card.

+ **Pay as you go, direct to third parties.** A handful of planners act more as referral services than full-blown brokers, providing you information about hospitals and physicians, airfares, and vacation opportunities, without doing much of the real legwork. They usually charge you a commission or set fee on any service you engage.

If you're dealing with a reputable agent, all these fee structures get you to much the same place. Beware, however, of agents asking 100 percent upfront. You want to see evidence of performance, meet all the parties personally, and know that your hard-earned dollars are going where they should. Always, always request and check at least two references or some other hard evidence of an agent's ability to produce results.

Bill Me Later

While a deposit of up to 50 percent of the total package cost is usually required, you should reserve at least 25 percent of the total bill for final payment. In other words, as with most other services, don't pay the entire bill until you're satisfied and all the services you've been promised have been provided. Most planners accept credit cards, but before you use yours, ask your agent about any surcharges associated with credit card payments. If paying with a credit card, be sure to alert your bank or credit card company to any overseas transactions, so their fraud department doesn't shut you down just when you most need your card.

What to Look for in a Health Travel Planner

The health travel agency industry is growing, and not all regions listed in *Patients Beyond Borders* are serviced by health travel planners. More are springing up monthly, with varied experience and credentials. Thus, if you decide to work with an agent, particularly one who's not been directly recommended by a trusted source, you should do some checking.

+ *How's the English?* As with physicians and other in-country contacts, if you're having trouble with translation or feel awkward communicating, move on.

+ *Request client references.* Any qualified agent should be able to furnish detailed letters of reference from at least two former clients. Agents may require you to keep such information confidential.

Check, Please

An agent's self-promotion on a Web site is not sufficient evidence of competence. Ask your agent for at least two references from treatment centers or former patients. You'll also see the better agencies popping up on hospital Web sites and in travel blogs. They'll be mentioned in newspaper and magazine articles and by in-country travel booster associations.

Obtain professional references. As you work with a potential planner but before you write your first check, you should contact one or two potential treatment centers and ask if they've worked with a given agency in the past and would recommend its services.

Request direct contact with your overseas physician. Just as a general travel agent isn't an airline pilot, a health travel is not a physician. Agents are facilitators, not doctors. Most agents are more than happy to put you in touch with one or more treatment centers and physicians. They'll work collaboratively to help you make the best choice among available options.

What services are provided? Of all the services a health travel planner offers, the most important are related to your treatment. Start your dialogue by asking the fundamental questions: Do you know the best doctors? Have you met personally with your preferred physicians and visited their clinics? Can you give me their credentials and background information? What about recuperation lodging? Do you provide transportation to and from the airport? To and from the treatment center? If an agent is knowledgeable and capable with these details, the rest of the planning usually takes care of itself.

What's all this cost? Don't wait until you get your final bill to discover the agent's fee structure. Ask the important money questions up-front: What are your fees? How and when are payments made? Which credit cards do you accept? Are there any extra or hidden costs?

How's the chemistry? Usually after the first couple of conversations and email exchanges and after you've done some checking around about your planner, either you'll reach a comfort level or you won't. If you're beginning to sense a good working rhythm and feel your planner genuinely has your interests at heart, you can feel confident about moving forward with the relationship.

Domestic or Abroad?

Some agents operate in-country, others in the US with in-country offices or point people. Either scenario is fine, so long as the good service that's promised on the Web site is actually being delivered.

> If you work with a US agency, make sure you'll have an in-country contact upon arrival.

Advantages of a US-based agency include local time zones, cultural familiarity, and better English. On the other hand, in-country agents give you the comfort of being on-the-scene, in close touch with treatment centers, physicians, lodging, and other third-party services.

If you choose to work with a US agency, make sure you'll have an in-country contact, one who's available to work out the details and smooth your trip.

When *Not* to Use an Health Travel Planner

Don't use an agent if your initial requests for information are not promptly answered, if the agent doesn't reasonably follow through on commitments, or if you aren't treated well. Difficulty deciphering your agent's English is a red flag, too.

If a trusted friend or other source has referred you to a specific clinic and physician, then half the work is done, and you may want to consider forgoing an agent's services, particularly if the hospital or clinic provides similar services.

However, even if you have a great direct reference, you might still experience difficulty communicating with a busy physician and staff. If so, it might be prudent to find an agent willing to work with your recommended physician and capable of providing a variety of services to help ease your planning burdens.

For Best Results . . .

Seek quality and service over price. While cost is a big reason most health travelers head abroad for treatment, avoid the "penny wise, pound foolish" trap. A few hundred dollars in additional fees can buy a wealth of experience, information, comfort, and quality service. If you're saving thousands on your treatment, the extra expenditure won't be noticed; in fact, in hindsight it will likely be appreciated.

As the medical tourism industry grows, new health travel services are popping up monthly, with all the usual promises of unmatched service and untold savings. When you find a planner whose references check out and with whom you appear to be striking up a good working relationship, that's a good time to quit shopping around and hunker down to serious trip planning.

Get it in writing. Prior to engaging an agent formally, get a good understanding of the services offered and the compensation expected. If your agent doesn't furnish a written agreement or letter of engagement, then a simple email from you, confirming roles, responsibilities, costs, and timelines will prevent disagreements down the road.

Avoid the "penny wise, pound foolish" trap. A few hundred dollars in additional fees can buy a wealth of experience, information, comfort, and quality service.

The Write Stuff

some planners use contracts or simple letters of engagement; others are less formal, and it's all word of mouth. Don't settle for a handshake; it may come back to haunt you! That said, agents are usually individuals or family businesses, and a 20-page contract backed by a bevy of lawyers won't be forthcoming. If you can't wangle a formal agreement, then take the time to send a confirming email that spells out work expectations, timelines, and financial arrangements. If you've already reached a comfort level with your agent's abilities and credentials, that's usually good enough.

Respect boundaries. Health travel planners are facilitators and information providers, not servants. Agents frequently complain about customers overstepping the bounds of courtesy, expecting concierge services for free or demanding medical advice and extra amenities not covered in their agreement. The best planners are also the busiest—and the most sensitive to your needs. Respecting the relationship will usually get you the best service.

Remember: the ultimate responsibility always rests with you to settle upon a physician and treatment center, and make key decisions about your trip.

Stay vigilant. Once you've decided to engage the services of an agent, you'll be doing yourself a disservice to let him or her do all the work. It's your health at stake. Whether at home or abroad, the buck stops with you.

Thus, continue to check and double-check everything. When your agent recommends two or three physicians, research their credentials, double-check their board affiliations, and ask for patient references. Confirm a hospital's standing and stature (e.g. accreditation, number of surgeries performed) and follow up any references supplied.

If you engage the services of a health travel planner, be sure to consult frequently Chapter Two, "Planning Your Health Travel Journey," and Chapter Five, "While You're There," to ensure that you and your agent share the same understandings about all aspects of your travel and treatment.

Follow up periodically. While a good planner can work wonders, relieving you of huge travel and planning burdens, even the best can fall behind or miss a beat. So check with your agent from time to time and always end your conversation with an understanding of the next steps. Be sure to find out when you can expect to hear from your agent again.

CHAPTER FIVE

While You're There

First Things First—Arm Yourself with Information

Now that you have settled on a destination, made appointments with one or more physicians, booked your airfare and hotel, and arranged transportation, the hard part is behind you—except of course for your treatment itself. You'll find that once you arrive in-country, you will be greeted graciously, with help and support from hotel and hospital staff, your health travel agent, or sometimes even a friendly bystander.

But before you travel, or at least on the airplane journey overseas, you should read, ask questions, and learn as much as you can about your destination. *Patients Beyond Borders* can't begin to provide all the important information you need about international travel—much less the specifics of your chosen destination. Yet we do want to point you to a few important basics to get you started. Everything else you need is readily available through a number of sources. (See "Getting the Information" below.)

If you've not done much international travel prior to booking your health trip, keep in mind that you don't need to be a seasoned travel veteran to have a successful trip. In fact, most American international tourists board their outbound flight in blissful ignorance of a destination's culture, customs, and language — and they do just fine. Armed with multiple credit cards, they rent a car or hire a limousine at the airport and head for a US-owned beach resort, without giving a thought to the country they're visiting. Many scarcely speak to a native, except perhaps to mumble a few words during shopping sprees or dining out.

> Knowing a little something about the culture, history, geography, and language of your host country will buy you boatloads of goodwill and appreciation.

Health travel is different. Unlike that dimly recollected junket to Las Vegas last summer, you're now far more concerned about practical matters. Getting things done cooperatively and efficiently will help you and your companion preserve your physical *and* mental health. And most health travelers are interested in saving money when it's prudent to do so.

By prearrangement, you'll be interacting closely with local physicians, staff, health planners, and others who live and work in-country. Knowing a little something about the culture, history, geography, and language of your host country will buy you boatloads of goodwill and appreciation. A small investment of time and effort in learning something about your destination will help you make the right choices and become more confident and proficient when you arrive in-country.

Getting the Information

Travel guides. You've probably seen at least one edition of *Lonely Planet, Insiders' Guide, Frommer's, Fodor's,* or some of the other more popular travel series. A host of travel guides have been published for every city and country featured in *Patients Beyond Borders.* Most of the general information (e.g. history, currency, banking, and transportation) is essentially the same in all the books. *Lonely Planet* books are generally written for a younger crowd, with information for backpackers as well as five-star travelers. *Frommer's* guides are aimed at an older audience, but like *Lonely Planet, Frommer's* is budget conscious, although somewhat stodgier then its hip counterpart.

It's a good idea to thumb pages of various guides in your local bookstore or library and choose the format and presentation that best fits your tastes. Avoid titles like *Rough Guide...*and *Off the Beaten Path. . . .* Save them for your dream adventure vacation.

Since books are not cheap, you might want to head to your local library to borrow three or four titles on your destination of choice. Or search the Amazon customer reviews, which offer individual readers' surprisingly erudite, accurate assessments of a book's strengths and shortcomings. Then purchase the one or two that sound best.

Be sure to take at least one travel book with you on the trip — it will become your travel bible — filled with notes, dog-eared pages, business cards, phone numbers, email addresses, and random scribblings. It's a good idea to purchase both a country guide and a city guide. The latter will contain a wealth of detailed information not found in a general reference. Of course, if you're planning a side trip or vacation, you might want a travel guide for those destinations as well. However, if you are a real lover of books, you may be wise to curb your enthusiasm. Books are heavy to carry, and seem to grow moreso the farther you travel.

Maps. While most travel guides contain country and city maps, they are often difficult to read. The print is small and the maps lack detail. If you want or need to know precisely where you are or if you are planning side trips, a small investment in an oversized street map or road map will yield large returns.

When in-country, bookstores are usually your best bets for high-quality maps and road atlases, but they can be difficult to find, and sellers are frequently out of stock. For that reason, it's often a good idea to buy a map before you travel. Some passport and visa services sell maps at a reasonable price (check online for various services). Amazon has a good supply; just go to www.amazon.com and search for **<city> map** or **<country> map**.

 Action Item: Buy a travel guide — and read it!

General Guidelines and Cautions

Here are a few general travel tips and guidelines that will help get you started.

Safety and security. The overriding concern of most patients new to global health travel is safety. That's understandable. In the past five years, this old world has seen (to mention only a few) several terrorist plots at UK airports (a frequent medical tourist stopover), a military coup in Bangkok (one of the most-traveled medical tourist destinations), peoples' rebellions in Oaxaca and Mexico City, rioting in Budapest (a popular dental and cosmetic surgery destination), and never-ending strife in Israel (an important destination for reproductive and infertility procedures).

> As a medical traveler, you'll be too busy achieving your health goals to be booking risky nights out on the town, hazardous wilderness tours, or adventurous side trips of uncertain outcome.

Obviously, we live in a troubled world. Yet, this fact remains: of the 400,000 Americans who traveled overseas for medical treatment in the last five years, not one has died as a result of violence or hostility. As you read this chapter, you'll learn that most health travelers are quite sheltered. They're chauffeured from the airport to the hospital or hotel, personally driven to consultations, given their meals in their rooms, and chauffeured back to the airport when it's time to go home. All with good reason, as the primary purpose of health travel is to undergo medical treatment. As a medical traveler, you'll be too busy achieving your health goals to be booking risky nights out on the town, hazardous wilderness tours, or adventurous side trips of uncertain outcome.

Currency, credit cards, and banking. Much has changed in our new era of electronic banking, and currency is no exception. Check your local travel guides for specifics. Check with your health travel broker and hospital beforehand to determine accepted forms of payment.

✢ *Cash.* Good old American greenbacks are usually the best way to get the most for your money, without all the surcharges and hassles that come with traveler's checks and credit cards. If you want to bring cold hard cash to cover your entire trip and treatment, be sure that you are confident about carrying that much money. Check with your hotel staff or hospital administration beforehand to determine whether they offer room or lobby safes.

Remember that most countries have restrictions on the amount of cash you are allowed to bring, or at least require that you declare it. Check beforehand.

✢ *Traveler's checks.* These somewhat outdated instruments are still accepted by most hotels, hospitals, and restaurants — but usually only for a fee. Be sure to check first with your treatment center on the types of traveler's checks accepted.

✢ *Credit cards.* As convenient as they are, avoid using credit cards overseas, particularly for large payments (such as settling your hospital bills). Some establishments tack on service charges that can run as high as 10 percent—negating the value of any frequent flyer miles you might want to earn. Then, adding insult to injury, upon your return, your bank statement may reflect an additional 2–5 percent on each transaction. If possible, avoid using your credit card for cash advances, as banks charge big commissions bites on each transaction. Check with your bank or credit card institution about its policies concerning international transactions.

✦ **ATMs.** Popping up on nearly every overseas street corner are the ubiquitous ATMs now so indispensable to Americans. ATMs usually offer exchange rates equal or close to the day's official rate. Prior to departing, check with your bank on its ATM surcharges, if any.

✦ *International wire transfers.* Avoid them. They are prone to frustrating bungled attempts at one end or the other. Also avoid black markets and moneychangers.

✦ *Hotel safes.* Most of the hotels and hospitals recommended in this book offer personal safes where you can stash your cash, passports, airline tickets, and other important belongings. Just remember to clean out your safe as you pack for departure! One dental patient, woozy on painkillers, reported getting to the airport, fumbling for tickets and money, and becoming hysterical before realizing he had forgotten to empty his safe. He made the plane, a little poorer and a little more gray-haired after a hectic taxi ride back to the hotel.

✦ When traveling on your own – as you might when shopping for gifts — be sure to take lots of small bills or coins. You don't want to be seen on the streets sorting through a pile of large bills, and most vendors can't or won't break them, leaving you standing there while they trot next door for change. Yet large bills are what you usually get from ATMs, banks, and money exchange offices. Ask for smaller denominations. Your hotel desk or hospital cashier can break big bills. Keep a change purse, and keep it full!

✦ **Water.** The last thing you need as a patient — pre- or post-treatment — is a case of green apple quickstep. Even in most parts of Europe, it's a good idea to request bottled water. Check to ensure that the cap's seal is unbroken, as plastic bottles are sometimes "recycled" by enterprising vendors, then filled with local tap water.

✦ **Food.** One of the most oft-heard comments from "on the road" patients is about the food. Surprisingly, the complaint isn't about the quality of the hospital meals. Indeed, the heart of the problem is the fact that institutional meals abroad tend to be *too* robust, particularly post-treatment. Patients just out of surgery, who are taking antibiotics, painkillers, and other pharmaceuticals, should not be sampling exotic new taste delights. Until you are well on your way to recovery, ask your hospital dietician for the blandest food possible, and pass the tray of spicy tandoori chicken to your companion!

Outside the hospital, avoid greasy spoons and street vendors. While veteran travelers and locals have no trouble with street food, American digestive systems are not primed to counteract the flora that thrives in native dishes. The better restaurants and best hotels are safer places to eat, but even there, it's best to choose only cooked foods. Fresh fruits and salads, as appetizing as they appear, may be washed in tap water. Say no to ice in drinks, also. It's often made with local water, and the last thing the health traveler needs is a case of vomiting or diarrhea to impede recovery.

Dress. If you're staying in a hospital, comfort is your first priority, and your gown will be about as elegant a fashion statement as you'll make. Once on the outside, you should respect local customs for dress. As a nearly universal rule, shorts are frowned upon except at the beach. And shirtless men are nearly never seen in town, even in the hottest climates. When walking the city, check out what the folks on the streets are wearing; if you're comparably dressed, you'll be fine.

Note for women: Make sure you take a scarf to Middle Eastern countries, India, and Southeast Asia, as well as some Mediterranean countries like Greece and Turkey. There may be times when you are expected to cover your head. Also, sleeveless garments, tank tops, and camisoles are frowned on; unless you're heading to the beach, leave them home. Cover your arms in-country.

Getting around town. Ground transportation varies depending upon your destination — from rickshaws and bicycles to motorcycles, buses, and stretch limousines. Generally, your best bet is a good old-fashioned motorized sedan taxi. They come in different shapes and sizes and are usually reliable. Be sure you used only authorized, licensed, or certified taxis. Your local

Note for women: Make sure you take a scarf to Middle Eastern countries, India, and Southeast Asia, as well as some Mediterranean countries like Greece and Turkey

travel guide or hotel concierge can give you specific information on finding the right services at the right price. Taxi drivers and honesty are often strange bedfellows. Agree on the price — or insist on using the meter — *before* getting into the car. Also, make sure your driver understands your destination. If not, find a driver who does. Carry the address and phone number of your hotel, hospital, or recovery resort with you at all times so you can show your driver where you need to go or phone your hotel if necessary.

Remember to tip, although in many countries the 15 percent that's customary in the US is not always expected.

Operator, Information: Staying in Touch While on the Road

When in-country, most folks want to communicate with friends, family, and coworkers back home, and good communications with your caregivers and medical staff are essential during your stay.

Gone are the days of postcards and telefax, now largely replaced by email, cell phones, instant messaging, and other helpful tools. If you're already using email and cell phones at home, you'll no doubt be comfortable in-country once you learn a few new ways of doing things.

Email. The most hassle-free and least expensive way to keep current with loved ones and coworkers is via email. Most countries featured in this book offer excellent Internet access, either free or very cheap. If you take your laptop, avoid traditional dial-up and modem. Dialing out from far-flung places can often be more trouble than it's worth, and high-speed access is available nearly everywhere you're likely to visit.

Before leaving on your trip, access your email account on the Web. Note your username and password, which may be different from those you ordinarily use. If you encounter difficulties, ask your email or Internet service provider how to log onto your email account using the Web. If you can't access your email using a Web browser (like Internet Explorer or Mozilla), consider setting up a temporary email account with one of the many free Web-based services. The three most popular are Hotmail (www.hotmail.com), Yahoo (www.yahoo.com), and Google (www.gmail.com). You can easily cancel the account after you return home.

You'll have no trouble finding Internet access abroad. Most hotels now offer high-speed wireless or Ethernet connections, either in your room or in the lobby. If you choose not to take a laptop, many hotels have terminals in their lobbies with Internet connectivity, but the price is often high and the wait

> If you take your laptop, avoid traditional dial-up and modem. Dialing out from far-flung places can often be more trouble than it's worth, and high-speed access is available nearly everywhere you're likely to visit.

may be long. It's usually cheaper and easier to find an Internet café on the street, if you're healthy enough to venture out.

Internet cafes. They abound abroad. They're usually inexpensive, with reliable, fast connections. Internet cafes can be a welcome refuge from your hotel or treatment center, and they'll sometimes afford you an opportunity to meet and chat with a fellow traveler. Your hotel or treatment center staff can tell you where the nearest Internet café is located. Or, you can do a Google search by entering the search terms **<internet café> <city> <country>**. Expect to pay $2-$6 an hour in an Internet café, with modest extra charges for printing.

> Internet cafes abound abroad. They're usually inexpensive, with reliable, fast connections, and sometimes afford you an opportunity to chat with a fellow traveler.

The more advanced or adventurous computer user can also deploy a wide range of telecommunications services including VoIP (Voice over IP), Instant Messenger, Web video chat, and more.

Mobile phones. If you want to hear your loved one's voices from afar, do a little research into the country you'll be visiting before you leave home. International telecommunications standards vary, as do costs and quality of service. Your best bets are purchasing or renting a "GSM-enabled" phone, buying an international calling card, or both.

The right mobile phone can be a great travel companion and medical assistant. Not only does a mobile phone allow you to circumvent the hassles of international telephone calling cards, it's usually the way physicians and other caregivers prefer to communicate with their patients. Thus, your in-country calls are likely to be as important as calls back home, making a cell phone nearly essential during your stay. But before you invest in an international mobile phone, check with your health travel agent or hospital. These folks often offer mobile phones as part of their service package, and it's much easier to use a phone that's provided for you than to go through the hassle of do-it-yourself.

If a phone is not provided for you, you may want to purchase or rent a "GSM-enabled" phone, along with a prepaid-SIM card for the country you'll be traveling in. Before you do, however, check the cell phone you already own to see if it is GSM-enabled. If it's less than a year old, chances are it is. Contact your mobile phone service provider to find out if your phone is GSM-enabled. If it is, ask to have it "unlocked." Insist if necessary. Unlocking your phone will allow you to use it much less expensively in any other country.

If you do not have a GSM-enabled phone and your stay abroad is a month or less, we suggest you buy an inexpensive, unlocked GSM phone. They are now available for under $100, along with a prepaid SIM card. That way, you can give your cell phone number to friends and loved ones *before* you leave. Although buying a phone is more expensive than other options, you can circumvent numerous hassles and the dauntingly steep learning curve that goes along with mastering the public pay phone system in many countries overseas. Also, purchasing a GSM-enabled phone is still cheaper than dialing from your hotel room, calling collect, or using a credit card.

To learn more about GSM phones, SIM cards, and traveling abroad with mobile phones, visit Telestial, Inc. at www.telestial .com. There you'll find a plain-English overview of international wireless phone use. Click on the "Getting Started" and "GSM SIM Tutorial" links.

Here are a few additional tips for using mobile phones internationally:

✦ Don't let your local mobile phone service talk you into using their GSM plan, which may well be expensive, without allowing you to make in-country, local calls to your physician and other caregivers easily. Insist that your service provider unlock your GSM-enabled phone.

✦ If you purchase a GSM phone abroad, be careful about signing up for a plan that might commit you to a year or more of service. Before you pull out your credit card, read the fine print.

✦ If you decide to rent a GSM phone, either in the US or abroad, you'll probably be tied into the rental company's calling plan, which can sometimes prove significantly more expensive — even for local, in-country calling. As a rule, if you plan to use your international phone *only* for emergencies, renting may be prudent. Otherwise, purchase a phone; it will come in handy on your next trip abroad!

✦ Even if you can't use your normal cell phone abroad, pack it anyway. Many folks find that upon return, a cell phone is useful in communicating from the airport or on the way home. Make sure to switch it off before packing, so the battery doesn't lose its charge.

International calling cards. If you've ever used international calling cards, you know there's a large and often bewildering array of options, with pros and cons for each.

If you choose to purchase a calling card in-country, chances are you'll be buying a card that you "swipe" through a pay phone, much as you swipe a credit card at your local grocery store. You'll be asked for your authorization code, and after giving it, you can dial the phone number. Other calling cards ask you to dial a local toll-free phone number and then enter your access code. While these cards are more versatile, you're faced with a whole lot of numbers to dial.

A more recent alternative to purchasing calling cards in-country is to sign up on the Internet for an international calling card service, prior to departing. After you register, calling card access information and a PIN code are emailed to you. You can also check your billing status online, add credit to your account, and utilize a host of other services. A simple Web search <**telephone calling cards**> will bring up dozens of such companies. We like Callingcards.com (www.callingcards.com). Unlike some of the geekier Web-based services, these folks are happy to help you set up your account over the telephone, and they'll walk you through their services step-by-step. Their customer service phone center stays open until 1:00 A.M. CST—handy if you need help from afar. You can reach them at 888 735.7467.

If you're having no success with calling cards, remember that you can always head to a pay phone, access the international operator, and call collect. While that's a much more expensive option, you'll at least get through. Or, as a last resort, you can call from your hotel room. It's extremely expensive, but it gets the job done. Just remember to keep calls from your room brief.

Additional tips for using telephones abroad:

✦ If you want to place international calls directly from your hotel room or use the phone line to dial out on your computer, inquire about the rates before you connect. As with US hotels, you'll pay a high premium for such services.

✦ Never call from a pay phone or other calling center that takes Visa or MasterCard without first checking the rates. They're usually ripoffs (including Verizon and other big names), and charges of $3-$5 a minute are common.

✦ When using an international calling card from a payphone, try to find a quiet place and avoid calling from the streets, particularly if you are hard of hearing or use hearing aid devices. Hotel lobbies are usually quieter.

✦ Many Internet cafes offer reasonably priced international telephone service, a great alternative to calling cards.

Communicating with Your In-Country Caregivers

Voice. Most folks who travel abroad for treatment are stunned to find that physicians and surgeons are generally far more easily accessible than are their doctors in the US. When you're in-country, your doctor's preferred method of communication may be the cell phone, which can be used for voice, voice messaging, and text messaging.

As part of your early planning and screening for the right doctor, be sure to ask for his or her cell phone number and ask if it's OK to call with questions or concerns. If it's not OK, then ask how the doctor prefers to stay in touch; ask also for the names and contact information of key staff members. While email is great during the early planning stages, once in-country you'll want to be assured of immediate direct contact and prompt responses to your queries.

Although all surgeries come with the same general precautions, take the time to learn the instructions *specific to your treatment.*

Remember that while caregivers abroad are generally friendlier and more accessible than their US counterparts, they are nonetheless quite busy. Keep your phone conversations concise and have a good idea what you want to say before you call.

Text messaging. Knowing how to use text messaging on your mobile phone is a real plus when communicating with your caregiver. In brief, text messaging is email for mobile phones. It's more widely used abroad than traditional email. Keep your text messages concise, e.g. "Doctor Alvarez, please call me back soon. I have a problem."

Going Under the Knife?
Pre- and Post-surgery Tips and Cautions

Be informed about general and specific pretreatment precautions. If your physician has not already briefed you (usually in writing), be sure to ask about food, alcohol, pharmaceuticals, and physical activities that may not be allowed prior to surgery. Ask also about the after-treatment regimen you will need to follow. Although all surgeries come with the same general precautions, take the time to learn the instructions *specific to your treatment.*

Get There Good to Go

Did you know that patients planning to undergo LASIK eye treatment must not wear contacts for two weeks prior to the operation?

Imagine disembarking from a 23-hour trip to Bangkok, walking into your doctor's office for your initial consultation wearing contacts, and hearing that for the first time!

The point is this: take the time to learn about the dos and don'ts for your procedure. Don't assume that your physician has told you everything you need to know—or that you heard, understood, and remembered all of the instructions your healthcare provider gave you. Ask about pre-treatment precautions specific to your procedure. And ask well in advance. As with passports and visas, the earlier the better.

The healthier you are before your treatment, the better your chance of a positive outcome. Prior to your procedure, follow these steps:

- **Stop smoking,** as it impedes the healing process. Smoking also damages your air passages, which makes lung infections more likely. If you're planning major surgery, and particularly cosmetic surgery, your physician will insist that you stop smoking prior to the procedure.

- **Maintain a healthy weight.** Overweight patients are more prone to infection.

- **Inform your doctor of any current or recent illness.** A cold or the flu can lead to a chest infection and other complications. Let your physician or health travel agent know if you don't feel well.

- **If you're diabetic,** make sure that your blood sugar levels are under control.

Ask questions; voice concerns. Too often, patients are timid about asking questions or raising concerns. Or, smitten by a nostalgic notion of yesterday's paternal, omniscient physician, patients trust their doctors to provide them with all necessary information. Remember, times have changed, doctors are busy, and being chronically over-booked is now a routine part of their work.

Thus, especially as a medical tourist, you or your companion has a right — and an obligation! — to ask questions. If things don't feel right, voice concerns politely and firmly. Don't allow a procedure to move ahead until you feel good about the answers you receive.

If your surgeon doesn't provide much information, ask questions like these:

✦ How long is my recovery period?

✦ How much pain will I experience?

✦ What kinds of physical therapy will I require?

✦ How will I know when it's safe to take a long flight home?

✦ When I return home, how will I know when it's safe to return to my normal routine?

Your doctor should welcome such questions. If you don't understand the answers, or if you don't clearly understand your doctor's English, ask that the explanation be repeated. It's OK to be something of an annoyance. It's your health at stake, and getting this information right is essential to your well-being.

Be germ-obsessed. Whether on the streets or in a deluxe hospital suite, cleanliness is a common worry among health travelers. And no wonder: overworked horror stories abound of children drinking sewer water; cows, camels, and monkeys fouling the streets; and kitchen personnel preparing food with unwashed hands and untreated water.

Food- and water-borne pathogens are a significant concern, both here and abroad. In the US, the Centers for Disease Control estimate that nearly 100,000 patients die each year from "hospital-acquired infections" (HAI) alone. That doesn't count the millions of cases of "food poisoning" acquired at home and while eating out. At least one-third of such cases are preventable, using simple measures and precautions. The good news is that — of all the patients, staff, and visitors who walk a given clinic's floors each year — less than 5 percent become infected, and far fewer die.

Although standards of cleanliness vary among countries (some, like Thailand, consider our hygienic standards inferior), infection rates in nearly all accredited hospitals abroad generally rank on par or a little lower than rates in the US.

Thus, whether here or there, risk does exist, however slight, and it pays to be vigilant, following a few simple precautions. When in the hospital, before and after treatment:

> Although standards of cleanliness vary among countries, infection rates in nearly all accredited hospitals abroad generally rank on par or a little lower than rates in the US.

✦ Make sure that you and your companion wash your hands thoroughly, particularly after using the toilet. Remind your companion, physician, nurse, and other hospital staff to do likewise before and after attending to you. They should wear gloves. If they don't, insist that they do.

✦ Inform your nurse if the site around the needle of an IV drip is not clean and dry.

✦ Ask that hair around the site of a surgical incision be clipped, not shaven. Razors cause tiny lacerations where infections can invade.

✦ Tell your nurse if bandages or other dressings aren't clean and dry or if they are sticking to wounds. Ask that discolored, wet, or smelly dressings be changed.

✦ Ask staff members to check on tubes or catheters that feel displaced or may be malfunctioning.

✦ Do deep-breathing exercises to prevent chest infections.

✦ Ask relatives or friends who have colds or are unwell not to visit. If your companion contracts a cold or flu, postpone visits or keep them as brief as possible. Watch out for unclean clothing, floors, or instruments, and bring such breaches of hygiene to the attention of physicians or staff.

✦ Eat only cooked foods, even in the hospital. Drink only bottled water and say no to ice.

Managing post-treatment discomfort and complications. You've been out of surgery for two days, you hurt all over, your digestive system is acting up, and you're running a fever. Was the dinner you just ate simmered in sewer water? Have you somehow contracted an antibiotic-resistant staph infection? Will you die here alone and unloved, a stranger in a strange land?

Coping with post-surgery discomfort is difficult enough when you're close to Mom's chicken soup. Lying for long hours in a hospital bed, far away from home, family, and Monday night football — that's often the darkest time for a health traveler.

Knowledge is the best antidote to needless worry. As with pre-surgery preparation, ask lots of questions about post-surgery discomforts *before* heading into the operating room. Be sure to ask doctors and nurses about what kinds of discomforts to expect following your specific procedure.

If your discomfort or pain becomes acute, local bleeding is persistent, or you suspect a growing infection, you may be experiencing a complication that is more serious than mere discomfort and that requires immediate attention. Contact your physician without delay.

Follow doctor's orders. That advice holds for post-treatment as well as pre-treatment. Physicians here and abroad complain long and loud about patient noncompliance. A large number of patients—40 percent or more according to some reports—simply will not follow the programs prescribed for them. Patients don't take pharmaceuticals, despite clear instructions on the bottle. They don't attend physical therapy sessions, despite inarguable research that shows dramatically improved recovery rates when physical therapy is deployed. Patients don't follow instructions for bed rest, choosing instead to head back to the office prematurely or hop onto a riding lawn mower before they should. If that sounds like you, rethink your strategies—and comply! Your body, mind, and loved ones will thank you. So will your doctor.

Before Leaving the Hospital: Get All the Paperwork

Wonderful. Your treatment was a success. You've rested a little and are now more than eager to leave the hospital for the comforts of home or of that five-star recovery retreat you booked on the Bay of Bengal. Not so fast! Impatient to be gone, and often suffering the woozy side effects of surgery and post-operative pharmaceuticals, patients too often find themselves back at home later, missing important documents that could have more easily been obtained on site. So before you hightail it out of your hospital or clinic, be sure that you have all of your important documents.

> Before you hightail it out of your hospital or clinic, be sure that you have all of your important documents.

Generally, larger hospitals provide complete medical documentation as part of the exit procedure. However, some smaller clinics may rely more on verbal instructions, and they are less likely to build and maintain a dossier on your case.

Regardless, be sure that you have the following in your possession before you walk out of the hospital (ideally prior to making final payment):

✦ *Any x-rays your surgeon and staff may have taken.* Try to get all x-rays and images in digital form (.jpg or .tif files), as well as hardcopy.

✦ *Any pre- or post-operative photographs.* If your doctor doesn't take them, you might ask your companion to snap a few close-ups. While not entirely complimentary, photographs provide additional visual information for your specialists back home, as well as backup should complications arise.

✦ *Any test results,* from exams, blood work or scans.

✦ *Post-operative instructions* (e.g. diet and physical activity precautions, bed rest, bandaging, bathing). If your doctor doesn't furnish you with such instructions, ask for them. If you can't obtain written instructions, arrange a time to talk with your doctor and take careful notes.

+ **Prescriptions, including instructions on dosage and duration.** If the pharmaceutical is a brand name manufactured in a country outside the US, be sure to ask your doctor what the comparable prescription is in the US. Your doctors at home may not know, but they'll feel more confident prescribing for you if you can provide them with documentation from your overseas practitioners.

+ **Physical therapy** recommendations or prescriptions, including full schedules and instructions.

+ **Exit papers** that indicate a discharge with a clean bill of health.

+ **Insurance claim forms,** if you've determined that your treatment is covered by a particular plan or for a particular hospital.

+ **Receipts for payment,** particularly if you paid in cash.

Action Item: **Alert your doctor prior to treatment that you'll be requesting copies of all images, instructions, and notes. Then a medical staffer can arrange to have duplicates made for you. Alerting your doctor serves notice that you're serious about wanting documentation, and the medical staff will be more likely to assemble and duplicate all materials as treatment proceeds.**

Speaking of paperwork, be sure to keep a journal near your bed, so that you or your companion can easily jot notes and keep them in a central place. Keep lists of questions so you don't forget to ask them. Record all verbal instructions and important observations for future reference.

Leisure Time: Before or After Treatment?

Since the recent dawn of contemporary medical travel, the media have had a field day promoting the image of sophisticated, devil-may-care patients jetsetting overseas for treatment, then heading to exotic resorts for two-week romps. Truth is, few health travelers match that description. The overwhelming majority of health travelers we interviewed focused on researching, locating, and receiving quality healthcare at significant cost savings. Vacation and leisure time played second fiddle.

The decision of when or whether to include a vacation as a part of a medical journey depends upon a number of important variables. The overwhelming number of health travelers we interviewed for this book were far more focused on researching, locating and receiving quality care at significant cost savings. Vacation and leisure time played second fiddle. Thus, before booking a week at that yummy-looking mountain rainforest spa retreat, consider the following:

Intensity of treatment and length of recovery period.
While promoters of health travel may imply otherwise, there's a big difference between tooth whitening and a hip replacement. Or, in the words of one physician, "Minor surgery

is what other people experience." When it's you, it's major, and even a simple tooth extraction or brow lift involves pain, swelling, post-treatment care, pharmaceuticals, and possible complications.

If you're undergoing surgery, focus on your recuperation. If your surgeon or health travel agent recommends a great beachside recovery setting nearby, then all the better. In any event, even if you're planning minor surgery (such as simple oral treatment or light cosmetic surgery), build in at least three days of recovery immediately following your treatment before heading out on a vacation.

> In the words of one physician, "Minor surgery is what other people experience."

Also remember that for many surgeries — and for *all* cosmetic treatment — you are required to avoid exposure to the sun for at least two weeks.

Remember also that air travel too soon after surgery increases the risk of deep vein thrombosis, a term that describes the formation of a clot, or thrombus, in one of the deep veins, usually in the lower leg. The immobility of long flights increases the risk, as does recent surgery. You can take preventive steps, including wearing compression stockings and moving about on planes and trains. Ask your doctor about how soon after surgery you can undertake a long, sedentary trip.

Your availability. Most health travel journeys take at least ten days: three or so for consultation and treatment and at least seven for recovery. Thus, if you or your companion works for a living, an extended stay may be out of the question. On the other hand, if you are retired or you have vacation days accrued, building leisure activities into the trip could be good medicine.

If you don't have at least three weeks to travel, reconsider combining treatment with pleasure and focus on what's important — your health!

Your pocketbook. The idea of saving a lot on airfare because "you're already there" is attractive. An added vacation may feel like a free bonus. But vacation expenses add up, and you're still spending real cash for every vacation day you take. Are you sure you want to spend the money you saved by getting healthcare overseas on a vacation you would never have taken otherwise? If money is tight, perhaps you're wiser to plan shorter, simpler, cheaper vacations at some other time, when you are feeling your best. Maybe the money you saved on treatment can be put to better use if saved for later. Patients who opt out of long, stressful trips tacked on to their health travel tend to return home in a better frame of mind — and with fewer complications.

> If you don't have at least three weeks to travel, reconsider combining treatment with pleasure and focus on what's important — your health!

Your personal preferences. Some health travelers we interviewed had no problem taking a week vacation in-country before heading into the hospital for treatment. Others worried the entire time. "All I did was fret about the procedure and all the unknowns before me," said one patient, who underwent a successful knee replacement in Malaysia. "I would have been better off postponing the fun part for another time."

Your companion. When planning your medical journey, consider your companion's interests as well as your own. One patient found that her companion—although a great friend and ally and a huge contributor to her successful heart surgery—was not the ideal fun mate. While in Austria, they had different notions about how to spend their leisure time. Carol liked playing the blackjack tables at Casino Wien; Jennifer preferred chamber music at the Conservatory.

> Patients who opt out of long, stressful trips tacked on to their health travel tend to return home in a better frame of mind—and with fewer complications.

We found the most successful health travel vacationers were either veteran medical travelers who knew the ropes or patients who had lots of time on their hands—at least a month to tag a vacation onto their treatment and full recovery.

If you fall into neither of those categories, consider earmarking some of your medical savings for some delayed gratification—in the form of an unfettered, fully relaxing vacation once you've successfully recovered. Why rush it, when in truth a successful medical treatment and a fun vacation usually make for strange bedfellows? For the moment, know that most successful health travelers focus their efforts on taking care of their bodies, recovering successfully, and returning home happy and well.

CHAPTER SIX

Home Again, Home Again

Beating Those Home-Again Blues

It's something of a paradox: arriving home from a long trip is at once joyful — and challenging.

After all, you've just been to a new and exciting place. Perhaps the richness of culture, the cordiality of the people, or the quality of healthcare you received surprised you. You may have delighted in learning a thing or two about a new land. Maybe you even picked up a bit of wanderlust on the road.

On the downside, you're probably experiencing the expected discomforts of surgery, the side effects of pharmaceuticals, and the annoyances of jetlag.

You'll likely return home exhausted, only to face backlogged bills, clogged email, endless voice mail messages, demanding kids, and a dirty house. Take a deep breath and try to relax.

It's important to pace yourself, particularly your first few days back home, allowing yourself time to settle back into a routine. That's even truer if you're not completely healed and you need additional recovery time.

Communicate Your Needs to Family Members

Yay! Dad's home! He went all the way to India for a knee replacement and came back alive to tell about it. In all the hubbub, family members also need to know that Dad or Mom might still need prescriptions, physical therapy, follow-up consultations with physicians, additional tests, x-rays, and lab work. You, the health traveler, may be unable to return to your full, pre-treatment load of tasks and responsibilities — at least not right away. Let family members know how they can help. Accommodations — as simple as a son who does his own laundry for a while or a mother-in-law who brings over a casserole — can make a world of difference.

Action Item: **Within a day or two after returning from your trip, review your exit documentation carefully with your family and loved ones and clearly communicate the help you need to complete a successful recovery. If possible, form a plan of who will do what, whether it's tracking down a prescription, giving you a lift to the local occupational therapy center, or simply loading the dishwasher after dinner.**

Touch Base with Your Local Doctor

If you followed our advice in previous chapters, you informed your local doctor or specialist about your health trip *prior* to departure. Now that you're back, pay a brief call (or send an email) to your healthcare provider's office and let everyone there know that you're back. Chances are you'll have specific needs, based on your overseas physician's instructions or recommendations. You might need an antibiotic prescription refilled or six weeks of physical therapy approved. Thus, it's best to touch base as soon as you reasonably can, both as a courtesy and for practical reasons.

Most physicians will be understanding and cooperative, particularly if you've brought home complete, accurate paperwork. If for some reason you find your physician uncooperative or uncommunicative, then consider seeking an alternative healthcare provider sooner rather than later. So make that call to your hometown doc soon after returning home.

Anticipate Longer Recovery Periods

Whether treated here or abroad, most patients can expect recovery periods of three months — sometimes even more — for large, invasive surgeries. For less stringent procedures, recovery periods range from a few days to several weeks. Regardless of the intensity of your treatment, don't be surprised if you find that you need what seems like a long time to feel fully yourself again, particularly after a long trip.

It's easy, for example, to underestimate the effects of jet lag.

In fact, seasoned travelers reveal that, for every one hour of time zone difference, travelers should allow one day to fully recover from jet lag. For a trip to Asia, that's nearly two weeks! Typical jet lag discomforts include feelings of disorientation, fatigue and general tiredness, inability to sleep, loss of concentration, loss of drive, headaches, upset stomach, and a general feeling of unwellness.

> Seasoned travelers reveal that, for every one hour of time zone difference, travelers should allow one day to fully recover from jet lag.

Add symptoms of jet lag to the list of unavoidable post-treatment discomforts, and your body's healing voices will be pleading with you to take things easy, at least during the first week after your return.

At home, some patients feel timid about asking for help, particularly if they managed to work a vacation or extended recovery period into the trip. Yet the fact remains that the body needs a great deal of rest and attention. Don't be afraid to voice a gentle reminder that you're still recuperating.

Hold on to Your Paperwork

Remember all that paperwork and assorted gobbledygook the hospital gave you prior to your departure? Forms, instructions, prescriptions, notes, and recommendations *ad nauseum.* Keep it all! Take it with you when you visit your local doctor, who's likely to find those documents more informative and reliable than your personal account of the trip. If your physician wants to keep one or more documents, ask for a copy for your files.

Stay with the Program

We've said it elsewhere in the book: pre- and post-procedure, it's all about compliance, compliance, compliance.

If you've just had dental surgery, you might be asked to use a special antiseptic rinse twice a day. Do so. Or for an orthopedic procedure, patients are usually required to undergo a rigorous physical therapy program. Do that, too. Nearly all procedures come with a regimen of antibiotics and other prescriptions, sometimes lasting weeks. That means you!

Granted, it's no fun to take those big horse capsules or drag yourself to that physical therapy appointment when you really need to clear those 400 emails sitting in your inbox. But consider the alternative: after all that work and investment and travel, do you really want to develop complications that could cost you extra time and money — if not your life?

Fully inform your family members and close friends about your post-treatment procedures and regimens. Loved ones should encourage you to do everything you can to get better, and they should help you follow your program in every way possible. Pepper your calendar and to-do list with reminders — of your prescriptions, appointments, therapy sessions, and other health-promoting activities.

> Granted, it's no fun to take those big horse capsules or drag yourself to that physical therapy appointment when you really need to clear those 400 emails sitting in your inbox. But consider the alternative.

Get Help or Farm Out the Work

If you've come this far in your health travel experience, chances are you are one of those people who "do it all." You're good at planning and problem-solving, juggling many balls at once, keeping myriad tasks and projects in the air, and managing to walk the tightrope of a complex contemporary life. That's why an otherwise challenging, difficult journey turned out so well. You managed it!

> For the first month or so after your trip, demand less of yourself and work back gradually into your normal routine.

Now that you're home, cut yourself some slack. Don't try to return immediately to your pre-treatment pace. If housecleaning was one of your daily chores, use some of your treatment savings to hire a temporary maid service. If you need to repair a lawn mower so you can cut the grass, send it into the shop. You get the idea. For the first month or so after your trip, demand less of yourself and work back gradually into your normal routine.

Stay Mentally and Socially Active

During long recovery periods, it's easy to become bored, isolated, and listless, falling into a rut of watching endless TV or horsing around on the Internet for hours on end. If your recovery doesn't allow you to be as physically active as you'd like or to return to work immediately, try to stay as emotionally fit as possible. Get a friend to bring you a stack of your favorite reading materials from the local library. Invite friends and family members to watch a good movie with you. Take up chess again, or Dungeons and Dragons, or whatever activity keeps you stimulated. Studies show that patients who stay mentally and socially active post-treatment recover better and faster than those who become couch potatoes.

If Complications Develop . . .

If your overseas doctors played your treatment by the rules, they probably insisted that you remain in-country for at least a few days following your procedure. The main reason was to observe your progress and monitor your condition for any signs of complications. More serious than the usual discomforts most patients experience post-surgery, most complications arise within a week after surgery. While 95 percent of all surgical patients experience no post-treatment complications, every patient should recognize the warning signs and promptly seek medical help.

> Studies show that patients who stay mentally and socially active post-treatment recover better and faster than those who become couch potatoes.

Post-treatment: Normal Discomfort or Something More Complicated?

Prior to your surgery, your doctor should thoroughly explain the procedure and tell you about discomforts you can expect after being wheeled out of the operating unit. Discomforts differ from complications. Discomforts are predictable and unthreatening. Complications, while rarely life threatening, are more serious and may require medical attention.

These are some common discomforts you can expect following your surgery:

- minor local pain and general achiness
- swelling (after dentistry)
- puffiness (after cosmetic surgery)
- bruising, swelling, and minor bleeding around an incision
- headaches (side-effect of anesthesia)
- urinary retention, or difficulty urinating (side-effect of anesthesia and catheters)
- nausea and vomiting, headache, dry mouth, temporary loss of memory, lingering tiredness (all common side effects of anesthesia)
- hunger and under-nutrition

Most surgically-induced discomforts recede or disappear altogether during the first few days after treatment, as the body and spirit return to normal. Be sure to report discomforts that persist or become more pronounced, as they might be early warning signs of more serious complications.

Complications vary according to each surgery, and you should know the more common ones. Complications are scary, and many doctors would rather not go into morbid detail about them unless pressed. Complications are rare; most arise in less than five percent of total cases—and generally among patients who are aged or infirm in the first place. So while it's wise to be informed and vigilant, there's no need to worry yourself sick anticipating the worst. Common symptoms of complications include:

- infection, increased pain, or swelling around the incision
- abnormal bleeding around an incision
- sudden or unexplained high fever
- extreme chest pain or shortness of breath
- extreme headache
- extreme difficulty urinating

If you experience any of the symptoms listed above, call your physician immediately.

For Companions

"Hold a true friend in both your hands."
— Nigerian proverb

Joining a friend, family member, or other loved one on a medical journey is truly a gift, but the rewards are many. Some companions simply appreciate the opportunity to travel. Others enjoy the chance to spend one-on-one time with a person significant to them, perhaps to deepen a relationship. With most companions, there's an element of "being in this together" — working through a unique experience and its inevitable surprises, then heading home with a great story to tell!

First Things First — Are You Up for the Job?

Before you overthink that question, here's some succinct advice: go with your first instincts:

✦ If you've already agreed to become a companion and fellow health traveler and you've not been bribed, railroaded, or otherwise coerced into the job, then chances are your first impressions were correct. While the journey won't always be a cakewalk, most memorable worthwhile experiences are less than easy, and they're the stuff of profound and lasting memories.

✦ If you've been asked to be a companion and are having strong reservations about it for any reason, then either talk it out with your friend or politely decline.

✦ If you're on the fence about becoming a companion, you might want to flip through Chapter Two, "Planning Your Health Journey," where you'll find important criteria for a successful companion-patient relationship. In brief, if you're reliable, organized, and like to have some fun, chances are good you and your partner will be enriched for the experience, despite — and often because of — the rough patches you'll inevitably encounter.

Know there are no magic formulas, but a good dose of common sense mixed with empathy and attentiveness is the main initial requirement. Each patient is different, as is each relationship between patient and companion. Use the sections below to get an idea of the broad requirements and milestones, and the rest will follow.

Before the Trip

The devil of any medical trip is in the details. The more of them you and your partner nail before boarding the plane, the more successful your trip and treatment will be. Patients are often distracted prior to the trip, not only by the usual family and professional concerns, but also by perfectly understandable worry about their upcoming treatment and travel. A good companion can help keep heads together, maintain calm in the household, and expedite trip planning greatly.

Use the checklist below to make sure that either you or your partner has addressed each important preparation:

✦ **Passports and visas.** At least a month prior to your departure, check to see that you and your partner either have them or they're on order. Just before your departure, make sure both of you have them on your person, not on the dining room table.

✦ **Medical documentation.** Make sure you've packed all written diagnoses, treatment recommendations, cost estimates, x-rays, lab reports, blood test results, and any other information related to the treatment. Your partner's in-country physician and staff will appreciate having these documents, and they'll save you time and money.

> The devil of any medical trip is in the details. The more of them you and your partner nail before boarding the plane, the more successful your trip and treatment will be

✦ **Kids, cats, and newspaper delivery.** Work with your friend to make sure all the family living arrangements are in order, and ask frequently how you can help. Examples of services you might provide include finding a pet sitter, making sure bills are paid in advance, and suspending newspaper delivery.

✦ **Confirm and reconfirm appointments and reservations.** A couple of days prior to departure, call or email the physician and treatment center to reconfirm all appointments and scheduled treatments. Do the same for your flight reservations, lodging, and any local transportation you've booked.

✦ **Read up on your destination.** If you can spare the time, become acquainted with your travel destination. Check your local library for travel guides, skim them for content, make notes, and then buy the one you and your partner like best. Or do an Internet search for the city and country where you'll be staying, print what interests you, and toss it into your travel bag.

> If you learn some facts about the culture and history, the locals will invariably appreciate your interest.

Although you need not be fluent in the language, at least one of you should know a little something about the local customs, protocol, transportation, restaurants, and historic sights. If you learn some facts about the culture and history, the local people will invariably appreciate your interest. That goes double if you take time to learn even a few words of the language.

✦ **Prescriptions and other essentials.** While you can purchase just about anything abroad that you might have forgotten to pack, it's always an extra hassle to do so, particularly on a medical trip. Be sure you and your partner have packed important prescriptions, an extra set of eyeglasses if you wear them, any creams, special soaps, hard-to-find ointments, and the like. Thoroughly check the medicine cabinet and bathroom counter to make sure you've packed all the creature comforts and necessities that might be difficult to purchase abroad. In these days of tight airport security, it's best to pack liquids and gels in checked luggage, but keep prescription medicines (in their original containers) in your carry-on.

✦ **Finances.** Sometimes even the best of friends can encounter misunderstandings about who pays for what. Avoid damaging a relationship by addressing financial questions early. Spell out expectations. For example, who's paying for the airfare? Lodging and meals? Sightseeing and tours?

Generally, with the more expensive surgeries (e.g. cardiovascular and orthopedic), the cost of a companion is factored into the overall savings of the procedure. However, a tooth cleaning and whitening that's more vacation than medical journey might entail a different set of financial parameters and expectations. In any event, get it straight before the trip, and you'll both breathe easier.

> Spell out expectations. For example, who's paying for the airfare? Lodging and meals? Sightseeing and tours?

While You're There

Once you've landed, a zillion challenges large and small will confront you, and they can be disconcerting, especially if you're not accustomed to traveling. That is where partners are either at their best or at their worst with one another. Keep your cool. Take a deep breath. Seasoned travelers know to "go with the flow" and have faith that all will turn out well. Usually does.

At the airport. Even if you are a seasoned international traveler, touchdown at your in-country destination is likely to be the most challenging part of your trip. You've just arrived in a strange land, full of oddly dressed people who are moving about with a lot more confidence than you are. The simplest of signs are a linguistic mystery: "Does *damas* mean restroom?" You're exhausted and grimy from the trip; the only things on your mind are a bed and a shower. But you have things you must do first. Keep your wits, snag some local currency from the airport money exchange, suffer your way through immigration and customs, gather *all* your luggage, find your transportation, and make a beeline for your hotel or treatment center.

After that, the worst is behind you.

Hospital check-in. As in the US, hospitals and clinics can be chaotic, bewildering places until you learn your way around. Two sets of eyes — and vocal chords — are better than one. Most often, you'll be surprised by the level of attention and care given to international health travelers. In the unlikely event you're not getting the service you need, gently, but firmly, find the right personnel and make sure you're noticed and served. If not, contact your physician or travel broker directly.

Pre-treatment. Once checked into the hospital or hotel, companions can turn their attention to providing emotional support, easing pre-treatment jitters, and doing little things to help the health traveler settle comfortably into unfamiliar surroundings and circumstances. Order flowers for the room? Draw a relaxing bath?

Probably more than any other time spent in-country, the period between the hospital check-in and the procedure is the time that requires the greatest vigilance and the largest number of quick decisions. During this brief time, both you and the patient will be meeting with doctors and staff, becoming acquainted with the facilities, and deriving a mutual understanding about what to expect in the coming days and weeks.

During this period, it's not uncommon for health travelers to experience doubts and second thoughts. It's natural to wonder if a huge life mistake has been made, particularly when far from the comforts of home and family.

Generally, if the surroundings are clean, the staff attentive, and the physicians and surgeons communicative, you and your partner have little to worry about. You'll find that your misgivings are like passing storms — turbulent and upsetting, and then followed by calm and bright light. However, if you and your partner have persistent concerns, particularly about hospital hygiene, staff competence, or treatment outcomes, voice them immediately. Or, if you feel that important facts have been misrepresented (such as physician's credentials, hospital accredita-

> Generally, if the surroundings are clean, the staff attentive, and the physicians and surgeons communicative, you and your partner have little to worry about.

tion, or surgery success rates), arrange additional consultations until you've resolved the problem. No patient should venture into treatment until reasonable trust has been established with the physician and other healthcare providers.

Post-treatment. Even after the least invasive procedures, patients experience discomfort, even pain. Your partner will also probably experience disorientation from prescription drugs, particularly if painkillers are involved. This is the time to be extremely sympathetic and attentive. During the first few days after treatment, patients often encounter discouragement, irritability, and sometimes unnerving mood swings. This is normal for any treatment and moreso when recuperating far from the comforts of home.

This phase passes. The trauma and discomfort of the treatment become more familiar and manageable, the pain recedes, and you both become more comfortable in your surroundings. During those initial days post-treatment, a little blind faith goes a long way.

Here's how you can help in the days immediately following treatment:

Have big ears. Listen carefully to advice and directives given by physicians and staff and then follow them. Your partner maybe unable to retain it all. You might need to head out and fill a prescription or two. Or maybe the respiratory therapist didn't show up, and you need to learn why. Or the doctor gave orders for two days of ice-pack treatment, but the ice hasn't materialized. Often medical directives in a hospital or clinic are verbal. The more of them that you remember and act on, the better the patient's prognosis.

Help stay in touch with friends and family. Just when loved ones at home are most concerned about the outcomes, your partner may not yet feel up to talking on the phone or sitting at a computer and tapping out a reassuring email. When you have a good grasp of how things are going, ask your partner if it's all right for you to get in touch with family and friends. Often, just a call or two will reassure loved ones back home, who will appreciate hearing news from afar.

> During the first few days after treatment, patients often encounter discouragement, irritability, and sometimes unnerving mood swings. This is normal for any treatment and moreso when recuperating far from the comforts of home.

Get away. As helpful and needed as you are, you're not super-human. You, too, require time for yourself — so take it! Find an hour or an afternoon to get away from the hospital or hotel. With a little research, you'll quickly find that most destinations offer a rich array of nearby, accessible excursions. If you're in India or Thailand, temples abound. They are wonderful refuges of beauty where you can usually find a quiet, contemplative corner. If in San Jose, Costa Rica, jump in a taxi and visit the Jade Museum.

In Kuala Lumpur, a stroll through one of the many parks, plazas, or markets will be relaxing and richly rewarding. These little sojourns will help rejuvenate you, and you'll return home with some colorful memories of your visit.

Back Home

Be in contact often. If you're a spouse or close family member who's gone along as a health traveler's companion, then you may resume living under the same roof when you return home, and maintaining contact isn't a problem. But friends who act as travel companions may need to make more effort. As life at home quickly gives way to daily routine, it's comforting for the patient to hear the travel companion's voice or see that friendly, reassuring face occasionally. So check in from time to time, ask if there's anything you can do, and simply be a friend. Recoveries are often lonely periods for a patient, who, despite all other indications, isn't yet quite ready to rejoin the real world.

> As helpful and needed as you are, you're not super-human. You, too, require time for yourself — take it!

Help promote compliance. As one who lived and breathed the patient's experience and heard doctor's orders first-hand, you're best equipped to prod your partner into maximal compliance with every part of the post-treatment program. Good post-treatment compliance is the best way to prevent complications and ensure a fast, full recovery.

Encourage family members and friends to participate. Even if you live under the same roof with the patient, you can't do it all. So, encourage those closest to your partner to participate. Spread out the work by assigning specific tasks, such as bathing, bandage changing, or transport to post-treatment consultations and physical therapy appointments. Sometimes friends and family want to be helpful, but they don't know what they can do. Understanding the patient's needs can work wonders during the important first weeks after the trip.

Help your friend stay physically, mentally, and socially active. After treatment, some patients lapse into relative isolation and inactivity, particularly if they weren't athletic or social in the first place. Get your partner up and out for a walk around the block, offer gentle reminders about church or school events, and do everything you can to keep the recovering health traveler functional and alert.

 Action Item: **Help your partner stay mentally and physically active during the recovery period.**

A Note to Patients about Your Companion

A person who joins you on a medical trip is the best friend you've got in the world. Respect the gift. Both of you are in a new land, trying to process a bewildering range of new experiences, while facing serious concerns about your health and your immediate future. During those challenging moments that confront every health traveler, take it easy on one another and keep the faith that all will turn out well.

When you have specific wants or needs, express them as clearly as you can to your companion. Take the time to verbalize your appreciation for your partner's presence. He or she made a big effort to join you — gave a large and true gift of love. Be as gentle and patient as possible with one another, and the deepened kinship fashioned from your travel experience will be its own reward.

Dos and Don'ts
for the Smart Health Traveler

Much of the advice in this chapter is covered in greater detail elsewhere in this book. Consider this a capsule summary of essential information, sprinkled with practical advice that will help reduce the number of inevitable "gotchas" that health travelers encounter. You may want your companion or family members to read this chapter, along with the introduction, so they better understand medical travel. They can use this information as a gateway to the more in-depth sections of this book.

✔ *Do* Plan Ahead.

Particularly if you'll be traveling at peak tourist season, the further in advance you plan, the more likely you are to get the best doctors, the lowest airfares, and the best availability and rates on hotels. Remember, you'll be competing for treatment with other health travelers. You'll also be competing with other tourists for hotels and amenities. If possible, begin planning at least three months prior to your expected departure date. If you're concerned about having to change plans, *do* be sure to confirm cancellation policies with airlines, hotels, and travel agents. For more information, see Chapter Two.

✔ *Do* Be Sure about Your Diagnosis and Treatment Preference

The more you know about the treatment you're seeking, the easier your search for a physician will be. For example, if you're seeking dental work, you should know specifically whether you want implants or bridgework. If the former, then you'll be narrowing your search to accredited implantologists. *Do* work closely with your US doctor or medical specialist, and make sure you obtain exact recommendations — in writing, if possible. If you are unsure or not confident of your doctor's diagnosis, seek a second opinion. Then, when you know your specific course of action, learn as much as you can about your procedure using textbooks, medical references, and reliable sites on the Internet. (For more information on recommended health research sites, see "Additional Resources" in the back of the book.)

✔ *Do* Research Your In-Country Doctor Thoroughly

This is the most important step of all. By following a few basics, you'll see the process is not daunting. When you've narrowed your search to two or three physicians, invest some time and money in personal telephone interviews, either directly with your doctor or through your health travel planning agency. *Don't* be afraid to ask questions, lots of them, until you arrive at a comfort level with a competent physician. For more information, see Chapter Two.

✘ *Don't* Rely Completely on the Internet for Your Research

While the online world has matured over the last few years, searching for information isn't yet on automatic pilot. Deeper digging — and more effort on your part — are usually required. While it's OK to use the Web for your initial research, *don't* assume that sponsored Web sites offer complete and accurate information. Cross-check your online findings with referrals, articles in leading newspapers and magazines, word of mouth, and your health travel agent. You'll begin to find the same names of clinics and physicians popping up. Narrow your search from there.

✔ *Do* Engage a Good Health Travel Planner

Most countries featured in this book are now served by at least one qualified health travel agent. Even the most intrepid, adventurous medical traveler is well served by the knowledge, experience, and in-country support these professionals can bring to any health journey. *Do* thoroughly research an agent before plunking down your deposit. Contact references, including clinics and former patients. Check for recommendations from hospitals and read articles from the local media. For more information, see Chapter Four.

✔ *Do* Get It in Writing

Cost estimates, appointments, recommendations, opinions, second opinions, air and hotel accommodations — get as much as you can in writing, and *do* be sure to take all documentation with you on the plane. Email is fine, so long as you've retained a written record of your key transactions. If you prefer to use the telephone, confirm your conversation(s) with a follow-up email: "As we discussed, it's my understanding that the cost for my treatment, including an extraction and two implants, will be $1,250. Is that correct? Could you please confirm that in a letter or email?" The more you get in writing, the less the chance of a misunderstanding, particularly when confronting language and cultural barriers.

✔ *Do* Insist on English

As much as many of us would like to have a better command of another language, the time to brush up on your Spanish is most definitely *not* when negotiating that new set of porcelain-on-titanium crowns in Costa Rica!

As you begin your research into a medical trip, consider the language barrier as an early warning sign in your screening process. If a clinic, physician, or health travel service that claims to serve international patients doesn't have a good grasp of English, then politely apologize for your lack of language skills and move on. There are plenty of English-speaking options in the global healthcare arena, and establishing a comfortable, reliable rapport with your key contacts is paramount to your success as a health traveler.

✗ *Don't* Plan Your Trip Too Tight

Most veteran health travelers admit that one of their biggest surprises was the efficiency of medical service they received while abroad. Staff-to-patient ratios are generally lower than in US cities, and the level of personal commitment is often better. Yet, it's best not to plan your trip with military precision. A missed consultation or an extra two days of recovery overseas can mean rescheduling that nonrefundable $1,300 airfare, with penalties. More important, scheduling a little leeway lets everyone breathe easier and gives you the flexibility of adapting seamlessly when things don't go precisely as planned.

A good rule of thumb is to add one day for every five days you've already scheduled for consultation, treatment, and recovery. If you're planning a facelift and tummy tuck, consultation and surgery might require three days, with a recommended recovery of ten days (totaling 13 days). Thus, you should add two or three days to your travel schedule to allow for weather delays, missed appointments, additional tests, and other unexpected events.

✗ *Don't* Forget to Alert Your Bank and Credit Card Company

The consumer fraud units of banks and credit card institutions have recently deployed hairpin triggers for unusual spending activity. Thus, overseas travelers — just when they need their credit cards and ATM cards the most — often find their accounts canceled immediately after using them in-country. Then the fun begins, as you try to connect with your bank's voice-activated customer service line, using your new overseas cell phone!

The easy fix is to contact your bank and credit card company (or companies) *prior to your trip.* Inform them of your travel dates, and tell them where you will be. If you plan to use your credit card for large amounts, alert the company in advance. Also, if you plan to use your credit card to pay for expensive treatments, this might be a good time to reconfirm your credit limits.

✔ *Do* Learn a Little about Your Destination

Once you've settled on your health travel destination, spend a little time getting to know something about the country you're visiting. You'll find a little knowledge goes a long way: the locals will differentiate you from less caring travelers and express sincere appreciation for your interest. *Do* buy or borrow a couple of travel guides, learn a little history, and a few basic phrases (such as hello, goodbye, please, thank you, excuse me). When in-country, pick up an English-language newspaper, which will get you up to speed on current events, happenings around town, and local gossip.

✔ *Do* Inform Your Local Doctors Before You Leave

Telling your doctor you're planning to travel overseas for treatment is a little like calling your auto mechanic to say you're taking your business to a competitor down the road. However, although you may never again see your former car mechanic, you *do* want to preserve a good working relationship with your family physician and local specialists.

Although they may not particularly like your decision, most doctors will respect your desire to travel overseas for medical care. Even if they privately question your judgment, they will appreciate learning about your plans *prior* to your trip. The pre-trip notification will pay off for you, too. When you return, you won't have to make an awkward call, just when you most need a prescription refilled. If your physician attempts to dissuade you, *do* be attentive and polite, but stay firm in your resolve if you've done your homework and made your choice. For more information, see Chapter Two.

✘ *Don't* Scrimp on Lodging

Unless your finances absolutely demand it, avoid hotels and other accommodations in the "budget" category. In foreign lands, particularly Asia and Central and South America, there's often a world of difference between "moderate" and "no-frills." The latter can land you in unsavory parts of town, with cold-water showers and shared bathrooms of questionable cleanliness. On the other hand, hospitals and travel agents tend to recommend deluxe hotels that charge astronomical rates even by US standards.

Press your health travel contacts to recommend a good, moderately priced hotel in the $100 per night range. While such affordability may not be possible or desirable in certain cities — some in India, for example — there's often a huge price difference at the "four-star" or "three-star" levels just below deluxe, where a range of perfectly comfortable, service-rich accommodations can be found.

✗ *Don't* Stay Too Far from Your Treatment Center

When booking hotel accommodations for you and your companion, make sure the hospital or doctor's office is nearby. This is doubly true in large cities. While in-town transportation costs are usually low, traffic and noise levels can be horrendous, and long, stop-and-start crosstown trips can be as stressful as a 24-hour flight. Simply check with your hotel, treatment center, or health travel planner for appropriately located lodging.

✔ *Do* Befriend Staff

Nurses, nurse's aides, paramedics, receptionists, clerks, and even maintenance people — consider each of them vital members of your health team! Often overlooked and always overworked, these professionals are omnipresent in the day-to-day operation of a hospital or clinic, and they wield a good deal of quiet power.

You and your companion might find you need one of these folks most in the wee hours when no one else is around. Invariably, it will be the second-floor lobby clerk who knows how to get in touch with your doctor or the nightshift nurse's assistant who fetches a clean bed sheet.

You and your companion should take the time to chat with medical staff members, learn their names, inquire about their families, and proffer any small gifts you might have brought. Above all, treat staff with deference and respect. When you're ready to leave the hospital, a heartfelt thank-you note and a modest cash tip makes a great farewell.

✗ *Don't* Return Home Too Soon

After a long flight to a foreign land, multiple consultations with physicians and staff, and a painful and disorienting medical procedure, most folks feel ready to jump on the first flight home. That's understandable but not advisable. Your body needs time to recuperate, and your physician will need to track your recovery progress. As you plan your trip, ask your physician how much recovery time is advised for your particular treatment. Then add a few extra days, just to be on the safe side.

✗ *Don't* Be Too Adventurous with Local Cuisine

Chicken vindaloo in Bangalore! Spicy prawn soup in Bangkok! Grilled snapper picante in Puerto Vallarta! Yes, it's true that most health travel destinations also have robust, tasty cuisine, with a variety of local culinary fare to tempt nearly any palate.

Yet one sure way to get your treatment off to a bad start is to enter your clinic with a rising case of traveler's diarrhea or even a mild dose of stomach upset due to local water or food intolerance.

Thus, when hunger calls, go easy with your food choices. Prior to treatment, avoid rich, spicy foods, exotic drinks (no ice!), and eat only cooked foods. If you can't survive without fresh fruits and vegetables, follow the international travel rule: "Boil it, cook it, peel it (yourself), or forget it!"

If you're staying in the hospital as an inpatient, don't be afraid to ask the dietician for a menu that's easy on your digestion.

Use only bottled water, even when brushing your teeth. *Insist on bottled water in developing countries throughout Asia, Central and South America, and even in most parts of Europe.* Make sure the seal is intact.

Finally, find out about drug interactions for any pharmaceuticals you're taking before or after your procedure. Some drugs carry cautions about food interactions. In short, play it safe on your medical trip; you and your digestive tract will thank you.

✔ *Do* Set Aside Some of Your Medical Travel Savings for a Vacation

You and your companion deserve it! If you're not able to take leisure time during your trip abroad, then set aside the extra dollars for some time off after you return home, even if for only a weekend getaway. You've demonstrated great courage and perseverance in making a difficult trip abroad, and you've earned some downtime with your cost savings.

✘ *Don't* Ever Settle for Second Best in Treatment Options

While you can cut corners on airfare, lodging, and transportation, always, always insist upon the very best healthcare your money can buy. Go the extra mile to find that best physician or surgeon. Although everyone likes a bargain, the best treatment doesn't always come from the lowest bidder. Focus on quality, not just price.

✔ *Do* Get All Your Paperwork Before Leaving the Country

Understandably, after you've undergone a treatment — whether a simple root canal or a hip replacement — you're eager to get home, go on vacation, or just get your life back. Too often and in too much of a hurry to leave, patients exit their treatment center lacking instructions, prescriptions, and other essential paperwork. Get copies of everything. For more information, see Chapter Two.

✔ *Do* Trust Your Intuition

Your courage and good judgment have brought you this far. Continue to rely on your sixth sense throughout your trip. If, for example, you feel uncomfortable with your in-country consultation, switch doctors. If you get a queasy feeling about extra or uncharted costs, don't be afraid to question them. Thousands of health travelers have beaten a well-worn path abroad, using good information and common sense. If you've come this far, chances are good you'll join the ranks.

Safe travels!

PART TWO

The Most-Traveled
Health Destinations

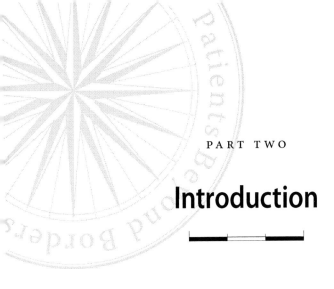

PART TWO

Introduction

Having read the first section, you now have a fair idea of what it takes to be a smart and informed health traveler. If you're reading this, chances are you've already reached a decision about your course of treatment, and you may have narrowed your search to several countries or a particular region.

Part Two: "The Most-Traveled Health Destinations" gives an overview of 22 destinations in 14 countries and includes important information about accreditation, leading hospitals and clinics, health travel agents, recommended accommodations, and cultural considerations.

As you read these pages, consider the following:

Things Change: While *Patients Beyond Borders* is the cumulative result of literally thousands of hours of research, keep in mind that contemporary medical travel is undergoing rapid changes. New hospitals gain accreditation by the month, and entire countries (for example, Dubai and the Philippines) are on the verge of emerging as leading medical travel centers. Moreover, travel and treatment prices fluctuate, countries become more or less stable, and exchange rates move in and out of favor. And, depending upon current events, even our domestic attitudes vary toward health travel—and travel in general.

If you stay informed, shop wisely, and always keep quality, reliable treatment at the top of your priority list, you'll be on a firm path to success as a global health traveler. If you've reached a decision to travel abroad for treatment, we hope you'll continue to look to us for guidance. For updates and additional services, visit our Web site at www.patientsbeyondborders.com.

Customer Service: Hospitals and clinics are busy places, and as much as these organizations would like to cater to medical travelers, truth is they're in the healthcare business, not the travel business. Thus, don't be surprised if some hospitals are slow to respond; and, despite their excellent reputation, accreditation, and references, some may not respond at all.

If you experience poor customer service from a hospital or clinic, try working through one of the health travel agents listed in this book. You may have learned about one from a friend or a Web search. Many agents have partnerships with hospitals, clinics, hotels, and airlines. All of the better agents have good contacts with the best physicians in a given treatment area. Unlike hospitals and other treatment centers, a health travel planner's job is to do just that—plan travel.

Accreditation: You may notice that for some countries we did not list all JCI-accredited hospitals. There are good reasons. For example, Brazil and Turkey, although they boast a high number of JCI-accredited hospitals, don't cater to North American health travelers. Their Web sites are generally not in English, and we found customer service to be poor to nonexistent. Similarly, if a hospital did not respond within a reasonable amount of time to our inquiries and requests for information, we excluded it.

While having JCI accreditation is a watermark for quality and an indication that patients should seriously consider when making their healthcare choices, it is not the only measure of quality. All the countries featured in this section impose internal accreditation standards on their hospitals and clinics. Requirements and oversight vary with each country: Mexico's standards and enforcement, for example, are far lower than Thailand's or Malaysia's, and there's no international body that rates accreditation standards by country or region.

If you're considering a hospital or clinic that's not JCI-accredited, double and redouble your research efforts. Has your hospital met its country's accreditation requirements? How many patients does your hospital see annually? How many surgeries have been performed for your specific procedure? What are the hospital's morbidity and success rates?

Medical Jargon: *Patients Beyond Borders* was written as a consumer book for you the layperson, not as a formal medical reference. Thus, while we've taken great pains to ensure medical accuracy throughout these pages, we often use lay terminology interchangeably with medical terminology, particularly when treatments themselves tend to be used interchangeably by physicians. For example, you might see "tummy tuck" instead of the tongue-twisting "abdominoplasty" or "gum disease treatment" in place of "periodontics." If you seek further clarification on a medical term, please consult the glossary in the back of this book. There we've listed and defined the medical terms most frequently used in *Patients Beyond Borders*. For more information on terms not covered in the glossary, consult a good medical dictionary or your physician.

Passports, Visas, Immunizations: Information listed on the following pages applies to US citizens. If you live outside the US, please check appropriate sources for requirements in your country.

Safety in Numbers: As you read this section, you'll see numerous references to specific numbers of procedures, surgeries, specialties, and super-specialties. As any medical professional will tell you, one of the best ways to gauge the success of a hospital or clinic is by learning the number of procedures performed at a given center. This statistic, combined with the success rate *of a specific procedure*, tells as much or more about a hospital's practices as any other number. Thus, a hospital that claims 2,700 angioplasties with a success rate of 98.4% should provide you more comfort than one that has performed 65 and cannot furnish a success rate. You'll do even better if you can find out the number of procedures performed by your specific physician or surgeon.

Old School, New School: The date a hospital was established is often a good clue to its appearance. A center such as Mumbai's Lilivati Hospital, which opened its doors in 1978, is an old building, despite providing excellent physicians and state-of-the-art equipment. Across town, Wockhardt's new Heart Institute is a gleaming testament to five-star healthcare, yet it lacks a history of treatment for that specific center. Patients should keep in mind that looks aren't necessarily an indication of quality care, or lack of it. A squeaky-clean, fully accredited hospital or clinic that only recently started offering services may not have garnered a sufficient history of procedures and success rates to satisfy you.

To help you navigate this section, we've provided a quick reference "Treatment and Country Finder." Consult this chart to locate the treatment you're seeking, and you'll quickly discover which countries specialize in your area of interest. Then hunker down and explore the destinations on the following pages.

Completeness: With all the changes occurring in the medical travel sector, *Patients Beyond Borders* cannot include every excellent dental clinic, cosmetic surgery center, or specialty hospital. Did you have a great experience at a clinic featured in the book? Did you have a poor experience? Did you have a successful treatment at a place we haven't yet mentioned? If so, we hope you'll visit our Web site (www .patientsbeyondborders.com) and inform us, so that we may further research your findings and broaden the base of information for our readership. You can choose to remain anonymous, and any information you provide will be kept completely confidential.

■ MAP OF THE MOST-TRAVELED HEALTH DESTINATIONS

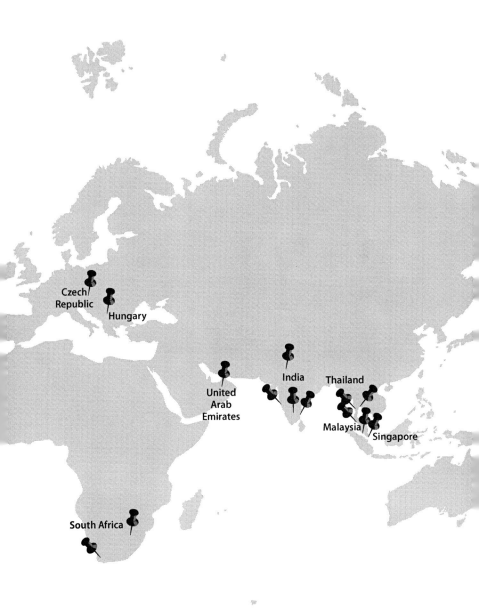

Czech
Republic

Hungary

United
Arab
Emirates

India

Thailand

Malaysia

Singapore

South Africa

■ THE MOST-TRAVELED HEALTH DESTINATIONS

TREATMENT	Brazil	Caribbean	Costa Rica	Czech Republic	Hungary
Cardiac:			■		
Cosmetic & Plastic Surgery:	■		■	■	■
Dentistry:	■		■	■	■
Fertility & Reproductive:	■				
Neurology and Spine:					
Orthopedic (all):			■		
Total Hip Replacement:					
Birmingham Hip Resurfacing:					
Oncology:			■		
Stem Cell Research:					
Sex Change & Cosmetic:	■				
Weight Treatment (Bariatric):	■		■		
Wellness/Alternative:		■			■

Legend:
- Primary destination for health travelers
- Secondary destination for health travelers

India	Malaysia	Mexico	Singapore	South Africa	Thailand	UAE/Dubai
P	P		P	S	P	P
	S	P	S	P	P	
S	S	P	S	P	P	
S			P	S	P	
P			P		P	
P	P	S		S	P	P
P	P		P		P	P
P			P		P	
P	S		P	S	P	
			P		P	
			S	S	P	
P	P	P	P	P	P	
P	P		P	P	S	

DESTINATION:
ANTIGUA AND BARBADOS

■ **AT A GLANCE**

St. John's, Antigua; Christ Church, Barbados

Language:	English
Time Zone:	GMT-4
Country Dialing Code:	Antigua: 268; Barbados: 246
Electricity:	Antigua: 230V, Plug types A & B; Barbados: 115V, Plug types A & B
Currency:	Antigua: East Caribbean Dollars (XCD); Barbados: Barbadian Dollars (BD)
Visa Required?	Not for stays shorter than 90 days
Required Immunizations:	None, although hepatitis A recommended; must show proof of yellow fever vaccination if traveling from a contaminated area
Treatment Specialties:	Addiction Recovery, Fertility/Reproductive Health
Leading Hospitals and Clinics:	Crossroads Clinic, Barbados Fertility Clinic
JCI Accredited Hospitals:	None
Standards and Accreditation:	National Association of Addiction Treatment Providers (NAATP), Association for Addiction Professionals, European Association for the Treatment of Addiction, American Society of Addiction Medicine, Human Fertilisation and Embryology Authority (UK), American Society of Reproductive Medicine

■ TREATMENT BRIEF

While *Patients Beyond Borders* generally places health considerations before vacations and leisure, it's easy to let one's guard down when addressing these two destinations. Picture miles of white sandy beaches, year-round mild temperatures, and balmy winds. The isolation and discretion offered by these two islands make Antigua and Barbados tailor-made for recovery and stress-free treatment. Thus, it's no wonder people with substance abuse challenges seek help there in recovering from addictions, or that couples find the setting ideal for addressing stressful, often emotionally charged fertility issues.

Contemporary music icon Eric Clapton founded the Crossroads Centre in Antigua to help people of the islands cope with their personal addictions. Soon the world heard about the clinic's success, and it wasn't long before the Barbados Fertility Clinic was on the map as well.

The islands also have several full-service hospitals that help visiting patients. Bay View Hospital, St. Michael, Barbados (www.info@bayviewhospital.com.bb), has a friendly English-speaking staff, including 50 physicians and surgeons.

The West Indies islands are located in the western Atlantic Ocean, east of the Caribbean Sea and relatively close to South America. It takes a few hours to fly from Miami to Antigua. From there, it's a short airplane ride to Barbados.

■ TYPICAL TREATMENTS AND COSTS

Addiction Recovery:

Residential Dependency Program (29-day live-in): $19,000

Renewal Programs (5-6 days): Price undetermined at publication

Sustained Recovery Program (per month): $3,900

Fertility/Reproductive Health:

See Barbados Fertility Centre for an explanation of the following procedures:

IVF: $6,000

IVF with ICSI: $7,000

IUI: $375

Related Medications: $2,000

■ HOSPITALS AND CLINICS

ANTIGUA

Crossroads Centre, Antigua
Willoughby Bay, St. Phillip's Parish
P.O. Box 3592
St. John's, Antigua, WEST INDIES
Tel: 888 452.0091 (US toll-free)
Tel: 800 783.9641 (UK toll-free)
Tel: 268 562.0035
Fax: 268 562.0036
Email: americas@crossroadsantigua.org
Web: www.crossroadsantigua.org

Founded by Eric Clapton in 1997, the 32-bed Crossroads Centre (CC) is a non-profit international center of excellence for the treatment of alcohol, drugs, and other addictive disorders. The center's mission is to help people and their families make the changes necessary to find new health, a new sense of well-being, and a new life of recovery. The center deploys the "whole-person approach" to healing and recovery by assisting each client in improving the quality of his or her relationships, career, and social, emotional, physical, and spiritual well-being.

CC specializes in medical detoxification, rehabilitation services, and discharge and aftercare planning. The 29-day residential chemical dependency program includes medical detoxification services, 12-step meetings and groups, individual and group therapy, individual assignments, nutritional counseling, and recovery lectures.

Extra benefits are provided as part of the package to enhance recovery: yoga, auricular acupuncture, spiritual counseling, fitness training, experiential therapy, and therapeutic massage. Included in the total cost is a four-day family outpatient program. Trained staff members help families understand the disease of addiction, improve family relationships, and support the recovery process. In 2006, 87 percent of the clients visiting Crossroads were international patients, with 73 percent from the US and Canada.

Family members attending the family outpatient program stay at one of several (pricey) local hotels approximately 30 minutes from the center, which is a boost for confidentiality.

Aftercare is an important part of the recovery program at Crossroads. CC is affiliated with the Sanctuary in Delray Beach, Florida, a transitional living home for men in recovery. In 2007, the center will also offer five- to six-day renewal programs for people in recovery, in which patients can reconnect with the program and receive help for problems they may be encountering.

English is the only language spoken among the 52 full-time staff members.

Unfortunately, the island has few moderately priced hotels and no business hotels. However, by the end of 2007, CC will have completed several reasonably priced on-campus cottages for visiting families.

Free transportation is provided to and from the airport, and patients and families are met at the airport by a staff member.

BARBADOS

Barbados Fertility Centre Inc.
Seaston House, Hastings
Christ Church
Barbados, WEST INDIES BB15154
Tel: 246 435.7467
Fax: 246 436.7467
Email: info@barbadosivf.org
Web: www.barbadosivf.org

While in vitro fertilization (IVF) is a serious issue for couples, the Barbados Fertility Centre (BFC) emphasizes that it needn't be a stressful experience. The more relaxed resort environment of Barbados plays a major role in keeping couples focused on the positive.

To reduce the stress even further, BFC accepts only a limited number of patients each month. As a day care unit, the center has just four recovery beds. Couples stay an average of 14 nights at nearby hotels and have their choice of comfort, luxury, premium, or elite packages.

The staff of ten includes one consultant gynecologist. All staff members speak English.

BFC has treated hundreds of local and international couples since becoming a full-time IVF unit in 2004. Approximately 80 percent of the patients who visit the clinic are from the US, Canada, and the UK. At least 20 to 30 US and Canadian couples are treated each year, and the numbers are growing.

Because the male factor is often significant in infertility, many of their clients require an intracytoplasmic sperm injection (ICSI), which is an injection of sperm into the egg. A high standard of care, relaxing atmosphere, and flexible embryo culture system (which permits blastocyst culture) all contribute to high success rates, which continue to improve each year.

To date, the center has performed the following procedures: 200 IVF, 700 IVF and ICSI, and 2,500 IUI (intrauterine insemination). BFC boasts cutting-edge technology in reproduction, and the center strives for the best personalized medical care.

BFC has better success rates at all ages compared to national statistics in the US and UK. The center's success is in part due to an individualized treatment program tailored to each patient's needs. In women 37 years and under, BFC's success rate is 54 percent compared to the average US rate of 41 percent and the average UK rate of 25 percent.

IVF costs are substantial, and the procedure is usually not covered by health insurance. IVF costs include medical consultations, private hospital fees, anesthesia, theater fees, laboratory services, scans, and blood tests. Medications are a separate cost. The Fertility Centre ensures that financial coordinators are available to assist in addressing related costs and financial packages and making payment arrangements that suit all needs.

■ ADDICTION RECOVERY ACCOMMODATIONS

The Sanctuary
PO Box 8463
Delray Beach, FL 33483
Tel: 561 843.7399
Fax: 561 278.2292
Email: tgentry@sanctuarydelraybeach.com
Web: www.sanctuarydelraybeach.com

Located in Delray Beach, Florida, the Sanctuary is now a subsidiary of Crossroads Centre. This accommodation brings men's transitional living to new standards. The three-house, 15-bed unit offers the highest quality of service and best possible start to a new life. The 24-hour staff supervision provides needed consistency and accountability in addition to random drug screening. The Sanctuary is located near Twelve Step clubs, where patients can integrate safely back into social settings.

Patients accepted into The Sanctuary must make at least a three-month commitment to recovery. The cost is $3,900 per month.

■ HOTELS: DELUXE

The Crossroads provides accommodations for patients, and in 2007 it will provide on-campus family housing. The Barbados Fertility Centre treatment packages include housing. Couples can choose from a range of prices.

ANTIGUA

Occidental Grand Pineapple Resort
PO Box 2000
Long Bay
St. John's, Antigua, WEST INDIES
Tel: 800 345.0356 (US toll-free)
Tel: 268 463.2006
Fax: 268 463.2452
Email: easst.pineapplebeachresort@
    candw.ag
Web: www.allegroantigua.com

The Inn at English Harbour
PO Box 187
English Harbour
St. John's, Antigua, WEST INDIES
Tel: 800 970.2123 (US toll-free)

Tel: 268 460.1014
Fax: 268 460.1603
Email: theinn@candw.ag
Web: www.theinn.ag

BARBADOS

The House
Highway 1
Paynes Bay, Antigua, WEST INDIES
Tel: 246 432.5525
Fax: 246 432.5255
Email: mbeckett@eleganthotels.com
Web: www.thehousebarbados.com

■ HOTELS: MODERATE

ANTIGUA

Trade Winds Hotel
PO Box 1390
Dickenson Bay
St. John's, Antigua, WEST INDIES
Tel: 268 462.1223
Fax: 268 462.5007
Email: twhotel@candw.ag
Web: www.twhantigua.com

BARBADOS

Allamanda Beach Hotel
Hastings
Christ Church, Bridgetown
Barbados, WEST INDIES
Tel: 246 438.1000
Fax: 246 435.9211
Email: gabriele.cummins@allamanda
    beach.com
Web: vacation@allamandabeach.com

DESTINATION: **BRAZIL**

■ AT A GLANCE

Rio de Janeiro, São Paulo

Language:	Portuguese, some English
Time Zone:	GMT-3
Country Dialing Code:	55
Electricity:	127 V and 220 V (Brazil's electricity is notoriously nonstandard.) Check your local destination for plug type.
Currency:	Real
Visa Required?	Yes
Required Immunizations:	None
Treatment Specialties:	Cosmetic, Dental Care, Ophthalmology, Weight Loss
Leading Hospitals and Clinics:	Albert Einstein Jewish Hospital, Ivo Pitanguy Clinic
JCI-Accredited Hospitals:	Albert Einstein Jewish Hospital
Standards and Accreditation:	Brazilian Society of Plastic Surgery, International Society of Aesthetic Plastic Surgeons, Brazilian Society of Aesthetic Dentistry, JCI

■ TREATMENT BRIEF

Brazilians take beauty seriously, perhaps to a fault. If, for example, you'd like perkier ears on Snoozie your family schnauzer, Dr. Edgado Brito, a São Paulo veterinarian of 20 years, has performed thousands of cosmetic alterations on pets worldwide. Un-doubtedly an extreme spillover from one of the world's most body-conscious countries.

Brazil boasts more than 4,500 licensed cosmetic surgeons, with the highest per capita number of practicing cosmetic physicians in the world. Most international patients head to São Paulo and Rio de Janeiro, Brazil's two largest cities. Smaller, cozier destinations, such as Porto Alegre and Santos, are also popular.

Prices vary widely. While the celebrity "surgeons-to-the-stars" command fees comparable to the highest found in the US, dozens of excellent, lesser-known clinics serve patients from all regions and income brackets.

Brazil is home to the internationally revered Ivo Pitanguy, the world's most renowned plastic surgeon. The clinic and institute bearing his name were established in 1963, and more than 4,000 surgeons have visited the center for training, workshops, and continuing education. Pitanguy and his protégés have set a standard for cosmetic and aesthetic surgery higher than anywhere else in the world.

Yet, for all its notoriety, Brazil lacks the medical travel infrastructure found in some smaller, less developed nations, such as Costa Rica. The Brazilian government has chosen not to follow the rise in international medical interest with corresponding investment, unlike many governments in Europe and Asia. In fact, Brazilian doctors are not allowed to advertise, and any commercialization of medical services is frowned upon by peers. Thus, Brazil's medical community has largely kept to itself, content to serve the apparently limitless local need for body beautification.

To further muddy the health travel waters, the language barrier looms large. While it's comforting to know that Brazil boasts eight JCI-accredited treatment centers, only one JCI-accredited hospital posts Web pages in English. All other sites are in Portuguese. It's one of medical travel's great mysteries that a hospital would endure all the expense and hardship of gaining JCI accreditation, only to serve English-speaking clientele inadequately.

Nonetheless, health travel services are gradually gaining ground, with the numbers of conscientious, reliable agents, recovery accommodations, and travel support services growing. Health travelers intent on Brazil should redouble their efforts to work from a base of reliable information or through a trustworthy, third-party agent

Prices vary widely, and travelers will find cosmetic surgery in Brazil generally more expensive than in Costa Rica, India, or Southeast Asia. The best-known treatment centers cater to high-profile clients, driving prices to nearly US levels. Thus, when considering Brazil, savings will likely take a backseat to a vacation or retreat.

Note: If you're planning to go to Rio, you may want to see (or avoid) the annual Carnaval festival. The *grand dame* of all street fairs occurs in late February or early March, and it makes our Mardi Gras look like a needlepoint convention. If you wish to avoid the chaos, steer clear of those dates. If you wish to enjoy the revelry, make sure you reserve air travel and lodging well in advance.

■ TYPICAL TREATMENTS AND COSTS

Cosmetic:

Pre-operative Doctor Consultation: $50

Arm Lift: $1,450

With Thigh Lift: $2,400-$3,400

Breast

Augmentation (no implants): $950

Augmentation (with implants): $3,900-$4,400

Implant Exchange: $950

Lift: $1,450

Lift/Reduction: $2,980-$3,500

Reduction (women): $1,450

Reduction (men): $950

Brow Lift: $950

Buttock Enhancement (injection): $1,450

Ear Surgery: $750

Eyelids

Upper or Lower: $750-$950

Upper and Lower: $2,850-$3,300

Facelift

Mini: $1,450

Major, with Mini-neck: $1,950

Major (face and neck): $3,000-$4,200

Implants

Buttocks: $1,450

Calves: $950

Cheeks: $950

Chin: $950

Pectoral: $1,450

Liposuction

One Area: $550

Two Areas: $750

Three Areas: $950

Four Areas: $1,150

Five Areas: $1,350

Small Body (all areas): $2,900-$3,200

Large Body (all areas): $4,500-$5,000

Nose Reconstruction: $950

Thigh Lift: $1,450

Tummy Tuck: $1,450

Mini: $3,000-$3,700

Silicone Implants:

Chin: $200

Cheeks (both): $400

Calves (both): $700

Breasts (both): $900

Buttocks (both): $1,000

Pectorals (both): $1,500

Hair Transplants:

Grafts

Up to 2,000: $3,000

Up to 3,000: $4,000

Dermatology:

Botox Injection (each session): $250

Chemical Peeling (each session): $200

Dermabrasion (each session): $150

Lymphatic Drainage (each session): $25

Laser

Hair Removal (each session): $150

Skin Resurfacing (each session): $200

Lip Injections (lip augmentation): $350

Thermage Lifting (without surgery): $2,500

Wrinkle Injections (around mouth): $350

Dental Care:

Crown
  Base Metal: $200
  Nobel Metal Porcelain: $250
  Porcelain: $200
  Gold: $300
Dentures
  Partial (each): $250
  Total (each): $300
Endo Post: $100
Extraction
  Each Tooth: $45
  Each Wisdom Tooth: $85
Filling (mercury-free): $45
Implant: $400
Root Canal
  One Tooth: $75
  Two Teeth: $125
  Three Teeth: $175
Teeth Cleaning (includes polishing): $35
Teeth Whitening (with laser): $300
Veneer (porcelain): $200
X-ray
  Diagnosis: $25
X-ray
  Panoramic: $25

Ophthalmology:

LASIK (per eye): $300-$400
Glaucoma (per eye): $1,500

Weight Loss:

LAP-BAND System: $600-$750

■ HEALTH TRAVEL AGENTS

Cosmetic Vacations
120 E. Oakland Park Blvd, # 105-1A
Fort Lauderdale, FL 33334
Tel: 877 627.2556 (US toll-free)
Tel: 305 433.8377
Fax: 954 565.8052
Email: mb@cosmeticvacations.com
Web: www.cosmeticvacations.com

Based in Fort Lauderdale, Cosmetic Vacations specializes in Rio de Janeiro and surrounding areas. Cosmetic Vacations boasts that all their physicians and surgeons are members of the Brazilian Society of Plastic Surgery—the national equivalent of the American Society of Plastic Surgeons and the largest organization of its kind in Latin America. For dentistry, all Cosmetic Vacations surgeons are members of the Brazilian Society of Aesthetic Dentistry.

Eighty percent of the clients of Cosmetic Vacations are from the US, due in no small part to an NBC *Today* show feature, which created the first stir of public awareness about cosmetic surgery in Brazil. All staff members and partner surgeons of Cosmetic Vacations speak English.

MedNetBrazil Concierge Services, Inc.
136 NE 4th Avenue
Deerfield Beach, FL 33441
Tel: 877 520.8597 (US toll-free)
Tel: 305 428.3701
Tel: 0 800 891.6428 (Brazil toll-free)
Fax: 305 402.2719
Email: concierge@mednetbrazil.com
Web: www.mednetbrazil.com

Christi de Moreas, Brazilian-American owner and president of MedNetBrazil (MNB), was once morbidly obese. Her journeys to Brazil for weight loss and plastic surgery eventually translated into a healthy lifestyle and a new career.

MedNetBrazil was founded in late 2002, after friends were encouraged by Christi's transformation. MNB now serves nearly 200 patients each year from the US and Canada. Christi recommends only physicians who speak English. All Brazilian staff, including Christi, speak English and Portuguese, in addition to some Spanish and French. All healthcare arrangements are made by the agency, although patients are free to call doctors and treatment centers on their own.

In addition to medical fees, MNB charges $300 per week for its medical concierge support system. Services include airport and doctor's office transportation, blood tests, five lymphatic drainage massages, a private nurse for the first 24 hours after treatment, daily home healthcare in your hotel room, cell phone use, plus a pre-operative spa date to prepare the skin.

Patients receive healthcare at one of two São Paulo hospitals in the Santos municipality: Hospital Frei Galvao or Santos Day Hospital. Afterwards, they recover in comfortable flats or apartments, which have a small kitchenette, living room, and bedroom.

Perfect Clinic
Av. Paulo Faccini, 1829
Guarulhos
São Paulo, BRAZIL 07111-000
Tel: 011 55 11.9490.9441
Fax: 011 55 11.6463.3301
Email: contato@perfect.com.br
Web: www.perfect.com.br

Serving Brazil's bustling city of São Paulo, Perfect Clinic caters mostly to Brazilian and European clientele, but some of its staff members and partner physicians speak English. If you don't speak Portuguese, insist on English up front.

Perfect Clinic has positioned its facilities for comfort, with offices, lodging, and partner clinics all within 20 minutes of the São Paolo airport — South America's largest. That's a good strategy, for São Paulo is a sprawling, largely commercial, somewhat impersonal megalopolis; patients interested only in healthcare can focus on the conveniences offered by Perfect Clinic.

Those choosing Perfect Clinic's full package (see Web site) receive lodging in a deluxe room near to the clinic; free transportation to and from airport, hotel and hospital; post-operative escort services between hotel and hospital; post-operative medications; and a post-operative massage in addition to referrals, consultations, and surgeries.

■ HOSPITALS AND CLINICS

Of Brazil's nine JCI-accredited hospitals, only one offers a Web site in English, and callers into these hospitals usually face a large language barrier. The same holds true for the renowned Hospital de Plastica in Rio. Patients who have selected Brazil as a destination should seek personal references, media references, or the services of a health travel planner.

RIO DE JANEIRO

Ivo Pitanguy Clinic
Rua Dona Mariana, 65
Botafogo
Rio de Janeiro, BRAZIL 22280-020
Tel: 011 21 25.2266.9500
Fax: 011 21 25.2539.0314
Web: www.pitanguy.com/clinic

Dr. Ivo Pitanguy, considered the father of plastic surgery, founded his world-famous clinic in 1963 after first studying in the United States and England. The clinic also houses the Pitanguy Institute, where plastic surgeons from 40 countries go to learn Pitanguy's techniques during a three-year master-apprentice study program.

In Brazil, 80 percent of all plastic surgery is cosmetic. In a country with a surplus of plastic surgeons, Pitanguy stands out. The clinic specializes in cosmetic/aesthetic surgeries, including those of the face, nose, and ears, in addition to body contouring and hair transplants. Reconstructive surgeries include scar revision, with skin grafts, skin expanders, and breast reconstruction.

The Pitanguy Clinic is the only known center where two patients receive surgery (even different procedures) simultaneously in the same operating room. Despite this, infection rates are a low 1 to 2 percent. Only local and regional anesthetics are used, and it is not uncommon for patients to converse during their surgeries.

It is a paradox that the most prominent treatment center in Latin America serving celebrity patients is situated in one of the largest and poorest shantytowns in Brazil. The crime rate is high in Rio de Janeiro, and the Pitanguy Clinic is located in a dangerous neighborhood.

SÃO PAULO

Albert Einstein Jewish Hospital
Av. Albert Einstein, 627/701
Morumbi
São Paulo, BRAZIL 05651-901
Tel: 011 55 11.3747.1301
Fax: 011 55 11.3747.1041
Email: capi@einstein.br
Web: www.einstein.br/ingles

The Sociedade Beneficente Israelita Brasileira Albert Einstein (SBIBAE, Albert Einstein Jewish-Brazilian Charitable Association) opened its doors in 1955 as a non-profit diagnostic and treatment center. The hospital's mission was based on four Jewish culture values: *mitzvot* (good actions), *refua* (health), *chinuch* (education), and *tsedaka* (solidarity).

Something must have worked. Today the hospital boasts more than 5,000 employees including 500 full time physicians. AEJH was the first hospital outside the United State to receive JCI accreditation (1999), which was successfully renewed in 2002.

Super-specialties include integrated cardiology, neurology, and oncology diagnostic and treatment centers. The AEJH Diagnostics Center prides itself on deploying the latest services and instrumentation. Recent acquisitions are their positron emission tomography (PET) and computer tomography (CT) scanners. The combined technology allows doctors to locate, at early stages and with great precision, minimal tumor lesions measuring up to 4 millimeters in length.

AEJH is Latin America's largest liver transplant center, performing some 120 transplants annually. The hospital boasts a consistent liver transplant success rate of 90 percent, on par with the best US and European hospitals.

Other specialties include coloproctology, dermatology, gastroenterology, hematology, neurology, ophthalmology, orthopedics, plastic surgery, and urology.

Einstein's International Patient Support Services department offers English translators, appointment and exam scheduling, help with nearby hotels and other lodging, and verification of domestic and international insurance coverage.

■ RECOVERY ACCOMMODATIONS

Independent recovery lodging is not yet available in Rio or São Paolo. Ask your hospital or health travel agent about recovery options. Most agents offer information on post-recovery services and accommodations.

■ HOTELS: DELUXE

We found that many hotel Web sites are in Portuguese, not English. If you are persistent, the hotels will connect you with a staff member who speaks English.

RIO DE JANEIRO

Le Méridien Copacabana
Avenida Atlantica 1020
Rio de Janeiro, BRAZIL 22010-000
Tel: 011 55 21.3873.8850
Tel: 0 800 25.7171 (Brazil toll-free)
Email: reservationsrio@lemeridien.com
Web: www.meridien-br.com/rio/
    portugues/index.shtml

Sofitel Rio de Janeiro
Avenida Atlantica 4240
Rio de Janeiro, BRAZIL 22070-002
Tel: 011 55 21.2525.1232
Fax: 011 55 21.2525.1200
Email: sofitelrio@accorhotels.com.br
Web: www.sofitel.com

SÃO PAULO

Caesar Park São Paulo Faria Lima
Rua das Olimpiadas, 205
São Paulo, BRAZIL
Tel: 011 55 11.3049.6622
Fax: 011 55 11.3049.6699
E-mail: arubbo@caesarpark.com.br
Web: www.caesarpark.com.br

Marriott Renaissance São Paulo
Alameda Santos, 2233
São Paulo, BRAZIL 01419-002
Tel: 011 55 11.3069.2233
Fax: 011 55 11.3064.3344
Email: reservas.brasil@marriott.com
Web: www.marriott.com

Parque Balneario
Avenida Ana Costa 55
Santos
São Paulo, BRAZIL 11060-003
Tel: 011 55 13.3289.5700
Email: reservas@parquebalneario.com.br
Web: www.parquebalneario.com/br

■ HOTELS: MODERATE

RIO DE JANEIRO

Hotel Promenade
Rua Teófilo Otoni 15/4° andar
Candelária
Rio de Janeiro, RJ BRAZIL 22090-080
Tel: 011 55 21.2106.2300
Fax: 011 55 21.2259.9030
Email: reservasbh@promenade.com.br
Web: www.promenade.com.br/ingles

SÃO PAULO

Comfort Hotel Downtown
Rua Araujo 141 Consolacao
São Paulo, BRAZIL 01220-020
Tel: 011 55 11.2137.4600
Fax: 011 55 11.2137.4601
Email: hotelhelp@choicehotels.com
Web: www.choicehotels.com

Hilton São Paulo Morumbi
Av. das Nacoes Unidas, 12901
Sao Paulo, BRAZIL 04578-000
Tel: 011 55 11.6845.0000
Fax: 011 55 11.6845.0001
Email: saomohifom@hilton.com
Web: www.hilton.com

Mendes Plaza Hotel
Avenida Marechal Floriano Peixoto 42
Gonzaga, Santos,
São Paulo, BRAZIL11060-300
Tel: 011 55 13.3289.4243
Fax: 011 55 13.3284.8253
Web: www.mendesplaza.com.br

Tryp Higienópolis Hotel
Rua Maranhao, 371 Higienópolis
São Paulo, BRAZIL 01402-002
Tel: 011 55 11.3665.8200
Fax: 011 55 11.3665.8201
E-mail: tryp.higienopolis@solmelia.com
Web: www.solmelia.com

DESTINATION: COSTA RICA

■ AT A GLANCE

San Jose and Escazu

Language:	Spanish (English widely spoken)
Time Zone:	GMT -6
Country Dialing Code:	506
Electricity:	120V
Currency:	Colon
Visa Required?:	No
Required Immunizations:	None
Treatment Specialties:	Cosmetic, Dental Care, Opthalmology, Orthopedics, Weight Loss
Leading Hospitals and Clinics:	CIMA Hospital, Rosenstock-Lieberman Center for Cosmetic Plastic Surgery, Prisma Dental Center, Meza Dental Care
JCI-Accredited Hospitals:	None
Standards and Accreditation:	Ministry of Health, Costa Rica

■ TREATMENT BRIEF

With so many Americans vacationing in, traveling to, or buying real estate in Costa Rica, many "Ticans" wonder if their country won't soon become the US's fifty-first state. Health travel is huge as well: some 14 percent of Costa Rica's international tourists visit this small, lush country to take advantage of its medical services, mostly cosmetic surgery and dental care. Costa Rica is one of the top five countries in the world most visited by Americans for medical treatment.

Three hospitals — CIMA, Clinica Catolica, and Clinica Biblica — are striving to Westernize and attract international patients. JCI accreditation is imminent. Yet, despite these advances, hospital Web sites are still in Spanish, and most physicians and staff are not yet ready for prime time with English-speaking patients. Lobbies are often overcrowded, with few international patient services facilities compared to the best hospitals in India, Malaysia, Singapore, and Thailand. Thus, travelers to Costa Rica should focus more upon the many fine private clinics, which can be found in the capital city of San Jose and its Americanized suburb Escazu.

Costa Rica boasts hundreds of board-certified physicians, surgeons, and dentists, mostly practicing in or near San Jose. Capitalizing on its success in cosmetic and dental surgery, Costa Rica's international medical offerings have expanded to include eye surgery and other elective procedures such as bariatric surgery for weight loss and even orthopedics.

One of Costa Rica's unique health travel specialties is the "recovery retreat," a hotel or ranch-style accommodation that serves recovering patients exclusively. Situated close to clinics, these retreats have all the amenities of a normal hotel, but they are staffed with nurses and interns who attend to the special needs of recovering patients. Transportation to and from the airport is usually included with the cost, as is transport to clinics for consultation and treatment. Guests in these retreats chat at breakfast and dinner about the latest treatment, and a snapshot of the clientele at any point in time usually reveals the progress of recovery—from the bruised and battered facelift of yesterday's procedure to the confident smile and gait of the patient heading home.

With its emphasis on ecotourism and its long history of relative political tranquility, Costa Rica can hardly be classified as a third-world nation. Perhaps no other country offers the recovering health traveler such easy access to leisure activities. Breath-taking national parks of volcanoes and cloud forests are less than an hour's drive from San Jose, and both the Pacific and Caribbean coasts are easily accessible, with plenty of local and westernized accommodations. For those planning minimally-invasive procedures, Costa Rica's proximity to the US and reputation as a tourist destination offer the best of both worlds to the medical tourist.

■ TYPICAL TREATMENTS AND COSTS

Cosmetic:

Breast Augmentation: $3,000-$3,400

Breast Lift/Reduction: $3,000 -$3,400

Eyelid Surgery (blepharoplasty, upper and lower): $1,500

Facelift: $2,800-$3,200

Liposuction (stomach, hips, and waist): $1,800-$2,400

Dental Care:

Bridge Units (per tooth): $180-$205

Crown (porcelain fused to gold): $350

Extraction (surgical, per tooth): $55

Implant (titanium with crown): $750

Root Canal (per tooth): $250

Weight Loss:

LAP-BAND® System: $8,000-$10,500

■ HEALTH TRAVEL AGENTS

Medical Tourism of Costa Rica
Costa Rica Office: A.P. 459-1260
Escazu, COSTA RICA
Tel: 011 506 353.6693
Email: info@medicaltourismofcostarica
.com
Web: www.medicaltourismofcostarica.com

US Office
2219 Delancey Place, #2
Philadelphia, PA 19103
Tel: 202 558.4619
Tel: 519 488.3129 (Canada)
Fax: 202 558 -8092
Email: info@medicaltourismofcostarica.
com
Web: www.medicaltourismofcostarica.com

Established in 2005, this newcomer was founded by Richard Feldman, who served for most of his career as a hospital administrator in the US and as the chief operating officer of the renowned CIMA Hospital in San Jose.

Serving around 20 patients a month, Medical Tourism of Costa Rica boasts the usual health travel amenities, including assistance with travel, hotel, tours, medical treatment, and surgical aftercare. An optional $300 concierge service provides 24/7 extras while the patient is in-country, plus airport and in-town transportation, restaurant reservations, sightseeing, rental cars, cell phones, and travel insurance.

According to Feldman, Medical Tourism of Costa Rica has sent more than 200 patients — mostly from the US — to Costa Rica for medical care since it opened its doors. Feldman and his team are at the forefront of expanding their Costa Rican treatment offerings to include addiction treatment, general surgery, opthalmology, orthopedics, weight loss (bariatrics) and wellness/preventive care.

A partnership with the deluxe Hotel Intercontinental Real offers private duty nurses and in-room day spa services for an extra fee.

Medical Tours International
6 Forge Gate Drive G-7
Cold Spring, NY 10516
Tel: 845 809.5254
Fax: 845 496.0350
Email: info@medicaltoursinternational.com
Web: www.medicaltoursinternational.com

Established in 2002, Medical Tours International opened its doors initially serving only Costa Rica. The agency has since expanded into Argentina, Brazil, South Africa, and Thailand. Founder Stephanie Sulger is a registered nurse of 30 years, and her staff is composed entirely of RNs. Before accepting a client, MTI screens all patients for health and "travelability."

MTI clients pay no additional fees; the fees are paid by MTI's approved short-list physicians and clinics. MTI refers patients only to accredited clinics and board-certified physicians and surgeons. Services include booking of air reservations, medical consultations, and in-country accommodations; assistance shipping medical records; and pre-op and post-op counseling.

Planet Hospital
23679 Calabasas Rd #150
Calabasas, CA 91302
Tel: 818 591.6681
Tel: 800 243.0172 (US toll-free)
Fax: 818 665.4810
Email: info@planethospital.com
Web: www.planethospital.com

Established in 2002, Planet Hospital primarily serves Asia and Latin America. Planet Hospital has established formal partnerships with CIMA and Clinica Biblica, two of Costa Rica's largest private hospitals. According to founder and head concierge Rudy Rupak, all physicians and surgeons recommended by Planet Hospital are either western board-certified or American educated.

All Planet Hospital's recommended physicians speak fluent English. Planet Hospital's formal relationship with Costa Rica's in-country Medical Tourism of Costa Rica helps ensure quality of service.

For more information on Planet Hospital, see Singapore.

■ HOSPITALS AND CLINICS

CIMA Hospital
Hospital Cima
San Jose, COSTA RICA
Tel: 011 506 208.1000
Fax: 011 506 208.1001
Email: cima@hospitalcima.com
Web: www.hospitalcima.com

The 44-bed CIMA Hospital is the first Costa Rican hospital to be accredited by the Costa Rica Ministry of Health. Affiliated with Baylor University Medical Center, CIMA has applied for JCI accreditation. Health travelers most often visit CIMA for cosmetic, eye, hip, and knee surgery.

As with many otherwise excellent Costa Rican hospitals (such as Clinica Biblica and Clinica Catolica), English is not the language of choice, and fluency is spotty among physicians and staff. Unless you're confident in your Spanish, you'll want to work with your companion or health travel agent to ensure that the language barrier doesn't slow you down.

Rosenstock-Lieberman Center for Cosmetic Plastic Surgery
P.O. Box 657-1005
San Jose, COSTA RICA
Tel: 011 506 223.9933
Fax: 011 506 223.9171
Email: info@cosmetic-cr.com
Web: www.cosmetic-cr.com

Founded in 1982 by Drs. Noe Rosenstock and Clara Lieberman (both still practicing!), the Rosenstock-Lieberman Center focuses on cosmetic surgeries. All its surgeons are members of the American Society of Aesthetic Plastic Surgery, the American

Academy of Cosmetic Surgery, the American Academy of Liposuction, or the International Society of Cosmetic Surgery.

Since 1997, the Rosenstock Institute has been offering courses on cosmetic surgery to selected physicians worldwide, under the sponsorship of the American Academy of Cosmetic Surgery.

Rosenstock offers procedures for nearly every imaginable cosmetic surgery desired, including hair transplant, facelift, blepharoplasty (eyelid surgery), otoplasty (ear surgery), rhinoplasty (nose surgery), fat transfer, lip embellishment, necklift, brachioplasty (arm lift), neck augmentation, breast augmentation, breast reduction/lift, liposuction, thigh lift, lower body lift, and tummy tuck.

Because most procedures at Rosenstock are done on an ambulatory basis, patients should plan to stay in one of the nearby recovery retreats or hotels. (See "Recovery Accommodations" below.)

Dental Implant Costa Rica

San Jose, COSTA RICA
Tel: 011 506.228 0141
Fax: 011 506 289.6984
Email: lobando@dentalimplant.com
Web: www.dentalimplantcr.com

Over the past two decades, the use of dental implants has grown in favor of traditional bridges and crowns, so much so that an entire dental sub-specialty—dental implantology—has made a huge mark on contemporary prosthetic dentistry. While general practitioners can—and often do—provide implantology services, the compexity of the practice and variety of implants warrant the services of a certified implantology specialist.

After several years of practice in two Costa Rican general dental clinics, Dr. Luis Obando opened his doors to offer implantology as a specialty. Services include dental implants, bone grafting, bone expansion, sinus lifts, single tooth implants, crowns and bridges (using implants as the base), and implant-supported overdentures.

The clinic's helpful Web site offers thumbnail summaries of various implant procedures, and a FAQ page counsels patients on post-op care.

Note: Traditional implantology requires two stages. The metal implant is first set into the lower or upper jawbone. In three-to-six months, after new bone has set around the implant, the patient must return for a post, crown and finish work. While the newer "immediate load" implant technique offers a one-step process, its application is still debated, and the procedure is limited by the patient's dental profile. Thus, if you're planning implant work abroad, budget the time and expense of at least one additional trip.

Prisma Dental Clinic

Rhomoser Boulevard, Banco Uno, 3rd floor
San Jose, COSTA RICA
Tel: 011 506 291.5151 or 011 506 291.5252
Fax: 011 506 291.5454
Email: dental@cosmetics-dentistry.com
Web: www.cosmetics-dentistry.com

Founded more than 20 years ago, highly publicized Prisma Dental Clinic is the *crème de la crème* of Costa Rican dentistry. Spacious quarters and a large staff cater to busy Americans and Canadians, which now make up most of Prisma's clientele. Its in-house laboratory, including panoramic x-rays and fully digitized imagery, saves on outside trips to the radiologist.

Prisma's founders, Drs. Thelma Rubenstein and Josef Cardero, received their advanced training in Switzerland and Montreal and at the University of Miami. Both are members of the International Congress of Oral Implantologists (USA). Nearly every type of dental procedure is performed at Prisma, including recent techniques in Invisalign® bracing (clear, removable braces), gingivoplasty (gum surgery), porcelain veneers, and inlays.

While Prisma's fees are still far less expensive than US prices, patients will nonetheless pay a comparative premium for the range of services offered by Prisma, as well for its extensive advertising and marketing campaigns.

Meza Dental Clinic

Condominium Torres del Campo
Barrio Tournon
San Jose, COSTA RICA
Tel: 011 506 258.5530
Email: info@mezadentalcare.com
Web: www.mezadentalcare.com

Founded in 1995 by Dr. Alberto Meza, this full-service clinic now employs seven dentists, surgeons, and implantologists. Clinic Director Meza is a member of the American Academy of Cosmetic Dentistry and remains very much in practice.

Meza Clinic offers a full range of dental procedures and services, including general dentistry (wisdom teeth extraction and root canal work), restorative surgery (porcelain dental bridges, complete and partial dentures, and full-mouth restoration), and cosmetic dentistry (aesthetic porcelain crown

■ RECOVERY ACCOMMODATIONS

CheTica Medical Recovery Ranch

San Jeronimo de Moravia
San Jose, COSTA RICA
Tel: 011 506 268.6133
Fax: 011 506 268.6133
Email: chetica@racsa.co.cr
Web: www.cheticaranch.com

Twenty minutes northeast of San Jose and Escazu, this 80-acre ranch was established in 1996, making it Costa Rica's longest-running recovery retreat. Since they opened the doors, hosts Ruben and Lorena Martin have served more than 2,000 international patients. Their guest register and associated patient kudos are truly impressive.

Medical and related services offered at CheTica include bathing and showering assistance, bandage changing, experienced injection care, dressing assistance, transportation to and from clinic and pharmacy, and patient monitoring (including blood pressure and temperature readings). A full-time nurse lives on the premises, and should complications arise, doctors visit the retreat regularly for patient checkups.

Las Cumbres Inn Surgical Retreat

P.O. Box 1335-1200
Pavas, COSTA RICA
Tel: 011 506 228.1011
Fax: 011 506 228.1011
Email: lacumbre@racsa.co.cr
Web: www.surgery-retreat.com

Nestled in the outskirts of the westernized San Jose suburb of Escazu, Las Cumbres offers specialty accommodations for patients recovering from cosmetic, dental, and eye surgery. Services include licensed nurses and complete medical support staff, special soft-cooked meals for dental patients, and transportation to and from the airport, hospital, and doctor's office. Staff members speak English, French, German, and, of course, Spanish.

A cozy lobby area and swimming pool offer panoramic views of the San Jose valley. Those who prefer the creature comforts of home will find Americanized shopping, dining, and fast food in Escazu's small and manageable downtown area.

Villa Plenitud

AP 165, Ciudad Colon 6100,
Santa Ana, COSTA RICA
Tel: 011 506 249.1339
Tel: 310 492.5529 (US)
Tel: 604 484.5285 (Canada)
Email: realme@racsa.co.cr
Web: www.villaplenitud.com

Canadian-born Ron Blache-Fraser founded Villa Plenitud in 1996. Twenty miles west of San Jose, the Villa offers full in-house, 24-hour medical assistance, transportation to and from the airport and clinics, and specialty meals to suit diet preferences and treatment requirements. The standard package includes all meals. The deluxe package includes a room with a view of the spectacular Virilla River Canyon, daily spa use (including massages), laundry service, two area tours, and complimentary manicure/pedicure.

■ HOTELS: DELUXE

Real Intercontinental

Prospero Fernandez Highway
San Jose, COSTA RICA 1000
Tel: 800 980.6429 (US toll-free)
Tel: 011 506 208.2100
Fax: 011 506 208.2101
Email: sanjose@interconti.com
Web: www.ichotelsgroup.com

Marriott Courtyard San Jose

Prospero Fernandez Highway
Calle Marginal N Plaza Itskatzu
San Jose, COSTA RICA 5024005
Tel: 011 506 208.3000
Fax: 011 506 298.0033
Email: See contact form on Web site.
Web: www.marriott.com

■ HOTELS: MODERATE

Hotel Parque del Lago
Baceocolon Ave. and 14th Street
San Jose, COSTA RICA

Tel: 011 506 257.8787
Email: info@parquedellago.com
Web: http://www.parquedellago.com

DESTINATION: CZECH REPUBLIC

■ AT A GLANCE

Prague

Language:	Czech (English not widely spoken)
Time Zone:	GMT +1
Country Dialing Code:	420
Electricity:	230V, Plug type E
Currency:	Koruny
Visa Required?	No
Required Immunizations:	None
Treatment Specialties:	Cosmetic, Dental Care
Leading Hospitals and Clinics:	Esthe Clinic, Esthesia Clinic, My Clinic Prague
JCI-Accredited Hospitals:	None
Standards and Accreditation:	The Czech Medical Chamber, The Czech Dental Chamber, The Czech Society of Plastic Surgery JEP, The Czech Society of Aesthetic Surgery

■ TREATMENT BRIEF

One of the most popular American tourist destinations in Eastern Europe is the Czech Republic's capital city, Prague, where health travelers will find most of the country's best clinics.

The Czech Republic's healthcare system is in transition. The Czech Republic enjoys long-standing healthcare oversight and strident requirements for physicians and surgeons. Cosmetic surgery in the Czech Republic is strictly regulated by the govern-ment and by the Czech Medical Chamber. Six years of study are required to become a plastic surgeon; three years are required for general surgery and six for cosmetic surgery. Yet, in a country where many phy-sicians in the public sector earn less money than office workers, health travelers must double their research to ensure quality of service.

Over the past decade, several privately funded clinics have opened that cater mostly to international patients from West-ern Europe and the UK. Staff and physicians speak English and provide care based on western-style models. Fees vary widely. Prague has recently seen a great increase in western-trained doctors opening private practices.

Health travelers generally head to Prague for either cosmetic surgery or dental care. Patients cite Prague as a favorite sight-seeing destination. They factor extra travel time into their trips, taking advantage of less invasive procedures and shorter recovery times to enjoy vacations, weekend get-aways, or Prague's endless urban activities.

Quoted prices usually include all pre-operative tests, examinations, surgery, medications, overnight stays, post-operative treatments, and an extra $200 for a friend or partner to accompany the patient. Health tourism packages often in-clude bike tours through the wine country, mountain exploration, hiking, horseback tours, and art and heritage festivals.

For those concerned about antibiotic resistant infections, the Czech Republic is reputed to have one of the lowest methicillin-resistant *Staphylococcus aureus* (MRSA) rates in Europe (meaning that un-like in the US, most staph infections in the Czech Republic can still be treated effec-tively with certain antibiotics).

■ TYPICAL TREATMENTS AND COSTS

Cosmetic:

Breast Augmentation: $3,500-$5,000

Breast Lift/Reduction: $3,200-$4,000

Facelift: $2,500-$3,850

Liposuction (stomach, hips, and waist): $2,700-$3,500

Tummy Tuck with Liposuction: $3,400-$4,500

Dental Care:

Implants: $650-$1.000

Crowns (all porcelain): $400-$470

Porcelain Veneers: $470-$550

Inlays and Onlays: $300-$375

Surgical Extractions: $30-$100

■ HEALTH TRAVEL AGENTS

Beauty in Prague
Skolska 32
Prague, CZECH REPUBLIC 1
Tel: 011 420 221.419.781or 011 420 221.419.731
Fax: 011 420 221.419.703
Email: beauty@beautyinprague.com
Web: www.beautyinprague.com

Founded in 2005 by Tamara Zdinakova, this Prague-based agency caters mostly to a European crowd taking advantage of low-cost healthcare in a great urban vacation setting. However, more North Americans began visiting after an article featuring Zdinakova and Beauty in Prague appeared in a 2006 issue of *Business Week*. All staff members speak English, as do all the physi-cians, surgeons, and dentists engaged by the agency.

Beauty in Prague's standard package includes full consultation with a plastic surgeon, pre-operative blood and ECG tests, full examination by an internist, surgery, all medications, up to five nights in the clinic, and free transportation between lodging and the clinic. Personal services include airport pick-up (although the client must pay a $30 fare) and arrangements for shopping and sightseeing.

Beauty in Prague lodges patients in apartments near Prague's trendy Old Town, a five-minute walk from some of the city's best restaurants and shopping. Apartments are equipped with high-speed Internet access. For families, Beauty in Prague offers babysitting and full day and night care.

■ HOSPITALS AND CLINICS

Esthe Clinic

Na Příkopě 17, 110 00
Prague, CZECH REPUBLIC 1
Tel: 011 420 2.2423.4824 (Plastic Surgery)
Tel: 011 420 2.2423.9738 (Laser Center)
Email: esthe@esthe.cz
Web: www.esthe.cz

Founded in 1996, Esthe has two centers, one devoted to cosmetic surgery and the other to laser resurfacing. Six plastic surgeons and four laser and dermatology specialists form one of Eastern Europe's largest cosmetic surgery centers.

The **Plastic Surgery Center** performs breast, eyelid, facial, nose, and outer-ear surgeries; lip enlargement; liposuction; and tummy tucks, often using endoscopic procedures.

Esthe Laser Center has amassed an impressive arsenal of the latest laser machines and instrumentation, including many of Candela Laser Corporation's high-end devices. Treatments include

■ **Wrinkle removal and lip enlargement:** Acne scars, facial wrinkles, and other irregularities in facial contours can be corrected by skin implant injections, which are applied into the upper layers of skin with ultra-thin needles. The volume of the injections and subsequent water retention smooth the skin's uneven surface and diminish wrinkles. The injections are most frequently used to fill the nose-mouth line and fine lip lines or to correct deeper forehead, cheek, and chin wrinkles.

■ **Spider veins:** Esthe uses a high-performance V-beam laser to treat spider veins on the face, thighs, or lower legs. The vascular laser is also helpful in removing warts and other dermal outgrowths.

■ **Pigmentation and tattoo treatments:** Tired of that "Robert Still Loves Me" tattoo? The Alexandrite laser focuses a 750-nm beam that pulverizes unsightly pigment into small segments, which are then washed away by the cellular system. Pigmentations resulting from age or sun, birthmarks, freckles, permanent make-up, scars, tattoos, and other hyper-pigmentations are treated using this technique.

■ **Depilation:** Permanent removal of unwanted hair from face, thighs, underarms, and other parts of the body is carried out with the Candela GentleLase™ laser.

■ **Acne treatment:** Esthe uses Candela's SmoothBeam™ laser to interrupt the cycle of acne scarring, caused by the hardening of the upper layer of skin around plugged pores (which become inflamed and then produce even more pore-clogging oil). This noninvasive procedure is used to treat ongoing acne, as well as old acne scars. Up to three sessions are usually required, combined with chemical peeling.

Esthesia Clinic

Trojská 163/28, 182 00
Prague, CZECH REPUBLIC 8
Tel: 011 420 2.8468.0530
Email: info@esthesia.cz
Web: www.esthesia.cz

Four doctors and a staff of six run this small clinic in the heart of Prague. Esthesia is one of the few clinics in Prague affiliated with the Czech Dental Chamber, Czech Orthodontic Society, and the Czech Society for Pediatric Dentistry. The clinic offers extractions, including wisdom teeth; implants; pediatric and adult orthodontics; periodontics; prosthetics, including ceramic veneer, crowns, bridgework, and dentures; restorative dentistry; and root canals.

Dentaktiv Clinic

Lumírova 21, 128 00
Prague, CZECH REPUBLIC 2
Tel: 011 420 2.2493.6589
Email: info@dentaktiv.cz
Web: www.dentaktiv.cz

Located in downtown Prague, Dentaktiv's claim to fame is its long workday—from 7 a.m. to 10 p.m., plus on the weekends (by request). The clinic's six doctors and sur-

geons handle the usual gamut, including bridges, cosmetic dentistry, crowns, dentures, fillings, implants, pediatric dentistry, periodontics, root canals, and teeth whitening. Dentaktiv also specializes in diagnoses and treatment of temporomandibular joint syndrome (TMJ), the troublesome jaw disorder often caused by trauma or stress.

MyClinic Prague

Panská 5, 110 00
Prague, CZECH REPUBLIC 1
Tel: 011 420 2.9682.7530
Fax: 011 420 2,9682.7532
Email: info@myclinic.cz
Web: www.myclinic.cz

Highly specialized, MyClinic deploys injectables to reduce the signs of aging skin. Procedures help to diminish skin irregularities and coarseness, increase skin tone, reduce the depth of wrinkle lines or size of pores, and unify color of irregular skin pigmentations. Other treatments help to diminish minor acne scars and improve acne-prone skin conditions.

The favored treatment is the highly touted Botox/Dysport™, used mostly to relax facial expression lines. Other injectables and treatments include

■ **Bio-Alcamid:** implants for cosmetic corrections, deep wrinkles, and folds.

■ **Restylane:** a naturally occurring acid, used for smoothing wrinkles and furrows and improving the contours of the lips.

■ **Silicon Oil/PMS:** implants applied by injection, used for fuller lips and filling minor wrinkles.

■ **Beautical:** temporary implant to correct deeper wrinkles, furrows, and reduced skin volume.

■ **Chemical Peeling:** application of fruit acids to improve skin tone and elasticity.

MyClinic is entirely outpatient; a typical visit lasts two to three hours, including consultation, "before" and "after" photos, and treatment. MyClinic employs two full-time staff physicians, both certified by the Czech Medical Chamber.

Prices are generally about half what you would expect to pay for similar treatments in the US or Canada. While it may not be worth a trip solely for a Restylane fix, while in Prague. . .

■ HOTELS: DELUXE

Hotel Constans
Břetislavova 309
118 00 Malá Strana
Prague, CZECH REPUBLIC 1
Tel: 011 420 2.3409.1818
Fax: 011 420 2.3409.1860
E-mail: hotel@hotelconstans.cz
Web: www.hotelconstanz.cz

Hilton Prague
Pobrezni 1
Prague, CZECH REPUBLIC 186 00
Tel: 011 420 2.2484.1111
Fax: 011 420 2.2484.2378
Email: guestcentre.prague@hilton.com
Web: www.hilton.com

Hotel U Prince
Staroměstské náměstí 11000
Prague, CZECH REPUBLIC 1
Tel: 011 420 2.2421.3807
Email: info@hoteluprince.com
Web: www.hoteluprince.cz

■ HOTELS: MODERATE

Golden Tulip Hotel
Hybernska 42
Prague, CZECH REPUBLIC 11000
Tel: 011 420 2.2410.0100
Fax: 011 420 2.2410.0180
Email: info@tulipinnterminus.com
Web: www.tulipinnterminus.com

Hotel Anna
Budecska 17
Prague, CZECH REPUBLIC 2 12000
Tel: 011 420 2.2251.3111
Fax: 011 420 2.2251.5158
Email: sales@hotelanna.cz
Web: www.hotelanna.cz

DESTINATION: NORTHWESTERN HUNGARY AND BUDAPEST

■ AT A GLANCE

Budapest; Northwestern Hungary (Gyor, Masonmagyarovar, Heviz, Szombathely)

Language:	Hungarian (little English spoken)
Time Zone:	GMT +1
Country Dialing Code:	36
Electricity:	230 Volts
Currency:	Forint (HUF)
Visa Required?	Not for stays shorter than 90 days
Required Immunizations:	None
Treatment Specialties:	Dental Care
Leading Hospitals and Clinics:	Villanyi Dent (Budapest), Gelenscer Dental Clinic (Heviz), Smile Dental Surgery (Gyor)
JCI-Accredited Hospitals:	None
Standards and Accreditation:	Hungarian Accreditation Council, Association of Hungarian Medical Societies, Hungarian Medical Chamber

■ TREATMENT BRIEF

Hungary is no stranger to health tourism; for centuries the well-heeled have been flocking to its restorative mineral springs, lakes, baths, and spas.

Since Hungary's admission to the European Union in 2004, travel and communications have grown easier. German and Swiss patients head to Hungary — literally by the busloads — for inexpensive, high-quality dental work, and patients from the US and Canada are beginning to catch on as well. Hungary boasts more dentists per capita than any other country, and post–Cold War Hungarian dentists pride themselves on their state-of-the-art equipment. Standards are changing as well. With its admission to the EU, Hungary has begun to upgrade accreditation and care standards to match those of Western Europe.

Hungary's cosmopolitan capital, Budapest, boasts the country's largest number of dental clinics—although they tend to be the region's most expensive. Dental travel agents also offer trips to smaller, sleepier (and more economical) towns such as Masonmagyarovar and Gyor, both near the Austrian border. Although a small town of 30,000 inhabitants, Masonmagyarovar is home to an incredible 160 dental offices!

While it's economical for Europeans to travel to Hungary for a dental checkup or a cleaning, most American patients traveling to Hungary are seeking more extensive care, including cosmetic oral surgeries, full-mouth restorations, and implants. Such work can be had at less than half the US price, including travel and accommodations.

Hungarian dentists must complete five years of dental training. In order to practice, a dentist must be registered with the Hungarian Medical Chamber. Accreditation and standards are set by the State National Health Commission and Medical Service, Hungarian Medical Chamber, and International Society of Aesthetic Plastic Surgeons. All that said, compliance to standards varies widely in Hungary, and health travelers should doubly rely on trusted sources, such as referrals or a reputable health travel agent.

As in so many other Eastern European countries that have suffered decades of repression and second-class treatment, the infrastructure remains spotty. The healthcare sector is no exception, so be sure to do your homework. Either engage the services of a health travel planner or check references carefully.

■ TYPICAL TREATMENTS AND COSTS

Dental Care:

Bridge Units (per tooth): $180-$205
Crown (porcelain fused to gold): $225-$260
Extraction (surgical, per tooth): $80-$125
Implant (titanium with crown): $950-$1,100
Root Canal: $80-$130

■ HEALTH TRAVEL AGENTS

Dental Value
Tel: 775 852.5105 (Posh Journeys in US)
Tel: 011 36 70.586.9600
Email: florian@dental-value.com
Web: www.dental-value.com

Based in Hungary and operated by founder Florian Scheuer, Dental Value serves US and Canadian patients in partnership with Posh Journeys of Reno, Nevada (see below).

Dental Value primarily works with Dr. Frank Kannmann and Dr. Alexander Schreiner, English-speaking German dentists who have moved their practices to Hungary (Masonmagyarovar and Budapest, respectively).

Scheuer will meet you at the airport, accompany you on your first visit to the dental office, and introduce you to the dentist and staff. He can arrange car rental, and he will provide patients with a mobile phone so the dentist and their family at home can reach them.

Hungarian Dental Travel
Manor Farm Offices
Aubourn, Lincoln
Lincolnshire, UNITED KINGDOM LN5 9DX
Tel: 011 44 1522.789.156
Tel: 707 751.1932 (US)
Fax: 011 44 1522.789.157
Email: customerservices@hungarian
dentaltravel.co.uk
Web: www.hungariandentaltravel.com

Established in 2005, Hungarian Dental Travel caters exclusively to health travelers heading to Hungary for dental work. Based in the UK, HDT sends approximately 30 patients to Hungary each month, including an increasing number of Americans.

After personally interviewing more than 100 dentists and clinics in Budapest and Northwest Hungary, founder Chris Hall selected seven, based on credentials, accreditation, emphasis on oral health, and patient satisfaction. All speak English, most have at least some training in Europe and the US, and most deploy state-of-the-art techniques and instrumentation. All major dental procedures are offered.

Both the US and UK offices can help Americans and Canadians with flight scheduling and airport transfers, transportation to and from airports, local transportation to and from surgery, hotel bookings, managing medical documentation (such as patient records, x-rays), and clinic and physician recommendations.

Posh Journeys
530 East Patriot Blvd.
Reno, NV 89511
Tel: 775 852.5105
Fax: 775 852.5105
Email: contact@poshjourneys.com
Web: www.poshjourneys.com

This Reno-based travel company, run by Jack and Helga van Horn, has been conducting international tours since 1987. Following their own positive dental treatment experience in Hungary, the couple has been arranging dental travel to Hungary for their clients since 2001.

Posh Journeys works with their Hungary-based partner Florian Scheuer of Dental Value (see above) to arrange airline tickets, airport transfers, lodging, and sightseeing. Posh/Dental Travel offers a wide range of accommodation options, from full-service spa hotels complete with hot springs to condominiums with kitchens, so patients can cook their own meals from food bought at a local market.

Posh Journeys/Dental Travel arranges health journeys to Budapest, as well as to selected towns in northwestern Hungary. A 15-minute videotape that explains procedures and processes is available upon request.

■ HOSPITALS AND CLINICS

Note: Dental clinics literally line the streets in northwestern Hungarian towns like Heviz, Mosonmagyarovar, and Gyor, with wide variations in service and expertise. Even the top clinics can vary in the amount of English spoken and the level of customer service. The clinics below represent the best Hungary has to offer. Travelers to Hungary should make an extra effort to attain the highest comfort level with their clinic and doctor. The services of a good health travel agent are recommended.

BUDAPEST

Villanyi Dent
6 Villanyi Street Room 1, First Floor
Budapest, HUNGARY 1114
Tel: 011 36 1.279.1184
Fax: 011 36 1.466.9566
Email: info@villanyident.hu
Web: www.villanyident.hu

Established in 1999, Villanyi Dent is located in the heart of Budapest. With seven practicing dentists and surgeons, this clinic's warm surroundings near the banks of the Danube are a plus for visitors. All dentists speak English.

Dental services include cosmetic, crowns and bridges, extractions, fillings, implants, inlays and onlays, orthodontics, and veneers.

The clinic conducts extensive previsit consultations and works closely with the highly regarded Hubi-Labi Technical Laboratory for all its imagery and lab work.

NORTHWESTERN HUNGARY

Eurodent Dental Clinic
Gyori Kapu u. 7
Mosonmagyarovar, HUNGARY H – 9200
Tel: 011 36 96.578.250
Fax: 011 36 96.217.200
Email: eurodent@eurodent.hu
Web: www.eurodent.hu

Established in 1993, six dentists and a staff of 20 serve mostly Europeans seeking to combine Viennese vacations with dental checkups and cleanings. Vienna is less than 90 minutes away, and border crossings have become much easier for tourists.

Treatments include closed sinus elevations; cosmetic and preservative fillings, inlays, and veneers; laser therapies; oral surgery (extractions, root canals); prosthetics (crown and bridge removal and a variety of metal and nonmetal crowns, including zirconium); and restorations.

Gelenscer Dental Clinic
Vorosmarty St. 75
Heviz, HUNGARY H-8380
Tel: 001 36 83.340.183
Fax: 001 36 83.540.253
Email: info@gelencserdental.hu
Web: www.gelencserdental.hu

Nine dentists, eight technicians and a total staff of 22 make up one of Heviz's largest dental clinics. Established more than 30 years ago, Gelenscer boasts its own lab, where most of the bridges, crowns, and other dental work are done onsite. Bone grafting and implants are specialties. All dentists speak English.

Isis Dental Clinic
Thokoly u. 16
Szombathely, HUNGARY H-9700
Tel: 011 36 94.339.155
Fax: 011 36 94.510.892
Email: isisdental@isisdental.hu
Web: www.isisdental.hu

Located at the foot of the Alps in Szombathely (one of Hungary's oldest towns, established in 43 AD by Roman Emperor Claudius), Isis Dental offers the full range of diagnoses, treatments, and surgeries. An onsite laboratory helps shorten wait periods for crowns, dentures, and implants. Implantolgists boast the use of products from Oraltronics and Nobel Biocare, two well-known European dental manufacturers.

Isis offers three-, six- and nine-day "Dental Week" packages that include free pick-up and drop-off to and from Vienna or Graz, consultations, and various treatments.

For those planning annual visits, the clinic offers a five-year guarantee on all prosthetic work with annual checkups.

Laserdent Dental Centre
2. Kolbai Str.
Mosonmagyarovar, HUNGARY 9200
Tel: 001 36 96.217.532
Fax: 001 36 96.217.532
Email: info@laserdent.hu
Web: www.laserdent.hu

Certified by the International Organization for Standardization (ISO), Laserdent was established in 1989 in Mosonmagyarovar, a scenic town near the Austrian border peppered with dental clinics catering to Western Europeans. In fact, many Europeans

(and increasingly Americans) first travel to Vienna to tour the city or catch a musical event, then rent a car to make the 90-minute drive across the border to Mosonmagyarovar.

Diagnoses and treatments are carried out by seven doctors and three specialists, all with more than 15 years' experience. Laserdent's oral surgeon has 30 years' experience, and has performed more than 3,000 implants. Seven dental technicians run Laserdent's extensive onsite laboratory, which helps speed the preparation of prosthetics.

Treatments include closed and open periodontal surgery, cosmetic dentistry and gum treatment, extractions, implants, periodontal treatment with lasers, prosthetic and prosthodontics, and root canals.

Laserdent provides written guarantees of three to five years on all work.

The comfortable lobby boasts an Internet connection, and Laserdent provides free transportation to and from the local airport.

■ RECOVERY LODGING

We found recovery accommodations in northwest Hungary drab, offering uninspired service. You're better off staying in hotels, many of which offer transportation, special diets, and other medical amenities to health travelers.

■ HOTELS: DELUXE

BUDAPEST

Gresham Palace Four Seasons Hotel
Roosevelt Ter 5-6
Budapest, HUNGARY H-1051
Tel: 011 36 1.268.6000
Fax: 011 36 1.268.5000
Email: budapest.reservations@fourseasons
.com
Web: www.greshampalace.com

NORTHWESTERN HUNGARY

Naturmet Hotel Carbona
Attila u. 1
Heviz, HUNGARY H-8380
Tel: 011 36 83.501.500
Fax: 011 36 83.340.468
Email: hotel@carbona.hu
Web: www.carbona.hu

■ HOTELS: MODERATE

BUDAPEST

Danubius Hotel Flamenco
Tas vezer u. 3-7
1113 Budapest, HUNGARY
Tel: 011 36 1.889.5600
Fax: 011 36 1.889.5651
Email: flamenco.reservations@danubius
group.com
Web: www.danubiushotels.com/flamenco

NORTHWESTERN HUNGARY

Hotel Arany Szarvas
Rado Setany 1
Gyor, HUNGARY H-9025
Tel: 011 36 96.517.
Fax: 011 36 96.517.454
E-mail: salidus.aranyszarvas@axelero.hu
Web: www.aranyszarvas-gyor.hu

Thermal-Hotel Mosonmagyarovar
Kolbai Karoly
Mosonmagyarovar, HUNGARY
Tel: 001 36 96.206.871
Fax: 001 36 96.206.872
Email: thermhot@axelero.hu
Web: www.thermal-movar.hu

DESTINATION: INDIA: DELHI

■ AT A GLANCE

Delhi

Language:	Hindi (English widely spoken)
Time Zone:	GMT +5
Country Dialing Code:	91
Electricity:	230 volts, 50Hz; two- and three-pin round plugs standard
Currency:	Rupee
Visa Required?:	Yes
Required Immunizations:	None
Treatment Specialties:	Cardiovascular, Cosmetic, Dental Care, General Surgery, Ophthalmology, Orthopedics, Transplants, Weight Loss
Leading Hospitals and Clinics:	Apollo Hospital, Escorts Heart Institute and Research Center, Max Healthcare
JCI-Accredited Hospitals:	Apollo Hospital
Standards and Accreditation:	Ministry of Health and Family Welfare, Indian Medical Association, Indian Health Care Federation, JCI

■ TREATMENT BRIEF

Note: This section serves as an introduction to India's medical services, as well as an overview of Delhi. Readers interested in the three other Indian destinations featured in this section (Bangalore, Chennai, and Mumbai) will find the information below of interest as well.

INDIA OVERVIEW

Who could have guessed ten years ago that India would grow into one of the world's most popular destinations for health travelers? Driven by a surging economy, a surplus of well-trained healthcare practitioners and a proven national penchant for international outsourcing of customer service, India now aims to be the leader in health travel. Serving more than 150,000 international patients annually, it's off to a good start.

India's official national health policy encourages medical travel as part of its economy's "export" activities, even though the services are performed within India. The government uses revenues generated from medical travel to increase its holdings in foreign currency.

With government and corporate investment solidly behind its healthcare system, more hospitals and super-specialty centers are in the works. The most recent example is "Medicity," a $250 million collaboration between India and General Electric, which will produce a multispecialty hospital in Gurgaon modeled after Mayo Clinic and Johns Hopkins in the US. The hospital will primarily serve an international clientele.

India's medical educational system produces nearly 30,000 physicians and nurses annually. Unlike its Asian counterparts, which have traditionally encouraged medical travel by aggressively recruiting foreign top-of-the-line physicians, India produces some of the world's finest physicians and surgeons internally, with excellent in-country teaching hospitals and research centers. (Many Indian physicians have joined American hospitals. At last count some 35,000 Indian specialists practice in the United States!)

India clearly has a two-tier health delivery system. Because of its widespread poverty, the Indian public healthcare system offers medical care to the poor at little or no cost. Few in India can afford treatments such as cosmetic surgery and other elective treatments that attract foreign patients.

The good news is that large, private hospitals are plowing profits from their international business into improved healthcare services for the indigent.

Currently, India's medical travel industry is clipping along at a 30 percent growth rate annually. Recently, those gains have come from increasing numbers of Americans, Canadians, and Europeans seeking treatment, particularly the more expensive cardiac and orthopedic surgeries, for which health travelers can save tens of thousands of dollars compared to the cost of treatment at home.

Most patients traveling to India stay in one of the larger cities, such as Bangalore, Delhi, Chennai, or Mumbai, where the best private hospitals are located. For more information, see those city entries.

DELHI

Most health travelers heading to India come to Delhi for super-specialty cardiovascular or orthopedic treatment. The city has more than its share of 200+-bed hospitals, including the JCI-accredited Indraprastha Apollo Hospital, Max Healthcare, and the acclaimed Escorts Heart Institute and Research Center. Apollo, India's largest healthcare provider, owns 37 hospitals and 7,000 beds. In Delhi, cardiac patients are often treated at the Escorts Heart Institute, headquartered there with eight centers throughout the subcontinent. Max Healthcare has several super-specialty centers, all located in New Delhi.

Health travelers willing to undergo the long flight and endure the bustling capital city will find nearly every treatment specialty available, including knee replacements, cosmetic surgery, heart bypass surgery, valve replacement, prostate surgery, spinal rehabilitation, dental care, cataract removal, bone marrow transplants, neurosurgery, radiotherapy for brain tumors, hair restoration, and preventative healthcare checks.

New Delhi is sprawling, busy, noisy, and, as the name implies, relatively new. Although startling cultural and economic contrasts exist, travelers are likely to find themselves more at home in Delhi than in other Indian cities such as Mumbai or Chennai. Delhi is the nearest medical center and point of departure for those patients willing and able to visit India's star tourist attraction, the Taj Mahal in Agra (about 200 kilometers, or 120 miles, away).

■ TYPICAL TREATMENTS AND COSTS

Cardiovascular:

Coronary Artery Bypass Graft: $7,300

Bypass + Valve Replacement (single): $9,850

Bypass + Valve Replacement (double): $11,600

Pacemaker:

Single-chamber: $5,400

Double-chamber: $7,500

Cosmetic:

Breast:

Augmentation: $2,750-$4,400

Lift/Reduction: $2,750-$4,200

Facelift: $4,750

Liposuction (stomach, hips, and waist): $825-$2,200

Dental Care:

Crowns (all porcelain): $300

Extractions (wisdom teeth): $675-$1,200

Implants: $925

Inlays and Onlays: $500-$900

Veneers (porcelain): $350

General Surgery:

Gall Bladder Removal: $1,500-$2,000

Prostate Surgery (TURP): $5,400

Ophthalmology:

LASIK (per eye): $675

Glaucoma (per eye): $875

Orthopedics:

Birmingham Hip Resurfacing: $8,250

Replacement:

Ankle Joint: $5,850

Total Hip: $7,850

Total Knee: $7,000

Total Shoulder: $6,950

Weight Loss:

LAP-BAND® System: $5,500

Gastric Bypass: $6,000

■ HEALTH TRAVEL AGENTS

IndUSHealth

7413 Six Forks Road

Raleigh NC 276143

Tel: 800 779.1314 (US toll-free)

Fax: 888 627.6492

Email: info@indushealth.com

Web: www.indushealth.com

Founded in 2005, this US-based firm sends its patients to leading medical destinations in India: Bangalore, Chennai, Delhi, and Mumbai. Founder Rajesh Rao claims to have sent 600 patients abroad to date.

Focusing on cardiovascular and orthopedic procedures, IndUSHealth has forged strong ties with super-specialty centers such as Apollo Hospitals, Escorts Heart Institute, Max Heart and Vascular Institute, and Wockhardt Heart Institute. IndUSHealth serves a wide range of treatments, including cosmetic surgery, dental care and vision.

Services include teleconference with physician, medical records conversion and transfer, travel reservations and ticketing, travel insurance, visa processing and financing assistance, if required. A cell phone for use in-country is provided prior to travel.

In addition to serving individual patients, IndUSHealth works with employers large and small to offer medical travel programs to employees. In July, 2006, Rao appeared as a witness before the US Senate Subcommittee on Aging, extolling the advantages of employer-assisted medical travel, and sparking a national debate over insurers' and corporations' roles in medical tourism.

MedRetreat
1121 Annapolis Road, PMB 160
Odenton, MD 21113
Tel: 877 876.3373 (US toll-free)
Fax: 847 680.0484
Email: customerservice@medretreat.com
Web: www.medtreatreat.com

For more information about MedRetreat, see Thailand.

Planet Hospital
23679 Calabasas Road, Suite 150
Calabasas, CA 91302
Tel: 800 243.0172 (US toll-free)
Fax: 818 665.4810
Email: rudy@planethospital.com

Web: www.planethospital.com

For more information about Planet Hospital, see Singapore.

Taj Medical Group
The TechnoCentre, Coventry University
Technology Park
Puma Way
Coventry UNITED KINGDOM
Tel: 877 799.9797 (US toll-free)
Tel: 011 44 2476.466.118
Fax: 011 44 2476.466.118
Email: info@surgeryindia.co.uk
Web: www.tajmedical.com

US Office
The Taj Medical Group
408 W 57th Street, Suite 9N
New York NY 10019
Tel: 877 799.9797 (US toll-free)
Email: info@surgeryindia.co.uk
Web: www.tajmedicalgroup.com

Taj Medical Group is the high guru of medical travel to India. Based in the UK with offices in the US and Canada, cofounders Jag and Dipa Jethwa have sent more than 600 patients to India over the past four years, mostly from Canada, Great Britain, and other parts of Europe. Taj's new US office, based in New York City, was opened to facilitate the special needs of American health travelers.

All Taj staffers speak fluent English, and Taj insists that all their recommended physicians and surgeons speak English as well. No up-front fees are required, and Taj provides all pretravel planning, pre-operative consultation, post-operative consultation and checkups, along with full, personal, in-country concierge service.

Taj sends most of its clients to JCI-accredited Apollo Hospitals. The agency uses its extensive physician contacts to match each patient with the best physician and procedure. Taj also has long-standing formal partnerships with Escorts Heart Institute and Max Healthcare.

■ HOSPITALS AND CLINICS

Max Devki Devi Heart and Vascular Institute
2 Press Enclave Road
Saket, New Delhi, INDIA 110017
Tel: 011 91 11.2651.5050
Fax: 011 91 11.2651.0050
Email: info@maxhealthcare.in
Web: www.maxhealthcare.in

Max Super-Specialty Hospital
1 Press Enclave Road
Saket, New Delhi, INDIA 110017
Tel: 011 91.11.2651.5050
Fax: 011 91 11.2651.0050
Email: info@maxhealthcare.in
Web: www.maxhealthcare.in

Six specialty clinics with more than 700 beds and 500 doctors make Max Healthcare Delhi's largest hospital network and one of the country's most influential health centers. International health travelers usually visit one of Max's two super-specialty centers, mostly for cardiac and orthopedic surgeries.

Max's International Patients Services department offers initial screening and diagnosis, telemedicine evaluation and recommendations, travel arrangements to Delhi (including visa, ticketing, airport pickup, money transfer and exchange, and ATM withdrawals), interpreters, lodging assistance, special return journey arrangements, and an exclusive help desk and dedicated relationship manager to ensure quality service.

Max also boasts a new vision clinic, **Max Eyecare**, which offers the full range of opthamological specialties and procedures. Its **Institute of Neurosciences** focuses on brain tumors, aneurysms, stroke, infectious diseases of the brain, spinal tumors and infections, and chronic spinal pain.

Indraprastha Apollo Hospital
Sarita Vihar
Delhi Mathura Road
Delhi, INDIA 110 044
Tel: 011 91 11.2692.5858 or 2692.5801
Fax: 011 91 11.2682.5536
Email: inquiry@apollohospitals.com
Web: www.apollohospitals.com/delhi

With more than 7,000 beds in 38 owned or managed centers, Apollo Hospitals is the largest healthcare group in Asia. Four thousand specialists and super-specialists and 3,000 medical officers span 53 clinical departments throughout the network.

Apollo New Delhi, with 692 beds and 14 operating theaters, treats more than 10,000 international patients annually. The Delhi center was the first hospital in India to receive JCI accreditation. As a result of the ensuing media coverage, American and Canadian patients are now more frequently seen, interspersed with princes, sheiks, and other VIPs in Apollo's Platinum international waiting lounge.

Apollo's treatment specialties include cardiology and cardiac surgery, pediatrics, orthopedics, neurology, oncology, and transplantation. Apollo is particularly proud of the latter, with more than 430 kidney transplants and 53 liver transplants to its name. Apollo's surgeons have also performed over 9,400 renal transplants and 130 bone transplants.

On the cardiac front, the hospitals have performed over 20,000 angiograms, 16,200 angioplasties, and 3,500 mitral balloon valvoplasties. Cardiac surgeries carry a 98.5 percent success rate across Apollo, higher than most brand-name US hospitals. A recently acquired 64-slice CT (computed tomography) scanner enables instantaneous, noninvasive angiography procedures at about half the cost of a similar procedure in the US.

Orthopedics is also huge here, and Apollo has pioneered procedures like total hip and knee replacements and the Birmingham hip resurfacing technique. While the Birmingham procedure was only recently approved in the US, Apollo specialist surgeons have performed hundreds over the past decade, with a 98+ percent success rates.

Partnerships with Mayo Clinic, Cleveland Heart Institute, and Johns Hopkins Medical Center help ensure best practices, thanks to a steady stream of Western influence and oversight.

Escorts Heart Institute and Research Center

Okhla Road
New Delhi, INDIA 110 025
Tel: 011 91 11.2682.5000
Tel: 011 98 11.268.5001
Fax: 011 91 11.2682.5013
Email: hospitality@ehirc.com
Web: www.ehirc.com

Note: The entire Escorts chain of hospitals was recently acquired by Fortis Healthcare

(now India's second largest healthcare and hospital network). Fortis has recently established a network-wide International Patients Center, which serves Escorts in New Delhi as well as other centers throughout India. Call 011 91 11.4229.5222 or email fipsc@fortishealthcare.com.

Cardiac care has become a specialty in India, with centers such as the Escorts, Wockhardt (Mumbai), Apollo (New Delhi and Chennai), and the Institute of Cardiovascular Diseases (Chennai) leading the way. Success and morbidity rates are on par with those found in the US and Europe, with major surgeries at 15-50 percent the cost. More Americans travel to India for cardiac and orthopedic procedures than for all other treatments combined.

Headquartered in New Delhi, with 11 heart command centers and associate hospitals throughout India, Escorts Heart Institute and Research Center now manages nearly 900 beds. The 332-bed New Delhi Institute has nine operating rooms and carries out nearly 15,000 procedures every year. Cardiac specialties include standard and specialty coronary bypass surgery; transmyocardial laser revascularization (TMLR); heart port surgery; robotic surgery for aortic aneurysms and dissections; carotid endarterectomy; valve surgery; and treatment of peripheral vascular disease.

The Institute's latest addition is its **Cardiac Scan Centre**, where state-of-the-art magnetic resonance imaging and computed tomography scans are used to diagnose coronary artery disease at its earliest stages.

Escorts International Services Department offers airport pickup and drop-off, travel arrangements, an interpreter, currency exchange, customized in-hospital cuisine, and sightseeing.

■ HOTELS: DELUXE

Note: As mentioned elsewhere in this book, good, safe, reliable, full-service hotels in India aren't cheap, and moderate hotels are often lacking in amenities that help any recovering patient feel more at ease. Thus, "deluxe" hotels listing below are in the $200+ per day range, and you'll find the "moderate" listings in the $100-$200 range.

Health travel planners, as well as hospitals' International Patient Centers, often offer hotel discounts through their partnerships. Check with your agent or clinic before paying full freight.

Hotel Intercontinental Nehru Place
Nehru Place
New Delhi, INDIA 110019
Tel: 011 91 11.4122.3344
Fax: 011 91 11.2622.4288
Email: del-nehruplace@interconti.com
Web: www.ichotelsgroup.com

Crowne Plaza New Delhi
New Friends Colony
New Delhi, INDIA 110 025
Tel: 011 91 11.2683.5070
Fax: 011 91 11.2683.7758
Email: crowneplaza@crowneplazadelhi.com
Web: www.ichotelsgroup.com

■ HOTELS: MODERATE

Hotel Savoia
Friends Colony, Mathura Road
Delhi, INDIA
Tel: 011 91 22.2404.2211
Fax: 011 91 22.2404.2242
Email: savoia@nivalink.com
Web: www.nivalink.com/savoia

Centrum Hotel
D-984, New Friends Colony
New Delhi, INDIA 110065
Tel: 011 91 22.2807.9270
Fax: 011 91 22.2806.5818
Email: travel@indiatravelite.com
Web: www.indiatravelite.com

DESTINATION: **INDIA: BANGALORE**

■ AT A GLANCE

Bangalore

Language:	Hindi (English widely spoken)
Time Zone:	GMT +5
Country Dialing Code:	91
Electricity:	230 volts, 50Hz; two- and three-pin round plugs standard
Currency:	Rupee
Visa Required?:	Yes
Required Immunizations:	None
Treatment Specialties:	Cardiovascular, Cosmetic, Dental Care, General Surgery, Neurology, Ophthalmology, Orthopedics, Stem Cell, Weight Loss
Leading Hospitals and Clinics:	Manipal Hospital, Wockhardt Hospital and Heart Institute
JCI-Accredited Hospitals:	Wockhardt Hospital and Heart Institute
Standards and Accreditation:	Ministry of Health and Family Welfare, Indian Medical Association, Indian Health Care Federation, JCI

■ TREATMENT BRIEF

Situated in southern India in the state of Karnataka, midway between the Arabian Sea and the Indian Ocean, this capital city of six million is India's fifth largest and fastest growing.

Bangalore has so many nicknames that one might suspect a public relations agency was working overtime. Its many local parks and abundant flora have earned it the name "The Garden City." As India's center for software production and outsourcing, Bangalore also qualifies as "India's Silicon Valley." Its rich array of produce, including grapes, mangoes, and guavas, has tagged Bangalore as "Fruit Market of the South." Bangalore is also known as the "Stone City" for its abundant granite deposits.

To this list one might add "Healthcare City," as Bangalore boasts the largest number of World Health Organization-approved systems of medicine in a single city. Patients will find a broad array of established treatment centers, including Manipal Hospital and Wockhardt Hospital's Center for Cardiovascular Surgery. Over the past five years, the average success rate for cardiac surgeries performed in Bangalore's eight cardiac care hospitals was 99.3 percent, on par with hospitals in US cities.

Bangalore is also India's unofficial seat of alternative treatments, and patients seeking help off the beaten medical path will find a wide array of choice, including ultramodern allopathy, Ayurveda, holistic naturopathy, spa-based rejuvenation, yoga, and more.

■ TYPICAL TREATMENTS AND COSTS

Cardiovascular:

Coronary Artery Bypass Graft: $7,300

Bypass + Valve Replacement (single): $9,850

Bypass + Valve Replacement (double): $11,500

Pacemaker:

Single-chamber: $5,400

Double-chamber: $7,500

Cosmetic:

Breast:

Augmentation: $2,750-$4,400

Lift/Reduction: $2,750-$4,200

Facelift: $4,750

Liposuction (stomach, hips, and waist): $800-$2,200

Dental Care:

Crowns (all porcelain): $290

Extractions (wisdom teeth): $675-$1,200

Implants: $925

Inlays and Onlays: $500-$900

Veneers (porcelain): $350

General Surgery:

Gall Bladder Removal: $3,300-$4,000

Prostate Surgery (TURP): $5,390

Ophthalmology:

LASIK (per eye): $650

Glaucoma (per eye): $875

Orthopedics:

Birmingham Hip Resurfacing: $8,250

Replacement:

Ankle Joint: $5,850

Total Hip: $7,850

Total Knee: $7,000

Total Shoulder: $6,950

Weight Loss:

LAP-BAND® System: $8,000-$9,500

■ HEALTH TRAVEL AGENTS

IndUSHealth

7413 Six Forks Road

Raleigh NC 276143

Tel: 800 779.1314 (Toll-free in the US)

Fax: 888 627.6492

Email: info@indushealth.com

Web: www.indushealth.com

For more information on IndUSHealth's services in India, see Delhi.

Taj Medical Group

The TechnoCentre, Coventry University

Technology Park

Puma Way

Coventry, UNITED KINGDOM

Tel: 877 799.9797 (US toll-free)

Tel: 011 44 2476.466.118

Fax: 011 44 2476.466.118

Email: info@surgeryindia.co.uk

Web: www.tajmedical.com

US Office

The Taj Medical Group

408 W. 57th Street, Suite 9N

New York, NY 10019

Tel: 877 799.9797 (US toll-free)

Email: info@surgeryindia.co.uk

Web: www.tajmedicalgroup.com

Note: Taj Medical Group is the best-known health travel agent representing India. For more on the Taj Medical Group's presence in India, see Delhi.

Health Tourism Bangalore

(Trans-European Express)

64 2nd Main, 1st Block, Koramangala

Bangalore, INDIA 560 034

Tel: 001 91 98.4527.6897

Email: info@healthtourismbangalore.com

Web: http://www.healthtourismbangalore
  .com/index.htm

This husband-and-wife team has been in the travel business since 1998. The pair specializes in patients heading to Bangalore for treatment. Fifty percent of its clientele are American and Canadian. The agency did not provide information on hospitals served.

■ HOSPITALS AND CLINICS

Manipal Hospital Bangalore
98, Airport Road
Bangalore, INDIA 560017
Tel: 011 91 80.2526.6646 (x 480 or 484)
Email: info@manipalhospital.org
Web: www.manipalhospital.org

Launched in 1990, the Manipal Hospital is owned by the giant healthcare management company, the Manipal Group. With 11 hospitals, 1,250 physicians, and 4,250 beds, this is one of Asia's largest and most respected hospital networks.

Manipal Hospital Bangalore is huge in its own right, with 600 beds and 39 specialties. Centers of excellence include

■ **Manipal Heart Foundation**, which performs 15 heart surgeries and 30 other cardiac procedures per day. The center specializes in patients with congenital heart diseases, such as atrial septal defect, ventricular septal defect, and patent ductus arteriosus. More than 14,000 cardiac surgeries have been performed in the past five years.

■ **Manipal Institute of Neurological Disorders,** which has 100 beds reserved for neurosurgery and neurology and four fully loaded operation theaters. It is one of India's largest centers for diagnosis and treatment of brain-related maladies. The department conducts around 1,000 major neurological operations annually, including surgery to treat brain hemorrhages and tumors, epilepsy, head injury, Parkinson's disease, spinal injury, spinal tumors, strokes, and congenital anomalies. Specialties include pediatric neuro-surgery, neurovascular surgery, functional and stereotactic surgery, and neuron endoscopy, in addition to craniofacial, skull-base, carotid, peripheral nerve, and spinal procedures.

■ **Manipal International Institute of Dental Medicine**, which boasts a wide range of general and surgical dentistry. The center also specializes in dentofacial orthopedics, where facial deformities are surgically corrected. MIIDM is equipped to treat patients who have multiple chronic diseases and complicated medical and drug histories. The center provides periodontics, oral surgery, and dental treatment for medically compromised and physically handicapped individuals.

■ **Manipal's Orthopedics Center** averages 160 surgeries a month. Its surgeons have conducted 350 knee replacements, 250 total hip replacements, 1,500 interlocking nailings, 1,000 arthroscopies, and 200 spinal instrumentation procedures. The center reserves one operation theater exclusively for joint replacement procedures. Success rates average 98+ percent.

■ Finally, **Manipal's Stem Cell Research Center**, launched in mid-2004, is one of India's few hospitals carrying on "bench to bedside" stem cell research, working with affiliated institutions in the areas of heart disease, bone marrow transplants, Parkinson's disease, diabetes, and spinal cord injury. Patients interested in this highly experimental area of research and application should contact Manipal's Stem Cell Research Center directly.

Wockhardt Hospital and Heart Institute
14, Cunningham Road
Bangalore, INDIA 560 052
Tel: 800 730.6373 (US toll-free)
Tel: 011 91 80.2226.1037
Fax: 011 91 80.2228.1149
Email: pthukral@wockhardtin.com
Web: http://www.whhi.com/

Bangalore is headquarters to the JCI-accredited Wockhardt Hospital and Heart Institute, one of Wockhardt's two super-specialty cardiac centers in India. (The other is in Mumbai.) In addition to its general treatment and surgery departments, Wockhardt has achieved global recognition as a pioneer in innovative cardiac surgery techniques to help patients termed inoperable.

Wockhardt's two linchpin specialty departments are the **Center of Cardiology**, which annually performs more than 500 angioplasties and 2,500 cardiac interventions; and the **Center of Cardiovascular Surgery**, which annually performs more than 1,200 cardiac surgeries. Both centers report a success rate of 99+ percent, matching international benchmarks.

The Center of Cardiovascular Surgery performed India's first minimally invasive coronary bypass surgery and has led the way in performing arterial grafts for bypass surgeries. The center has three cardiovascular operating rooms equipped with monitoring and resuscitative technology and the latest instrumentation for performing beating-heart cardiac surgery.

Wockhardt has performed more than 15,000 heart operations and 40,000 interventional cardiology procedures since opening its doors in 1989.

For further information on Wockhardt Hospital, see Mumbai.

Wockhardt Super-Specialty Hospitals
154/9, Bannerghatta Road
Opp. IIM-B
Bangalore, INDIA 560 076
Tel: 011 91 80. 6621.4444
Tel: 800 730.6373 (US & Canada toll-free)
Email: pthukral@wockhardtin.com
Web: www.wockhardthospitals.net

Expanding on the success of its sister center on Cunningham Road, Wockhardt's newly opened (November, 2006) 400-bed super-specialty hospital centers its services around cardiovascular, orthopedics, neurosciences, minimal access surgery, and women's and children's services. Fully JCI-accredited, this center works in close partnership with physicians, surgeons, and staff at the Wockhardt Hospital and Heart Institute across town.

As with Wockhardt's super-specialty hospital in Mumbai, an exclusive partnership with Harvard Medical International, a division of Boston's Harvard Medical School, gives Wockhardt access to top-flight international medical expertise, along with standards oversight and best practices discipline. Through its Harvard partnership, Wockhardt physicians and staff are afforded opportunities to consult with hospitals of excellence throughout the US and the world.

Wockhardt's medical services include

■ **Adult Cardiology and Cardiac Surgery Center,** which specializes in closed-heart surgeries such as a Blalock-Taussig (BT) shunt; simple open-heart surgeries such as septal defect repairs; and complex open-heart surgeries. Super-specialties include

■ **Interventional Cardiology:** coronary angiography, angioplasty, and stenting; angiography and angioplasty of arteries in neck, leg, arm, and kidney; permanent pacemaker (single- and double-chamber); heart failure device and implantation; and endovascular aneurysm repair.

■ **Cardiothoracic and Vascular Surgery:** off-pump bypass surgeries, valve surgeries and repairs, and left ventricle size restoration surgery. (Nearly all of their bypass surgeries are now done off-pump.)

■ **Wockhardt's Center for Bone and Joint Care** provides up-to-date diagnostic facilities and treatment in orthopedics, joint replacement surgeries, hip resurfacing, and musculoskeletal problems ranging from minimally invasive arthroscopic surgeries to complex trauma services. The center employs the minimal access surgery approach for fractures, which until recently have required more invasive surgeries. Super-specialties include

■ **Total Knee Replacement: unicondylar knee replacement** (which requires only a small incision to rapid recovery); failed, infected, or revision joint replacements; extra corporeal irradiation; and total joint replacement.

■ **Total Hip Replacement:** cementless total hip replacement (which is less complicated in the fixation of prosthesis); hip resurfacing/surface replacement artroplasty; cementless bipolar/partial hip replacement in elderly with fractures; shoulder replacement; and revision joint replacement (for patients whose earlier replacements have failed).

Other services include pediatric orthopedics, orthopedic oncology (including custom-made prosthetics), and sports medicine.

■ The **Neurology and Neurosurgery Super-Specialty Center** addresses head trauma, complex brain and spinal surgeries, and other conditions. Its **Brain and Spine Center** provides advanced microsurgical techniques to conduct precision-driven complex microsurgeries. Endoscopic techniques are being developed for complex brain and spinal surgeries, along with the most recent minimally invasive procedures. Operative services include

■ **Microsurgery for Brain Tumors: endoscopic brain surgery, skull base** surgery, surgery for brain trauma and congenital cranial deformity; brain surgery for abnormal blood vessels, epilepsy, and removal of blood clots; pre-operative embolization of spinal lesions.

■ **Slipped Disc in the Neck or Lower Back:** microscopic lumbar discectomy or decompression, microscopic anterior cervical discectomy, and endoscopic discectomy.

■ **Degenerative Disc Disease:** minimally invasive spinal fusion, total disc replacement surgery, corrections of spinal deformities (congenital and acquired), and osteoporosis.

■ For those who desire alternatives to the "big knife," Wockhardt's specialists are particularly proud of their **Center for Minimal Access Surgery**. The center is dedicated to performing surgical procedures using the latest minimal access techniques, allowing patients to enjoy faster recovery and fewer postsurgical complications. The procedures minimize surgical trauma, pain, and blood loss. The center has recruited leading surgeons in the fields of laparoscopic, endoscopic, and robotically assisted surgeries in a wide range of super-specialties, including

- **Laparoscopic Surgery:** appendectomy, gall bladder removal, hernia, spleen, colorectal, adrenalectomy, pancreatic, and obesity.

- **Other Minimal Access Surgeries:** TURP (transurethral resection of prostrate), PCNL (percutaneous nephrolithotripsy), laparoscopic urology, thoracoscopic surgery, and minimal access cardiac surgeries

■ HOTELS: DELUXE

Note: As mentioned elsewhere in this section, good, safe, reliable, full-service hotels in India aren't cheap, and moderate hotels are often lacking in amenities that help any recovering patient feel more at ease. Thus, "deluxe" hotels listed below are in the $200+ per day range, and you'll find the "moderate" listings in the $100-$200 range.

Health travel planners, as well as hospitals' International Patient Centers, often offer hotel discounts through their partnerships. Check with your agent or clinic before paying full freight.

Royal Orchid Hotel
1, Golf Avenue
Bangalore, INDIA , 560 051
Tel: 011 91 80.2520.5566
Fax: 011 91 80.2520.3366
Email: royalorchid@baljeehotels.com
Web: www.baljeehotels.com

The Leela Palace Kempinski
Tel: 011 91 80.2521.1234
Fax: 011 91 80.2521.7234
Email: reservations.bangalore@theleela
.com
Web: www.theleela.com

■ HOTELS: MODERATE

Buena Vista Guest House
Wilo Crisa Apartment,
14 Rest House Crescent Road,
Bangalore, INDIA
Tel: 011 91 80.5112.2757
Fax: 011 91 80.5112.2957
Email: travel@indiatravelite.com
Web: http://www.indiatravelite.com

■ AT A GLANCE

Chennai

Language:	Hindi (English widely spoken)
Time Zone:	GMT +5
Country Dialing Code:	91
Electricity:	230 volts, 50Hz; two- and three-pin round plugs standard
Currency:	Rupee
Visa Required?:	Yes
Required Immunizations:	None
Treatment Specialties:	Cardiovascular, Cosmetic, Dental Care, General Surgery, Ophthalmology, Orthopedics, Transplants, Weight Loss
Leading Hospitals and Clinics:	Apollo (Corporate Headquarters), Apollo Dental Clinic, Institute of Cardiovascular Diseases, Sankara Nethralaya Eye Hospital
JCI-Accredited Hospitals:	Apollo Hospital
Standards and Accreditation:	Ministry of Health and Family Welfare, Indian Medical Association, Indian Health Care Federation, JCI

■ TREATMENT BRIEF

Located on India's southeastern Bay of Bengal coast, Chennai (formerly Madras) is the capital city of the state of Tamil Nadu and the fourth largest city in India. Known for its numerous temples and classical Indian dance, Chennai is also the corporate headquarters of Apollo Hospitals, India's largest hospital network. Much medical activity has grown around Apollo, and Chennai is now one of India's most important medical centers. Apollo has more than 7,000 beds in 32 locations, and its broader network includes nursing and hospital management colleges, pharmacies, diagnostic clinics, and a dental center also located in Chennai.

In Chennai a host of specialty clinics and research centers have followed Apollo's example, and standards are steadily rising. In

2006, Apollo/Chennai became the second hospital in the Apollo network to receive JCI accreditation. According to hospital officials, Americans use its services mostly for cardiovascular and orthopedic procedures.

As with most other Asian destinations, larger surgeries are the focus for international patients. Cardiac specialties and orthopedics abound, particularly knee and hip replacements. More talked about is the popular Birmingham hip resurfacing procedure, only recently FDA-approved in the United States, and often a better choice than total hip replacement surgery for patients requiring such treatment.

■ TYPICAL TREATMENTS AND COSTS

Cardiovascular:
Coronary Artery Bypass Graft: $7,300
  Bypass + Valve Replacement (single): $9,850
  Bypass + Valve Replacement (double): $11,600
Pacemaker:
  Single-chamber: $5,400
  Double-chamber: $7,500

Cosmetic:
Breast:
  Augmentation: $2,750-$4,400
  Lift/Reduction: $2,750-$4,200
Facelift: $4,750
Liposuction (stomach, hips, and waist): $820-$2200

Dental Care:
Crowns (all porcelain): $300
Extractions (wisdom teeth): $675-$1,200
Implants: $925
Inlays and Onlays: $500-$900
Veneers (porcelain): $350

General Surgery:
Gall Bladder Removal: $3,300-$4,000
Prostate Surgery (TURP): $5,400

Ophthalmology:
LASIK (per eye): $675
Glaucoma (per eye): $875

Orthopedics:
Birmingham Hip Resurfacing: $8,250
Replacement:
  Ankle Joint: $5,850
  Total Hip: $7,850
  Total Knee: $7,000
  Total Shoulder: $6,950

Weight Loss:
LAP-BAND* System: $8,000-$9,400

■ HEALTH TRAVEL AGENTS

IndUSHealth
7413 Six Forks Road
Raleigh NC 276143
Tel: 800 779.1314 (US toll-free)
Fax: 888 627.6492
Email: info@indushealth.com
Web: www.indushealth.com

For more information on IndUSHealth's
services in India, see Delhi.

MedRetreat
1121 Annapolis Road, PMB 160
Odenton, MD 21113
Tel: 877 876.3373 (US toll-free)
Fax: 847 680.0484
Email: customerservice@medretreat.com
Web: www.medtreatreat.com

For more information about MedRetreat,
see Thailand.

Planet Hospital
23679 Calabasas Road, Suite 150
Calabasas, CA 91302
Tel: 800 243.172 [AU: Missing digit]
Fax: 818 665.4810
Email: rudy@planethospital.com
Web: www.planethospital.com

For more information about Planet Hospital, see Singapore.

Taj Medical Group
The TechnoCentre, Coventry University
Technology Park,
Puma Way
Coventry, UNITED KINGDOM
Tel: 877 799.9797 (US toll-free)
Tel: 011 44 2476.466.118
Fax: 011 44 2476.466.118
Email: info@surgeryindia.co.uk
Web: www.tajmedical.com

US Office
The Taj Medical Group
408 W. 57th Street, Suite 9N
New York NY 10019
Tel: 877 799.9797 (US and Canada toll-free)
Email: info@surgeryindia.co.uk
Web: www.tajmedicalgroup.com

Note: Headquartered in the UK, Taj Medical
Group is the longest-running health travel
agent representing India. For more on Taj
Medical Group's presence in India, see Delhi.

■ HOSPITALS AND CLINICS

**Apollo Hospitals/Chennai —
International Patient Service Center**
21, Greams Lane (off Greams Road)
Chennai, Tamil Nadu, INDIA 600 006
Tel: 011 91 44.2829.6569
Fax: 011 91 44.2829.5463
Email: enquiry@apollohospitals.com
Web: www.apollohospitals.com

Apollo's Chennai Hospital, with more than 1,000 beds and an international service center, received its JCI accreditation in February 2006. Seventy percent of Apollo Chennai's physicians and surgeons have trained, studied, or worked in institutions and hospitals in the US or Western Europe.

Apollo Chennai is one of only four Apollo Centers of Excellence in India. Specialties include cardiology and cardiothoracic surgery, cancer care, cosmetic surgery, nephrology and urology, orthopedics, and radiology and imaging sciences.

Best-known for its orthopedics and cardiology super-specialties, Apollo has performed thousands of hip resurfacing surgeries with a success rate of 98.3 percent. Similarly, Apollo has performed more than 27,000 heart surgeries with a current success rate of 99.6 percent (higher than most US hospitals' success rates).

For patients interested in alternative therapies, Apollo Chennai offers the world's only comprehensive, hospital-based Wellness Center, occupying a full floor of the hospital. Holistic healing therapies such as Ayurveda, aromatherapy, pranic healing, yoga, meditation, and music therapy are offered to international patients as part of Apollo's complementary recovery package.

Apollo Dental Centre
21, Greams Road
Opp. M.R.F
Chennai, INDIA 600 006
Tel: 011 91 44.2829.4080
Tel: 011 91 44.5212.1111
Fax: 011 91 44.2829.2013
Email: contact@apollodentalcentre.com
Web: www.apollodentalcentre.com

An affiliate of JCI-accredited Apollo Hospital/Chennai, with main offices adjacent to the corporate headquarters and hospital, the center offers a full range of dental care, including crowns and bridges, inlays and onlays, dentures, dental implants, root canals, restorative surgery, cosmetic dentistry, and pediatric dentistry. Restorations are guaranteed for two years; advanced crowns and bridges and injection-molded dentures are guaranteed for five years.

Institute of Cardiovascular Diseases
4-A, Dr. J. Jayalalitha Nagar
Mogappair
Chennai, INDIA 600 037
Tel: 011 91 44.2656.1801
Fax: 011 91 44.2656.5510
Email: admin@mmm.org.in
Web: www.icvd.org

This 179-bed facility is one of India's top cardiovascular centers. Its surgeons performed south India's first heart transplant and India's first bilateral lung transplant, first pediatric heart transplant, and first simultaneous heart and lung transplant. The parents of ailing children will be happy to learn that the center specializes in pediatrics; 25 percent of the center's patients are kids.

ICVD's **Department of Cardiac Surgery** functions through two independent, but mutually linked, adult and pediatric units. Together, they perform approximately 2,000 operations annually.

The **Adult Cardiac Surgical Unit** performs 1,500 operations yearly, mostly coronary artery bypass procedures, deploying off-pump methodology. Valve replacements are a big specialty, and ICVD gives special emphasis to repair techniques that preserve native valves wherever possible. New and traditional repair techniques such as chordal shortening, quadrangular resection, and artificial chordae are used as needed.

The **Pediatric Cardiac Surgical Unit** handles a wide spectrum of congenital cardiac abnormalities in patients ranging from newborns to adults. The unit has worked on more than 7,500 cases of congenital cardiac abnormalities. Besides operating on the "simpler'" anomalies such as atrial septal defect, ventricular septal defect, and patent ductus arteriosus, the pediatric unit handles the more complex anomalies, including hypoplastic left heart syndrome, transposition of great arteries, complete atrioventricular canal defect, and total anomalous pulmonary venous drainage. ICVD has performed more than 150 aortic valve repairs on infants as well as octogenarians.

Sankara Nethralaya Eye Hospital
"The Temple of the Eye"
18, College Road, Nungambakkam
Chennai, Tamil Nadu, INDIA 600 006
Tel: 011 91 44. 4227.1816
Tel: 877 393.7666 (US and Canada toll-free)
Fax: 011 91 44.2825.4180
Email: mrf@snmail.org
Web: www.sankaranethralaya.org

Established in 1978, the Sankara Nethralaya Eye Hospital has been recognized by leading Indian media and government sources as one of the country's finest. Daily, the hospital sees 1,200 patients and performs 100 eye operations in 22 operating theaters.

Sankara Nethralaya's ophthalmic subspecialties include cataract and refractive corneal surgery, glaucoma, uveitis, vitreoretinal surgery, pediatric ophthalmology, squint, and neuro-ophthalmology.

Sankara is particularly proud of its **Ocular Oncology Department**, which diagnoses and treats eye cancer, retinal tumors, and cancers in surrounding structures. Deploying recent innovations such as transpupillary thermotherapy (TTT) has enabled the clinic to save eyes and lives, according to its founder. The department treats choroidal melanoma and has the expertise and instrumentation to perform complicated surgical procedures such as total eyewall resection brachytherapy, which can salvage — instead of removing — affected eyes.

■ RECOVERY RETREATS

Taj Fisherman's Cove
Kovelong Beach
Kanchipuram District 603 112
Tamil Nadu, INDIA
Tel: 011 91 44.6741.3333
Fax: 011 91 44. 6741.3330
Email: fishcove.chennai@tajhotels.com
Web: www.tajhotels.com

■ HOTELS: DELUXE

Note: As mentioned elsewhere in this book, good, safe, reliable, full-service hotels in India aren't cheap, and moderate hotels are often lacking in amenities that help any recovering patient feel more at ease. Thus, "deluxe" hotels listed below are in the $200+ per day range, and you'll find the "moderate" listings in the $100-$200 range.

   Health travel planners, as well as hospitals' International Patient Centers, often offer hotel discounts through their partnerships. Check with your agent or clinic before paying full freight.

Taj Connemara
2, Binny Road
Off Anna Salai
Chennai, INDIA 600 002
Tel: 011 91 44.5500.0000
Web: www.tajhotels.com

The Park Chennai
601 Anna Salai
Chennai, INDIA 600 006
Tel: 011 91 44 5214.4000
Web: www.theparkhotels.com

■ HOTELS: MODERATE

The Residency Towers
115, Sir Theagaraya Road
T. Nagar
Chennai, INDIA 600 017
Tel: 011 91 44.2815.6363
Email: resmds@vsnl.com
Web: http://www.theresidency.com

Comfort Inn Marina Towers (II064)
2A Ponniamman Koiil Street
Egmore
Chennai, INDIA 600 006
Tel: 011 91 44.2858.5454
Fax: 011 91 44.2858.5454
Email: hotelhelp@choicehotels.com
Web: www.choicehotels.com

DESTINATION: INDIA: MUMBAI

■ AT A GLANCE

Mumbai

Language:	Hindi (English widely spoken in professional and medical circles)
Time Zone:	GMT +5
Country Dialing Code:	91
Electricity:	230 volts, 50Hz; two- and three-pin round plugs standard
Currency:	Rupee
Visa Required?:	Yes
Required Immunizations:	None
Treatment Specialties:	Cardiovascular, Cosmetic, Dental Care, Fertility/ Reproduction, General Surgery, Ophthalmology, Orthopedics, Weight Loss
Leading Hospitals and Clinics:	Asian Heart Institute and Research Center, Jaslok Hospital, Dr. L. H. Hiranandani Hospital; Wockhardt Hospital and Heart Institute, Lilivati Hospital, Rotunda: The Center for Human Reproduction, Shroff Eye Hospital and LASIK Center
JCI-Accredited Hospitals:	Jaslok Hospital, Shroff Eye Hospital and Laser Center; Wockhardt Hospital and Heart Institute
Standards and Accreditation:	Ministry of Health and Family Welfare, Medical Council of India, Indian Medical Association, Indian Health Care Federation, JCI

■ TREATMENT BRIEF

India's most populous city, Mumbai, and its surrounding area are home to 20 million, making it the world's fifth most populated urban center. Formerly Bombay (Portuguese for "good bay"), Mumbai is the economic and entertainment hub of India.

With six large private hospitals serving international patients and a number of specialty treatment centers, Mumbai now counts healthcare as one of its most important economic assets, along with engineering, information technology, and film. ("Bollywood" is king in India, and any hospital visitor with a television will be treated to some lively and colorful cinematic productions.) Mumbai is India's New York, bristling with commercial activity and cultural diversity, extreme in every imaginable way.

Mumbai is headquarters to two large, multispecialty hospitals, including the JCI-accredited Wockhardt Hospital and Heart Institute and the renowned Jaslok Hospital. Wockhardt's treatment center in Mumbai has established five super-specialty clinics for cardiology, neurology, orthopedics, ophthalmology, and minimal access surgery. One of Wockhardt's two super-specialty heart Institutes is here, offering a full range of cardiovascular diagnostics and surgeries.

Jaslok Hospital, one of India's oldest and most venerated, offers 35 specialties, with a fully loaded International Patient Services Center.

Mumbai also hosts smaller, prestigious, single-specialty clinics, such as the JCI-accredited Shroff Eye Hospital and the Rotunda Center for Human Reproduction.

■ TYPICAL TREATMENTS AND COSTS

Cardiovascular:

Coronary Artery Bypass Graft: $7,300

    Bypass + Valve Replacement (single): $9,850

    Bypass + Valve Replacement (double): $11,600

Pacemaker:

Single-chamber: $5,400

Double-chamber: $7,500

Cosmetic:

Breast:

    Augmentation: $2,750-$4,400

    Lift/Reduction: $2,750-$4,200

Facelift: $4,750

Liposuction (stomach, hips, and waist): $825-$2,200

Dental Care:

Crowns (all porcelain): $300

Extractions (wisdom teeth): $675-$1,200

Implants: $925

Inlays and Onlays: $500-$900

Veneers (porcelain): $350

General Surgery:

Gall Bladder Removal: $3,300-$4,000

Prostate Surgery (TURP): $5,400

Opthalmology:

LASIK (per eye): $650

Glaucoma (per eye): $850

Orthopedics:

Birmingham Hip Resurfacing: $8,250

Replacement:

Ankle Joint: $5,850

Total Hip: $7,850

Total Knee: $7,000

Total Shoulder: $6,950

Weight Loss:

LAP-BAND® System: $8,000-$9,400

■ HEALTH TRAVEL AGENTS

Global Surgical Solutions

PO Box 631278

Irving, TX 75063-1278

Tel: 888 234.1361 (US toll-free)

Fax: 888 234.1361

Email: customerservice@globalsurgical
solutions.com

Web: www.globalsurgicalsolutions.com

Global Surgical Solutions founder Medhavi Balachandran is a former Mumbai resident now living in Texas. Her agency specializes in Mumbai, focusing on two of its top hospitals, L.H. Hiranandani and the Asian Heart Hospital and Research Center.

This agency's services include a detailed medical/surgical estimate, detailed information about hospitals and selected physicians, transport to and from the airport via chauffeur-driven car, an English-speaking "relationships manager" who acts as the patient's guide while in-country, and assistance with travel arrangements through a local agency.

For additional fees, Global Surgical Solutions can also help with vacation and sight-seeing, special meals and dietary plans, the use of private nurses during your recovery period, and a prepaid mobile telephone for in-country and international calls.

IndUSHealth

7413 Six Forks Road

Raleigh NC 276143

Tel: 800 779.1314 (US toll-free)

Fax: 888 627.6492

Email: info@indushealth.com

Web: www.indushealth.com

For more information on IndUSHealth's services in India, see Delhi.

Meditours

1055 Gibson Road

Kelowna, BC CANADA

Tel: 866 717.6565 (US and Canada toll-free)

Tel: 250 717.6565

Email: shaz@meditours.org

Web: www.meditours.org

Established in 2005 and run by two brothers, Shaz and Milind Pendharkar, this Vancouver-based agency serves US as well as Canadian clientele, primarily patients heading to Mumbai. Meditours is the exclusive agent for Jaslok Hospital. The agency also serves other established Mumbai-area centers, including the JCI-accredited Shroff Eye Hospital (see below). Ninety-five percent of Meditours patients are US or Canadian.

For more tourist-minded patients, Meditours maintains good relations with Kerala-based hospitals, including the Kerala Institute of Medical Sciences and the Malabar Institute of Medical Sciences. One advantage to treatment in Kerala is its superb resort facilities on the Arabian Sea and along its dozens of scenic rivers. Kerala is also the reputed home of Ayurvedic medicine, with clinics in every nook and cranny of Kerala.

All Meditours-recommended physicians are either US-trained or are US board-certified.

Taj Medical Group
The TechnoCentre, Coventry University Technology Park
Puma Way,
Coventry, UNITED KINGDOM
Tel: 877 799.9797 (US toll-free)
Tel: 011 44 2476.466.118
Fax: 011 44 2476.466.118
Email: info@surgeryindia.co.uk
Web: www.tajmedical.com

US Office
The Taj Medical Group
408 W. 57th Street, Suite 9N
New York, NY 10019
Tel: 877 799.9797
Email: info@surgeryindia.co.uk
Web: www.tajmedicalgroup.com

Note: Taj Medical Group is the best-known health travel agent representing India. For more on Taj Medical Group's services in India, see Delhi.

In Mumbai, Taj sends patients to the Wockhardt Hospital and Heart Institute and Dr. L.H. Hiranandani Hospital (see below).

■ HOSPITALS AND CLINICS

Asian Heart Institute and Research Center
Bandra Kurla Complex, Bandra (E)
Mumbai, INDIA 400 051
Tel: 011 91 22.6698.6666
Fax: 011 91 22.6698.6506
Email: customer.care@ahirc.com
Web: www.ahirc.com

Asian Heart Institute (AHIRC) was established by Contemporary Healthcare Pvt. Ltd. and six of India's top cardiac specialists. A 15-minute drive from Mumbai's domestic and international airports, the hospital forms part of the new Bandra-Kurla Complex (BKC), a $250 million business-shopping-healthcare-living complex in northern Mumbai.

Notably, AHIRC formed an early relationship with the renowned Cleveland Heart Clinic, which worked with the center to establish guidelines that would ensure international standards from the day it opened its doors--rather than inching up to such standards over time, as is the case with many overseas hospitals.

In 2005, the surgeons at the hospital performed 1,337 coronary surgeries and procedures with a mortality rate of less than 0.5 percent. All coronary procedures at AHIRC deploy the beating-heart technique, which reduces post-operative complications and the length of hospital stays.

The surgeons' education encompasses medical training and fellowships completed in the US (at the Cleveland heart Clinic), the UK, and Australia.

In addition to coronary artery surgery, AHIRC specializes in the Maze procedure for atrial fibrillation, valve repair and replacement, and aneurysm surgery of the aorta and other blood vessels. A special pediatric team operates on all types of cardiac conditions in children.

Asian Heart Institute's International Patients Department offers airport pickup and drop-off, hotel accommodations and local travel arrangements for companions, consultations with physicians and surgeons, prayer rooms, and Internet facilities.

Jaslok Hospital and Research Centre
15 - Dr. Deshmukh Marg
Pedder Road
Mumbai, INDIA 400 026.
Tel: 011 91 66.573.333 or 011 91 66.573.240
Email: info@jaslokhospital.net
Web: www.jaslokhospital.net

Jaslok Hospital and Research Centre is a private, multispecialty hospital with 376 beds, 124 full-time resident physicians, and around 100 consulting physicians. Jaslok has its own department of nursing, employing 495 nurses and 60 students.

Jaslok is one of India's top independent private hospitals, with 35 established specialties. Of interest to the international health traveler are radiation oncology, cardiovascular and thoracic surgery, advanced dental surgery, dermatology, ophthalmology, orthopedics, urology, oncosurgery, and nuclear medicine radiation oncology. Jaslok also boasts a **Neuroscience Division**, a **Department of Chest Diseases**, and a **Department of Infertility Management and Assisted Reproduction**.

International patients are asked to contact its exclusive agent, Meditours (listed under "Health Travel Agents" above). The hospital's International Services Depart-

ment provides airport pick-up, translator, an onsite coordinator for appointments and consultations, locker facilities, and customized cuisine.

Dr. L.H. Hiranandani Hospital
Hill Side Avenue, Hiranandani Gardens
Powai
Mumbai, INDIA 400 076
Tel: 011 91 22.2576.3300
Fax: 011 91 22.2576.3311
Email: wecare@hiranandanihospital.org
Web: www.hiranandanihospital

A newcomer to the Mumbai healthcare scene, the Dr. L. H. Hiranandani Hospital opened its doors in early 2004 with 130 beds. More than 30 specialties and subspecialties are offered. HLL's Centres of Excellence include cardiology (including primary angioplasty), joint replacement and hip resurfacing, human reproduction, bariatric surgery, hair rejuvenation surgery, dental surgery, and ophthalmology.

HLL aggressively promotes its "International Health Checks." Overseas patients can choose silver, gold, or platinum check packages for liver, diabetic, pulmonary, osteoporosis, renal, thyroid, ophthalmology, and cholesterol tests. Cancer marker tests and mammographies are also offered. You can find detailed information on each health check on the HLL site under "Overseas Patient Care Center."

Lilavati Hospital and Research Centre

A - 791, Bandra Reclamation

Bandra (W)

Mumbai, INDIA 400 050

Tel: 011 91 98.2132.0065

Fax: 011 91 22.2640.7655

Email: lilaworld@lilavatihospital.com

Web: www.lilavatihospital.com

Established in 1978, this 300-bed hospital in the heart of Mumbai is known for its cardiovascular and oncology surgeries and orthopedics. Lilavati's LilaWorld Assistant Cell was established as a special wing of the hospital to accommodate international patients. Amenities include a yoga center, 24-hour pharmacy, temple, and meditation center.

Rotunda: The Center for Human Reproduction

672, Kalpak Gulistan

Perry Cross Road Bandra (W)

Mumbai, INDIA 400 050

Tel: 91 22.655.2000

Fax: 91 22.655.3000

Email: drkaushi@gmail.com

Web: www.rotundaivf.com

Fertility consultation and treatment are usually long and emotionally arduous processes. As most couples know, they are also expensive and not covered by health insurance. Many couples choose to get started abroad, then return to the US to continue treatment and hook up with support groups and ongoing counseling.

Founded in 1963, Rotunda is India's most respected fertility treatment facility. In-house pathology, endoscopy, and sonography services allow a couple to undergo all tests under one roof. In addition

to the standard fertility services, Rotunda also provides sex preselection, assisted egg hatching, and a Recurrent Pregnancy Loss Clinic.

Shroff Eye Hospital and LASIK Center

222 V. Road Bandra (West)

Mumbai, INDIA 400 050

Tel; 011 91 22.5692.1000

Fax: 011 91 22.5694.9880

Email: safalas@yahoo.com

Web: www.lasikindia.in

Established in 1919 and family-run since its ineption, the Shroff Eye Hospital and LASIK Center is the one of the world's only JCI-accredited vision hospitals. It is one of only five JCI-accredited hospitals in all of India.

Drs. Rahul Ashok and Anand Ashok Shroff, along with 23 other physicians and consultants, provide full-service vision diagnosis and treatment, catering to international travelers from 35 countries.

Treatments include phacoemulsification cataract surgery, vitreoretinal surgery (for treating advanced diabetic retinopathy, retinal detachment, macular hole, and other retinal diseases), LASIK surgery, glaucoma surgery, squint surgery, keratoplasty and other corneal surgery, oculoplastic surgery, and other cosmetic treatments.

Shroff Hospital also runs seven super-specialty clinics including

■ **Diabetic Retinopathy Clinic, which is** dedicated to the identification and long-term care of diabetics at risk for diabetic retinopathy. The clinic is equipped with digital angiography systems, retinal sonography, various lasers and advanced vitreoretinal surgery equipment to provide treatment to patients with even advanced forms of the disorder.

■ **Macular Degeneration Clinic,** for treatment of this common disorder among older people. Digital flourescein angiography and indocyanine green angiography are used to diagnose the condition. Treatment is provided in the form of photodynamic therapy.

■ **Glaucoma Clinic,** offering a full range of diagnostics, including the Humphrey computerized visual field analyzer to help prevent further damage to vision.

■ **Uveitis Clinic,** including a pathology laboratory that provides the complete range of exams and tests.

■ **Cornea Clinic, providing** therapeutic and diagnostic capabilities for corneal disorders, including all aspects of anterior segment imaging such as corneal topography and pachymetry.

■ **Squint/Pediatric Ophthalmology Clinic,** a subspecialty clinic specializing in children with strabismus ("crossed eyes") and amblyopia ("lazy eyes"), with prescription of glasses and full-eye exams of infants and children. Adults with strabismus who desire strabismus surgery or eye muscle surgery are also seen here.

■ The Shroffs are particularly proud of their **LASIK Clinic,** which deploys the latest wavefront-guided LASIK technology. Also known as custom LASIK, the treatment involves new technologies that measure distortions in the eye, providing the physician with the information needed to chart a treatment plan customized to each patient.

Wockhardt Hospital and Heart Institute
Wockhardt Towers
Bandra Kurla Complex
Bandra East
Mumbai, INDIA 400 051
Tel: 800 730.6373 (US and Canada toll-free)
Tel: 011 91 22.2659. 4444
Email: pthukral@wockhardtin.com
Web: www.wockhardt.com

Known throughout Asia and the rest of the world for its specialty centers, Wockhardt is one of India's shining healthcare stars, particularly in the area of heart disease and surgeries. Established in 1990 in Bangalore and headquartered in Mumbai, Wockhardt is building and refining major specialty "clusters" in Calcutta (Wockhardt Hospital and Kidney Institute) and Bangalore (for cardiac, orthopedics, and neuroscience). Its Mumbai center boasts four super-specialty clinics, including its world-renowned Heart Institute, where dozens of landmark operations have been performed.

An exclusive partnership with Harvard Medical International (a division of Boston's Harvard Medical School) gives Wockhardt access to top-flight international inedical expertise, along with standards oversight and best practices discipline. Through its Harvard partnership, Wockhardt physicians and staff are afforded opportunities to consult with hospitals of excellence throughout the US and the world.

In addition to accreditation by the International Standards Organization, Wockhardt/Mumbai became the first hospital in southern India to receive JCI accreditation. Specialties include

■ **Orthopedic Clinic,** which recently introduced the Birmingham hip resurfacing procedure to its Mumbai center. One of the most sought-after procedures by international tourists, the popular Birmingham treatment is not yet allowed in the United States.

■ **Wockhardt Eye Hospital,** with clinics in cataract, glaucoma, vitreoretina and retinovascular, uveitis, squint, orbital diseases and oculoplasty, cataract and intraocular surgery, diabetic retinopathy, and neuro-ophthalmology.

■ **Wockhardt Brain and Spine Hospital:** A team of ten super-specialists, trained mostly in the UK and US, have created an internationally recognized center for the diagnosis and treatment of brain and spinal conditions. Specialties include stereotactic brain surgery (deploying brain scans, image guidance, and minimally invasive techniques); cerebrovascular surgery (aneurysms); movement disorder surgeries (including Parkinson's disease, dystonia, and multiple sclerosis); and neuromuscular disorders. Its new **Specialty Epilepsy Clinic** deploys new methods for diagnosing and treating epilepsy and other seizure-related conditions.

As with many other Indian private hospitals, Wockhardt's outpatient rooms are the lap of luxury compared to most US facilities; they include attached washroom, companion sofa bed, laundry service, color TV with DVD player, and computer terminal with Internet connection.

Wockhardt's International Patient Service Center offers airport pickup and drop-off, travel arrangements, coordination of all appointments, arrangements for accommodating companions and family, locker facilities for valuables, and cuisine tailored to suit individual palates.

■ HOTELS: DELUXE

Note: As mentioned elsewhere in this book, good, safe, reliable, full-service hotels in India aren't cheap, and moderate hotels are often lacking in amenities that help any recovering patient feel more at ease. Thus, "deluxe" hotels listing below are in the $200+ per day range, and you'll find the "moderate" listings in the $100-$200 range.

Health travel planners, as well as hospitals' International Patient Centers, often offer hotel discounts through their partnerships. Check with your agent or clinic before paying full freight.

Fariyas Hotel
25 off Arthur Bunder Road
Mumbai, INDIA
Tel: 011 91 22.2204.2911
Fax: 011 91 22.2283.4992
Email: info@fariyas.com
Web: www.fariyas.com

Taj President Hotel
90, Cuffe Parade
Mumbai, INDIA 400 005
Tel: 866 969.1825 (US toll-free)
Tel: 011 91 22.6601.1825
Fax: 011 91 22.6665.0303
Email: president.mumbai@tajhotels.com
Web: www.tajhotels.com

■ HOTELS: MODERATE

Sea Princess
Juhu Beach
Mumbai, INDIA 400 049
Tel: 011 91 22.2661.1111
Fax: 011 91 22.2661.1144
E-mail: seaprincess@vsnl.com
Web: www.seaprincess.com

Best Western Emerald
Juhu Tara Road, Juhu
Mumbai, INDIA 400 049
Tel: 011 91 22.2661.1150
Fax: 011 91 22.2660.3475
Email: hotelfrontoffice@greatemerald.com
Web: www.bestwestern.com

DESTINATION: **MALAYSIA**

■ **AT A GLANCE**

Kuala Lumpur and Penang

Language:	English widely spoken
Time Zone:	GMT+8
Country Dialing Code:	60
Electricity:	240V
Currency:	Ringgits
Visa Required?	Not for stays shorter than 90 days
Required Immunizations:	None
Treatment Specialties:	Cardiovascular, Cosmetic, Dental Care, Fertility/ Reproductive Health, General Surgery, Ophthalmology, Orthopedics, Stem Cells, Transplant
Leading Hospitals and Clinics:	Gleneagles Intan Medical Center, Kuala Lumpur; Gleneagles Medical Center, Penang; Pantai Medical Center; Prince Court Medical Center; Subang Jaya Medical Center
JCI-Accredited Hospitals:	None
Standards and Accreditation:	Association of Private Hospitals of Malaysia (APHM); Malaysian Medical Society for Quality of Health (MSQH). All private medical centers must be approved and licensed by the Malaysia Ministry of Health.

■ **TREATMENT BRIEF**

While most Asia-bound health travelers head to India or Thailand for treatment, Malaysia is probably the international medical community's best-kept secret. Facilities and expertise are on par with India and Thailand, with sometimes even lower costs, particularly for the more elaborate cardiovascular and orthopedic procedures. A comparative skip from neighboring Singapore, Malaysia offers excellent facilities and care, with prices 30-50 percent lower.

At least a dozen of Malaysia's 49 private

hospitals, including the acclaimed Gleneagles Hospital Group, now serve international patients.

Because Malaysia was a long-time British colony until 1957, Western culture is ingrained throughout the country. English is universally and comfortably spoken. Tourist attractions abound, particularly in the squeaky-clean capital of Kuala Lumpur and on the island of Penang, a favorite international beach resort and medical travel center in its own right.

Aside from these many allures, Malaysia remains somewhat impenetrable. Despite a rise in publicity, in-country services for the aspiring health traveler are disappointing. No recovery facilities exist, and in-country health travel planners are scarce.

For those who wish to research Malaysia further, two excellent Web sites provide ample data and easy searching. First, check out the Association of Private Hospitals of Malaysia Web site, www.hospitals-malaysia.org. There, you'll be able to search by region for all accredited hospitals; then, within each hospital, drill down to individual physician credentials.

At the Malaysia Healthcare Web site, www.malaysiahealthcare.com, you can use the drop down menus to access the procedure that interests you, then read about an array of comparative packages offered by the various treatment centers. The site also carries animated tutorials that are easy to understand and impressively presented.

While getting treatment, many international patients take advantage of the exceptional, thorough, and inexpensive physicals offered by most Malaysian private hospitals. A dazzling array of tests and exams, including blood work, bone density scan, chest X-ray, and treadmill can be had for around $500. Malaysian hospitals were the creators of "well-man" and "well-woman" packages — extensive, inexpensive physicals, and tests promoting preventive care. Packages include pre-employment, executive screening, maternity, and more. Health travelers can choose from a wide array of diagnostic packages, including heart, stroke, cancer, and bone scan.

An example of where Malaysia's international health travel industry is heading is the Prince Court Medical Center. As Malaysia's newest super-hospital, which will open its doors in late 2007, Prince Court will cater primarily to high-end and international patients. Financed by Malaysia's Petronas Company (builders of Kuala Lumpur's famed twin Petronas Towers), the hospital was built in partnership with the prestigious Medical University of Vienna, which supplied the chief medical officer in a three-person leadership team.

The nine-story, 300-bed hospital boasts 12 operating theaters and 15 consulting suites. In addition to covering all medical specialty fields, five "centers of excellence" will include cardiovascular, cosmetic surgery, oncology, pediatrics, and urology.

■ TYPICAL TREATMENTS AND COSTS

Cardiovascular:

Coronary Artery Bypass Graft: $12,000-$13,500

Bypass + Valve Replacement (single): $12,000-$13,500

Bypass + Valve Replacement (double): $9,000-$10,500

Pacemaker:

Single-chambered: $6,500-$8,000

Double-chambered: $7,000-$9,000

Cosmetic:

Breast:

Augmentation: $4,300-$4,500

Lift/Reduction: $4,300-$4,500

Facelift: $4,200-$4,800

Liposuction (stomach, hips, and waist): $4,200-$5,000

Tummy Tuck: $4,500-$6,000

Dental Care:

Crowns (all porcelain): $1,000-$1,500

Extractions:

Surgical: $175-$220

Wisdom Teeth: $80-$100

Implants: $2,720-$3,000

Inlays and Onlays: $100-$125

Root Canals: $700-$1,100

Veneers (porcelain): $950-$1,150

Orthopedics:

Replacements:

Ankle Joint Replacement: $4,000-$8,500

Total Hip: $6,800-$8,150

Total Knee: $6,300-$8,000

Total Shoulder: $8,000-$10,500

■ HEALTH TRAVEL AGENTS

Gorgeous Getaways
34 Fenwick Street
Melbourne VIC AUSTRALIA 3068
Tel: 011 61 394.100.153
Fax: 011 61 394.100.153
Email: info@gorgeousgetaways.com
Web: www.gorgeousgetaways.com

Although headquartered in Australia, Gorgeous Getaways regularly caters to an American clientele seeking cosmetic surgery in Malaysia and Thailand. Founder Louise Cogan and her staff have sent more than 400 patients to Malaysia and Thailand, and they now handle around 40 patients per month, increasingly from the US.

One of the huge attractions of medical treatment in Malaysia is price, and cosmetic surgery is no exception. Gorgeous Getaways carries a number of packages at eye-popping deals. For example, GG offers a package that includes breast augmentation, liposuction to abdomen, hips and thighs, 14 nights in a one-bedroom apartment for two adults, and airport transportation for $5,580. The same treatment, including a facelift, is $8,160. Treatments are carried out in two of Kuala Lumpur's finest healthcare centers, Ampang Puteri Specialist Hospital and HUKMSC Hospital (see below for descriptions). For those seeking treatment in a more resort-like setting, GG enjoys a partnership with Bangkok Phuket Hospital on Phuket Island in Thailand.

While you're at the business of improving your body, GG also advocates improving lifestyle habits, and thus offers packages that include a personalized diet program, personal fitness training, or a choice of facial and body packages and massage treatments.

Malaysia Healthcare Networks
Cameron Towers, Blk. B, Unit 1006
Jalan 5/58B, Petaling Jaya
Selangor, MALAYSIA
Tel: 011 60 377.853.727
Fax: 011 60 377.853.727
Email: info@malaysiahealthcare.com
Web: www.malaysiahealthcare.com

A newcomer to the health travel agent arena, Malaysian Healthcare has formed partnerships with Malaysia's largest hospital networks, such as KPJ Healthcare, the National Heart Institute, and Twin Towers Medical Centre. Malaysian Healthcare works with seven private, accredited hospitals offering 70 different procedural specialties.

A destination manager is assigned to accompany each patient throughout the visit. Malaysian Healthcare offers the usual amenities, including identification and booking of desired medical treatment, all travel booking, pre-treatment medical consultations, customized holiday planning, and a 24-hour toll-free number.

Malaysia Healthcare Networks' impressive Web site (www.malaysiahealthcare .com) allows patients to plan, arrange, and manage their treatment and holiday in Malaysia. Besides selecting a hospital in Malaysia, health travelers can conduct due diligence on a doctor or a specialist that would be performing the required treatment. The portal also allows patients to directly contact a selected physician, and seek consultation on treatment options.

One extra we've not seen elsewhere is Malaysian Healthcare's commitment to

making the patient's Malaysian physician available by phone or email to the home country physician upon request. Should post-operative complications or pre-op questions arise, this is a reassuring service.

MedRetreat
1121 Annapolis Road, PMB 160
Odenton, MD 21113
Tel: 877 876.3373 (US toll-free)
Fax: 847 680.0484
Email: customerservice@medretreat.com
Web: www.medtreatreat.com

For more information on MedRetreat, see Thailand.

■ HOSPITALS AND CLINICS

Gleneagles Medical Centre (Kuala Lumpur)
282 & 286 Jln Ampang
Kuala Lumpur, MALAYSIA 50450
Tel: 011 60 3.4255.2786
Fax: 011 60 3.4257.9233
Email: gimc-info@gleneaglesintan.com.my
Web: www.gimc.com.my

Established in 1996, this 330-bed private hospital is a subsidiary of Parkway Group Healthcare, Asia's second largest hospital network, based in Singapore. All of its 103 physicians and surgeons speak English, as do most of the staff. New to the medical travel industry, Gleneagles treated more than 400 US and Canadian patients last year. Treatment specialties include orthopedics, cardiovascular, and general surgery.

Gleneagles's amenities for international patients now include in-room therapeutic spa treatments, such as facials, body massages, and beauty treatments. The goal is to ease the stress of recovery and pamper the recuperating patient.

For the deluxe-minded, Gleneagles offers its presidential suite, fit for royalty, at a hefty $1,000 per day. Rooms and suites for mere mortals are modern and spacious, at less than $125-$300 per day.

Gleneagles Medical Center (Penang)
Pulau Pinang Clinic Sdn Bhd
1, Jalan Pangkor
Penang, MALAYSIA 10050
Tel: 011 60 4.220.2109
Email: enquiry@gmc.po.my
Web: www.gleneagles-penang.com

Established in 1973 and now a subsidiary of the giant Parkway Group Healthcare, Gleneagles was the first private hospital in Penang to be awarded three years full accreditation by the Malaysian Society for Quality In Health (MSQH). The hospital underwent full renovations in the late 1990s, and it is now one of Malaysia's most modern facilities.

Specialties include cardiovascular surgery (adult and pediatric), gastroenterology, gynecological oncology, nephrology, neurosurgery, general oncology, ophthalmology and vitreoretinal surgery, orthopedics, and pediatrics.

Pantai Medical Center
8, Jalan Bukit Pantai
Kuala Lumpur, MALAYSIA 59100
Tel: 011 60 3.2296.0888
Fax: 011 60 3.2282.1557
Email: pmc@pantai.com.my
Web: www.pantai.com.my

The Pantai Medical Center (PMC) is owned by the giant Pantai Group, with seven hospitals throughout Malaysia. Established in 1974 in the heart of Kuala Lumpur, PMC is its flagship hospital, with 264 beds and more than 130 specialists. The hospital has stepped up its efforts to raise its international profile, forging recent partnerships with Johns Hopkins, Duke University Medical Center, the Cleveland Clinic, and Massachusetts General Hospital.

A general hospital, Pantai offers nearly every type of general diagnostics and treatment, including specialties in urology, cardiology, orthopedics, gastroenterology, endocrinology, and ophthalmology. Pantai's Web site features an impressive roster of specialists, with email addresses for all listed physicians and surgeons.

PMC and the Pantai Group have also forged relationships with a dozen insurance providers worldwide, including Prudential/Cigna and BUPA.

Subang Jaya Medical Centre (SJMC)
Sdn. Bhd, 1, Jalan SS 12 / 1A,
47500 Subang Jaya
Selangor Darul Ehsan, MALAYSIA
Tel: 011 60 3.5630.6466
Fax: 011 60 3.5630.6075
Web: www.sjmc.com.my

Opened in 1995, Subang Jaya Medical Centre is a privately owned and internationally accredited tertiary care medical center near Kuala Lumpur, a half-hour drive from Kuala Lumpur's international airport. With the addition of its north wing and **Cancer and Radiosurgery Centre** in 2001, SJMC now has 375 beds and 14 operating theaters, with 89 specialty suites.

SJMC offers the full range of treatments, with sub-specialties in cardiovascular and thoracic surgery, oncology and radiosurgery, vascular interventional radiology, blood and marrow transplant, liver transplant surgery, urology, and infertility management.

SJMC's centers of excellence include

■ **Blood Diseases Centre,** which provides a full range of laboratory hematological services for diagnosis of blood disorders; comprehensive treatment for hematological malignancies, such as leukemia, lymphoma, and myeloma; cryopreservation and stem cells storage services for patients undergoing blood/marrow transplants; and blood/marrow transplant using matched unrelated donor for pediatric patients. SJMC is currently the only private hospital in Malaysia to offer blood/marrow transplant services.

■ **Heart Centre,** which is a one-stop treatment center that comprises the *Coronary Care Unit* (CCU), the adjacent *Cardiac Ward*, and the *Cardiovascular Laboratory*. Together they make SJMC's Heart Centre the largest in Malaysia. More than 2,000 angiograms and angioplasties have been performed since its inception. Noninvasive beating-heart techniques are promoted and practiced by SMJC's Heart Centre specialists.

■ **Vascular Interventional Radiology Centre,** where specialists practice a branch of radiology that combines new catheterization and imaging technologies. Vascular interventional radiology offers precise, accurate diagnoses and minimally invasive treatments for blood vessel disorders and diseases of the internal organs. Also known as pinhole surgery, the surgical incision, which is guided by high resolution imaging equipment, is as small as the tip of a pencil. Procedures performed using VIR generally involve less time, pain, and trauma and lead to shorter hospital stays.

■ **Subang Fertility Centre,** formerly the Pivet Laboratory Malaysia, which is a private fertility unit now based at SJMC. Couples who are having difficulty conceiving now have the benefit of the hospital's ancillary support staff and facilities, all under one roof. The center boasts many of Malaysia's firsts, including the first in-vitro fertilization (IVF) and first intracytoplasmic sperm injection (ICSI) births in the country. The center is also one of the first units in the country to successfully deliver babies conceived through the ICSI technique (using frozen-thawed and freshly retrieved testicular sperm). It was also the first center to provide treatment with recombinant drug technology, resulting in Malaysia's first IVF and ICSI births resulting from these medications.

■ **Nuclear Medicine and PET/CT Centre,** where radioactive materials are used safely in the diagnosis and treatment of various diseases. The computed tomography (CT) scan is a non-invasive, safe, and relatively painless procedure, usually involving a small injection. Positron emission tomography (PET) is another imaging method used to detect small metabolic changes in diseased tissue. With these techniques, information about various organs can be obtained quickly with little or no pain. SMJC utilizes these sophisticated techniques for bone, lung, renal (kidney), brain, and heart scans in diagnosing cancer, heart disease, neuro-logical conditions, and brain abnormali-ties.

SJMC's milestones include Malaysia's first related-donor pediatric liver transplant (1995); Malaysia's first liver transplant from a non-blood relative (1995); first open-heart surgery in a Malaysian private hospital (1985); and Malaysia's first in-vitro fertiliza-tion and embryo transfer (1999).

■ HOTELS: DELUXE

Crown Princess
City-Square Centre, Jalan Tun Razak
Kuala Lumpur, MALAYSIA 50400
Tel: 011 60 3.2162.5522
Fax: 011 60 3.2162 4492
Email: reservations@crownprincess
.com.my
Web: www.crownprincess.com.my

Hotel Nikko Kuala Lumpur
165, Jalan Ampang
Kuala Lumpur, MALAYSIA 50450
Tel: 011 60 3.2161.1111
Fax: 011 60 3.216.1122
Email: info@hotelnikko.com.my
Web: hotelnikko.com.my

E&O Hotel (Penang)
10 Lebuh Farquhar
Penang, MALAYSIA 10200
Tel: 011 60 4.222.2000
Fax: 011 60 4.261.6333
Email: reservations@e-o-hotel.com
Web: www.e-o-hotel.com

■ HOTELS: MODERATE

Lanson Place Hotel and Residency
1, Jalan Ampang Hilir
Kuala Lumpur, MALAYSIA 55000
Tel: 011 60 3.4253.2888
Fax: 011 60 3.4253.1773
Email: enquiry.lpar@lansonplace.com
Web: www.lansonplace.com

Sucasa Service Apartment
222, Jalan Ampang
Kuala Lumpur, MALAYSIA 50450
Tel: 011 60 3.4251.3833
Fax: 011 60 3.4252 1096
E-mail: sucasa@pd.jaring.my
Web: www.sucasahotel.com

DESTINATION: **MEXICO**

■ AT A GLANCE

---

(1) California and Arizona borders, (2) Texas and New Mexico borders, (3) coastal

Language:	Spanish; some English
Time Zone:	GMT-6, GMT-5
Country Dialing Code:	52
Electricity:	127 V, Plug type A
Currency:	Mexican Peso
Visa Required?	No
Required Immunizations:	None
Treatment Specialties:	Cosmetic, Dental Care, Ophthalmology
Leading Hospitals and Clinics:	Hospital Angeles, Tijuana: Christus Mu guerza
JCI-Accredited Hospitals:	None at this writing
Standards and Accreditation:	Mexican Academy of Dermatology; Mexican Association of Plastic, Reconstructive, and Aesthetic Surgery; Mexican Counsel of Aesthetic and Reconstructive Plastic Surgery

■ TREATMENT BRIEF

At first blush, Mexico is a mystery to the aspiring health traveler. Few world-class hospitals exist in Mexico, unlike less-developed India or neighboring Costa Rica. Mexican accreditation standards are weak, and to date Mexico can boast no JCI-accredited institutions. (In contrast, Brazil has six, Singapore has eleven, and Turkey has eight!)

However, JCI accreditation may be in the offing for two of Mexico's large healthcare systems. Hospital Angeles, which has five hospitals throughout Mexico, recently applied for accreditation. The other large network, Christus Muguerza, is now part of Christus Health in the US, which serves eight US states, mostly along the US-Mexican border. The merger has made Christus Muguerza the largest healthcare provider in Mexico. JCI accreditation at Hospital Christus Muguerza is expected by the end of 2007.

Along the US-Mexican border or the beautiful Mexican coast or in developed expatriate communities, you'll find dozens of smaller, established clinics that reliably treat tens of thousands of Americans each year. Many of these patients return annually for checkups, dental cleanings, physicals, and a host of other treatments that can be had far less expensively than in Europe and many Asian countries — without the rigors of trans-oceanic travel.

Mexico-bound health travelers usually encounter smaller clinics, run by two or three physicians, often second- and even third-generation families. Unassuming, yet clean and efficient, they're often as not run by either expatriate US physicians or practitioners trained in the US or Europe.

Quality clinics can be found in nearly every major city and resort, yet finding them can be fraught with frustration, and the few health travel agents serving Mexico tend to be partnered with a particular clinic or hospital. Moreover, the health traveler is likely to encounter less English in Mexico than in Malaysia or South Africa, tens of thousands of miles away.

Mexico City, with 26 million inhabitants, has the best and worst of everything, including several world-class hospitals (such as Hospital Angeles and Hospital Espanol). These centers offer state-of-the art specialties and super-specialties, including cardiology, oncology, and orthopedics.

Unfortunately, most Web sites remain in Spanish, and English-speaking physicians are not always available, nor are translation services. English-speaking patients may need to seek the assistance of health travel agencies to arrange the care they are seeking.

Convenience is the big motivation for most Mexico-bound health travelers, and it's no wonder that more than 70 percent of Mexico's US patients reside in California, Texas, or Arizona. Nearby patients from San Diego, Los Angeles, Phoenix, Tucson, and Brownsville simply make the two- to six-hour drive across the border to their clinic of choice, stay for a night or two in a hotel, then drive back. Comments one veteran multinational patient: "A three-hour drive across the border saves me $700 in physicals and dental work every year. That's a no-brainer."

Yet, for folks farther away from the border and particularly those east of the Mississippi, Mexico may be less of an option, unless you have plenty of time to search for a dentist or cosmetic surgeon, or you are traveling to Mexico anyway.

Perhaps more than any other health travel country, Mexico's leading medical destinations each serve a different type of patient. Thus, we've grouped clinics and accommodations into three destinations:

1) *Along the Border: California and Arizona* — for patients driving from those and nearby states, as well as international health travelers. This area includes Tijuana. Nearby San Diego, La Jolla, and Oceanside offer accommodations to suit any budget.

2) *Along the Border: Texas and New Mexico* — mostly for Texans and New Mexicans. Getting to El Paso International Airport sometimes requires two or more hops, even from larger urban airports, and upscale accommodations are scarce. This area includes Chihuahua and Monterey.

3) *Along the Coast*—for those seeking resorts and recreation to complement their medical treatment. This area includes Cabo San Lucas and Mazatlan. Puerto Vallarta is also a popular destination.

■ TYPICAL TREATMENTS AND COSTS

Note the wide range of prices in some treatment areas. The prices given are based on quotes received from phone calls, emails, and Internet sites. As always, when choosing a healthcare provider, check qualifications carefully.

Cardiovascular:
Abdominal Aneurysm Repair: $33,000
Cardiac Catheterization: $12,000
Coronary Artery Bypass Graft: $32,500
Valve Replacement
   Aortic or Mitral: $35,000

Cosmetic:
Breast
   Augmentation: $825-$5,000
   Lift/Reduction: $900-$3,900
   Reduction (female): $1,300-$7,650
   Reduction (male, one): $900-$3,650
   Reduction (male, two): $1,600-$5,850
Eye Lift
   Upper or lower: $2,030
   Both Upper and Lower: $2,750
Facelift: $1,000-$4,000
   Face and Neck Lift: $7,350
Liposuction (stomach, hips, and waist): $800
Nose Reconstruction: $3,800
Tummy Tuck: $1,100-$6,300

Dentistry:
Crowns (porcelain on gold): $300-$425
Dentures (upper or lower): $700-$1150
Extractions (surgical): $90-$150
Implants (per tooth): $1,250-$1,800
Inlays and Onlays: $150-$250
Porcelain Veneers: $90-$150
Root Canals: $225-$300

General Surgery:
Gall Bladder (laparoscopic): $6,400
Hernia Repair
   One (general): $3,600
   One (laparoscopic): $5,450
   Two (general): $4,400
   Two (laparoscopic): $4,550

Orthopedics:
Carpal Tunnel Release: $2,800
Joint Replacement
   Knee (one): $14,650
   Hip (one): $17,300
Meniscus Repair (both knees): $10,950

Vision:
Cataract
   One eye: $2,550
   Both eyes: $3,900
Glaucoma: $1,500
LASIK (per eye): $300-$400

Weight Loss:
LAP-BAND System: $500-$600
Gastric Bypass: $800

Wellness:

Colonoscopy

With Biopsy: $1,500

Virtual: $1000

Wellness Exam

Men (< 40 yrs): $875

Men (> 40 yrs): $1,200

Women (< 40 yrs): $1000

Women (> 40 yrs): $1,550

■ HEALTH TRAVEL AGENTS

Third-party travel planners for Mexico are scarce, offset by the fact that hospitals and clinics generally offer full services to patients and Mexican phone numbers are readily available to Americans. Similar time zones to the US are also a plus for contacting healthcare providers. We caution you to check out Mexican healthcare referrals carefully.

Global Choice Healthcare

9200 San Mateo Blvd NE

Albuquerque, NM 87113

Tel: 800 392.5189 (US toll-free)

Tel: 877 858.0123 (US toll-free)

Fax: 818 665.4810

Email: info@planethospital.com

Web: www.info@gchcare.com

Global Choice (GC) orchestrates complete medical procedure packages to Monterrey, Mexico (Christus Muguerza Hospital), and Singapore. GC caters to uninsured and underinsured patients, small businesses, and benefit brokers.

GC focuses on episode-of-care packages, which can be treated in a finite time period. They have a predictable start and stop date, so that clients know how much time will be involved.

Medical procedures covered include cardiovascular bypass grafts, cosmetic surgery (tummy tucks), dental care, infertility care, general surgery, orthopedics (hip resurfacing), bilateral knee replacements, vascular surgery, and wellness clinics.

PlanetHospital

23679 Calabasas Rd #150

Calabasas, CA 91302

Tel: 800 243.0172 (US toll-free)

Fax: 818 665.4810

Email: info@planethospital.com

Web: www.planethospital.com

Established in 2002, PlanetHospital primarily serves Asia and Latin America, although it is expanding to Cyprus, Dubai, and Israel. The agency recently included Mexico in its itinerary. PlanetHospital has sent more than 1,000 people to other countries for healthcare, and the agency services more than 80 clients each month.

For more information on Planet Hospital, see Singapore.

Plastic Surgeons Mexico

San Diego, CA

Tel: 888 732.2314 (US toll-free)

Tel: 760 731.0624

Web: www.plasticsurgeons-mexico.com

Plastic Surgeons Mexico (PSM) is a part of Surgical Care International (see below). The agency provides general information on plastic surgeons in Tijuana, but only after you register on its Web site. Most of its referrals are to the Aesthetic Plastic Surgery Institute. Patients working with PSM are responsible for their own travel arrangements.

Surgical Care International LLC
2385 NW Executive Center Drive
Suite 100
Boca Raton, FL 33431
Tel: 866 712.6166 (US toll-free)
Tel: 760 731.0624
Fax: 561 450.8284
Web: www.surgicalcareinterantional.com

Surgical Care International (SCI) arranges healthcare to Guadalajara, Mexico, where shopping sprees, sightseeing, cultural pursuits, and trips to nearby beaches and spas can be arranged around a medical appointment schedule. Many US cities have nonstop flights directly to Guadalajara, and flights often take four hours or less. SCI provides full-service arrangements of health providers, financing, and accommodations.

■ HOSPITALS AND CLINICS

ALONG THE BORDERS: CALIFORNIA AND ARIZONA

For better or worse, the most accessible clinics in this region are located in Tijuana, just over the border from San Diego. With a nearly insurmountable reputation for illicit drugs, prostitution, and nonstop revelry, Tijuana is also the state of Baja's largest city and a huge cultural and commercial center. Dozens of well-established and reputable dental and cosmetic surgery clinics exist alongside the fly-by-nights and hangers-on. We caution you to choose your healthcare center carefully. Use a reputable health travel agency or a recommendation from a trusted friend.

Aesthetic Plastic Surgery Institute
(Tijuana)
Jose Clemente Orozco 2468
Plaza Medical Zona Rio
Tijuana, B.C., MEXICO 22320
Tel: 866 846.4144 (US toll-free)
Tel: 011 52 664.634.2310
Email: drsergio@sergiosoberanes.com
Web: www.drsergiosoberanes.com

This small clinic, with one surgeon and a staff of six, treats patients from the US and Canada, often referred by Plastic Surgeons Mexico. The clinic's beautifully appointed offices provide comfort amidst the less elegant backdrop of downtown Tijuana.

Head surgeon Dr. Sergio Soberanes received his degree at Universidad Autonoma de Baja California's School of Medicine in 1984 and completed his internship at Hospital General de Tijuana. The clinic is board-certified through the Mexican Board of Aesthetic Plastic and Reconstructive Surgery, and Dr. Soberanes is a member of the Mexican Counsel of Aesthetic and Reconstructive Plastic Surgery.

APSI's specialties include Botox treatments, brow lifts, eyelid surgery, facelifts, and nose reconstruction. Body contouring procedures include arm, hip, and thigh lifts; breast lifts, augmentation, and reduction; tumescent liposuction; tummy tucks; and vaginal reconstruction and rejuvenation. Weight-loss treatments include LAP-BAND surgery, gastric bypass surgery, and post-bariatric body contouring.

Baja Oral Center (Tijuana)
Jose Clemente Orozco St. 10122-Suite 408,
4th floor
Plaza Pacifico Building, Zona Rio
Tijuana, B.C., MEXICO
Tel: 800 601.3795 (US toll-free)
Tel: 011 52 664.634.7626
Email: smile@bajaoralcenter.com
Web: www.bajaoralcenter.com

Six specialists and a staff of 12 run this
clinic, located on the fourth floor of a large
downtown Tijuana office building. Specialties include cosmetic and restorative
dentistry, implants, oral and maxillofacial
surgery, orthodontics, pediatric dentistry,
periodontics, and root canals. The clinic
claims to be 100 percent mercury-free.

Baja Oral's lobby is equipped with a
courtesy Internet connection and free calls
to the US. For those who wish to see what
the dentist sees, treatment rooms carry
intra-oral cameras and monitors.

Free taxi transport from the twin town
of San Ysidro helps patients avoid border
hassles.

Clinica Dental Estrella (Tijuana)
Av. Niños Heroes No. 995 between 3rd and
4th street
Zona Centro
Tijuana, B.C., MEXICO 22000
Tel: 619 308.7989 (US toll-free)
Tel: 011 52 664.688.1651
Fax: 011 52 664.685.0494
Email: info@clinicadentalestrella.com
Web: www.clinicadentalestrella.com

Specializing in implants and prosthodontics (including bridges, crowns, dentures
[partial and complete], inlays, and veneers),
family-run Clinic Dental Estrella, with four
doctors and a staff of ten, claims more than
30 years combined dentistry experience.

Prosthodontist Jaime Estrella received
his three-year specialty in advanced prosth-
odontic dentistry from California's Loma
Linda University, where he also completed
a one-year internship in implant surgery.

Implantologist Miguel Estrella received
a three-year specialty in advanced implant
dentistry from Loma Linda University, and
training in esthetic restorations at the Nobel Biocare Training Institute in Yorba Linda,
California. He is licensed with the Dental
Board of California, and is a Member of the
American Academy of Implant Dentistry,
and the American Academy of Osseointe-
gration.

The facility offers onsite deep bleaching
light system, digital and panoramic x-rays,
digital photography, implant tomography,
and a sterile surgical suite.

Codet Aris Vision Institute (Tijuana)
Codet Aris Vision Institute Ave.
Padre Kino 10159
Tijuana, B.C. MEXICO 22320
Tel: 888 265.6567 (US toll-free)
Tel: 011 52 664.682.9250
Email: info@codetlaser.com
Web: www.codetarisvision.com

Codet Aris Vision Institute enjoys a good reputation, owing mostly to its founder Dr. Arturo Chayet. In 1994, he attracted worldwide attention as the first surgeon in western North America to perform corrective laser eye surgery, and he has since gone on to achieve several worldwide milestones in refractive surgery. A past president of the Mexican Society of Refractive Surgery, Chayet has been published in dozens of scholarly journals. In 2000 the US-based International Society of Refractive Surgery awarded him its highest-honor, the Lans Award, for outstanding and innovative research in the field of refractory surgery. Chayet received his degree in corneal and refractive surgery at the University of California, San Diego.

Codet's eye surgeons have performed more than 14,000 eye surgeries since 2002. Most patients arrive from outside Mexico. Although LASIK treatments are by far the most requested treatments, specialties include cataracts, corneal treatments, glaucoma, ocular plastics, pediatric ophthalmology, and retinal surgery.

For those who want to be on the forefront of vision techniques, Codet is usually years ahead of the US. For example, in September 2004, the FDA approved the Verisyse implantable lens, which was heralded as a milestone. Yet the announcement was no surprise to Chayet, whose clinic had been deploying this procedure since 1998.

CosMED Plastic Aesthetic Surgical Center (Tijuana)
Calle Mision de San Diego #1527-301
Zona Rio
Tijuana, B.C., MEXICO
Tel: 877 426.7633 (US toll-free)
Tel: 011 52 664.634.1903
Fax: 011 52 619.330.3744
Email: cosmed@infosel.net.mx
Web: www.cosmedtj.com

Although smaller than some of its counterparts with a staff of 15, CosMED is one of Mexico's most acclaimed cosmetic surgery clinics. Its three surgeons see more than 400 Americans and other international travelers each month for consultation or surgery.

CosMED's surgeons claim more than 30 years of combined practice in cosmetic surgery, and all are board-certified. Specialties include

- **Facial Rejuvenation**: cheek and chin enhancement; collagen injections; ear modification; facial lifts including eyes, eyebrows, forehead, and neck; lip treatments; and nose reconstruction

- **Cosmetic Dermatology**: chemical peels, dermabrasion, laser skin resurfacing, and wrinkle and scar improvement

- **Body Contouring**: Botox injections; breast enlargement, lift, and reduction; buttock implants; liposuction and ultrasonic liposuction; tummy tuck; and spider vein therapy

■ **Hair Transplants:** mini-grafts and micro-grafts

CosMED also boasts a full-service spa, housed in the same offices, which offers a 60-minute facial treatment, 35-minute "lunchtime peel," 80-minute four-layer facial, eight-minute deep-cleansing intensifying facial, 35-minute manual lymphatic drainage (recommended before and after facelifts), and skin resurfacing.

CosMED's Web site features an all-video testimonials page. In addition to hearing the expected accolades, prospective patients can view the clinic's impressive surroundings.

Hospital Angeles Tijuana (Tijuana)
Av. Paseo de los Heroes #10999
Zona Rio
Tijuana, B.C. MEXICO 22010
Tel: 011 52 664.635.7806
Fax: 011 52 664.634.2251
Web: www.hospitalangelestijuana.com
.mx/new

Hospital Angeles Tijuana is part of the large Hospital Angeles group that has applied for JCI accreditation. The five-story hospital tower hosts 94 patient rooms and six operating rooms in addition to specialty operating areas.

The hospital has more than 60 specialist physicians, most of whom are US or UK board-certified or have US or UK fellowships. Specialties include cardiovascular, cosmetic surgery, general surgery, infertility treatment, neurology, and orthopedics.

Health tourist agency Planet Hospital refers patients to this facility for cardiovascular care.

Pacific Dental (Tijuana)
Ignacio Comonfort #9317 Suite F Zona Río
Tijuana, B.C. MEXICO
Tel: 877 752.5132 (US toll-free)
Tel: 011 52 664.634.0835
Email: pacificdental@hotmail.com
Web: www.mexicotijuanadentist.com

Most patients coming to Pacific Dental are Americans seeking the 60 percent dental discount often found in Mexico.

The clinic boasts its own crown and bridge laboratory, specializing in porcelain fused to metal and all-ceramic restorations. The latest dental materials are used: Express 2, Finesse, Optec, and Procera.

Services include cosmetic and general dentistry, crowns, dentures, implants, porcelain veneers, restorations, root canals, and tooth bonding.

ALONG THE BORDERS: TEXAS AND NEW MEXICO

Somewhat less accessible to the international traveler, several reputable clinics serve Dallas, Houston, San Antonio, El Paso, Albuquerque, Santa Fe, and other nearby US population centers. Health travelers may choose to fly into El Paso or Dallas, then rent a car and drive across the border.

Rio Dental (Chihuahua)
3970 Rio Chompoton
Cd. Juarez,
Chihuahua, MEXICO
Tel: 800 635.7462 (US toll-free)
Tel: 011 52 915.760.8773
Fax: 011 52 915.975.8257
Email: office@riodental.com
Web: www.riodental.com

Owned and run by Americans, Rio Dental Clinic opened its doors in 2005, peopled by a young, talented staff of dentists and specialists. Lead dentist (and co-owner) Dr. Jessica Andel graduated in 2000 from Universidad Autonoma de Ciudad Juarez, and has been practicing since that time. Three additional specialists focus on oral surgery, periodontics, and root canal. Rio Dental requires that all dentists and specialists speak English, and more important, that they complete biannual continuing education seminars in Mexico and the US.

Services and specialties include crowns and bridges, dentures and plates, implants, tooth whitening, and routine checkups. Rio Dental provides free transportation to and from most El Paso hotels and from the airport for patients heading directly to their office.

Christus Muguerza Conchita Hospital
(Monterrey)
Christus Muguerza Alta Especialidad Hospital
Hidalgo 2525 Pte. Col. Obispado
Monterrey, Nuevo Leon, MEXICO
Tel: 011 52 8399.3400
Web: www.christusmuguerza.com

Christus Muguerza Sur Hospital
(Monterrey)
Carretera Nacional 6501 Col La Estanzuela
Monterey, Nuevo Leon, MEXICO
Tel: 011 52 8155.5000
Web: www.christusmuguerza.com

Christus Muguerza Hospitals are part of the US Christus Health Group, a nonprofit health system that serves more than 44 hospitals in the US and Mexico. Christus Health is ranked as one of the ten best Catholic health systems in the US.

Conchita Hospital is a 110-bed hospital connected with the University of Monterrey. It provides cardiology, hemodialysis, and neurology services. Larger Alta Especialidad Hospital, which has 200 beds, specializes in cosmetic and weight-loss surgeries. Sur Hospital has 100 beds and a full pediatric unit.

Global Choice Healthcare offers healthcare packages to Christus Muguerza for cardiovascular care, cosmetic and general surgery, ophthalmology, and orthopedics.

ALONG THE COAST

We've focused on the most popular resorts, most accessible by air (one-stop or less from most major US airports, with ample accommodations for every lifestyle). Health travelers heading for these destinations have usually budgeted additional time to allow for recovery as well as a week or more sightseeing or relaxing.

Mexican Dental Vacation (Mazatlan)
Olas Altas #1
Centro Historico
Mazatlan, Sinaloa, MEXICO 82000
Tel: 780 701.2507 (from Canada)
Tel: 011 52 669.981.8236
Fax: 011 52 669.981.8236
Email: nkonev@yahoo.com
Web: www.mexicandentalvacation.com

Mexican Dental Vacation (MDV) was founded by Canadian businessman Nick Konev to provide first-class dental care at huge savings. The clinic has two dentists: Dr. Lino Guzman is an oral surgeon and endodontist. His wife, Dr. Arcelea Mesa, is a general dentist. Both attend annual continuing education courses and conferences in the US.

MDV specializes in implants, and the office performs seven to ten implants each day. Other specialties include bridges, root canals, and cosmetic work such as bleaching and crowns. Prices at MDV are slightly higher than the average dental prices in Mexico, but the prices are still at least 50 percent less than in the US. Why the higher prices? MDV offers the newest state-of-the-art equipment, an autoclave to clean all equipment (which not every office in Mexico has), and a two-year guarantee on dental work done at the clinic.

A word of caution: As in the US, there are often delays in dental work, so plan a few extra days in Mazatlan, just in case. In addition, treatments such as implants are a two-step process, with several months of healing between procedures, meaning two visits to the land of the sun. MDV rents timeshares to health travelers, who can choose from some of Mazatlan's finest for around $300 per week.

Miguelangelo Plastic Surgery Clinic

(Cabo San Lucas)
Transpeninsular Highway MK 6.7
Cabo San Lucas, B.C. Sur, MEXICO 23454
Tel: 800 386.2226 (US toll-free)
Tel: 011 52 624.104.3853
Fax: 011 52 624.104.3587
Email: info@miguelangeloclinic.com
Web: http://miguelangeloclinic.com

One of Mexico's top cosmetic surgery clinics, the one-doctor Miguelangelo clinic is renowned mostly for its founder, owner, and head surgeon, Dr. Miguelangelo Gonzalez. The clinic has a staff of ten. Up to 90 percent of its patients come from the US or Canada.

A new recovery center is scheduled to open in 2007 in Cabo San Lucas's upscale Pedregal neighborhood. Currently, patients spend one or two nights recovering at the center, attended 24/7 by clinic personnel.

Angel's Touch Dental Clinic (Cabo San Lucas)

Plazas Doradas Building Local #10 & #11
Carretera Transpeninsular
Cabo San Lucas, B.C. Sur, MEXICO
Tel: 866 331.3996 (US toll-free)
Tel: 011 52 624.142.6192 or 011 52 624.142.2459
Fax: 011 52 624.142.2459
Email: info@angelsdental.com
Web: www.angelsdental.com

Owner and head dentist Dr. Rosy Peña opened her clinic in 1981, in the central plaza of Cabo San Lucas. Angel's Touch now has a staff of five, including a general dentist, dental surgeon, endodontist, orthodontist, and periodontist. The clinic sees more than 120 US patients each month.

Services include amalgam/mercury filling removal (price includes tooth color-matching resin replacement fillings), bridges, crowns (porcelain over metal), dentures, extractions, fillings, implants (traditional or one-day [for laterals only]), partials (traditional and ValPlast or Teflon), periodontal (including gum reduction, osseous treatment, and deep periodontal cleaning), and root canals.

■ HOTELS: DELUXE

Although the deluxe hotels listed are at the higher end of accommodations given, featured amenities vary by location.

ALONG THE BORDERS: CALIFORNIA AND ARIZONA

Grand Hotel Tijuana (Tijuana)
Blvd. Agua Caliente 4500
Col Aviacion, CP 22420
Tijuana, BC, MEXICO
Tel: 866 472.6385 (US toll-free)
Fax: 011 52 624.681.7016
Email: reservations@grandhoteltij.com.mx
Web: www.grandhoteltij.com.mx

Hotel Del Coronado (San Diego)
1500 Orange Avenue
Coronado, CA 92118
Tel: 800 468.3533 (US toll-free)
Tel: 619 435.6611
Fax: 619.522.8262
Email: delinquiries@hoteldel.com
Web: www.hoteldel.com

ALONG THE BORDERS: TEXAS AND NEW MEXICO

Fiesta Inn Ciudad Juarez (Juarez)
Paseo Triunfo de la Republica 3451
Colonia Circuito Pronaf
Ciudad Juarez, Chihuahua, MEXICO
Tel: 011 52 656.686.0700
Email: rinternet@posadas.com
Web: www.fiestainn.com

Hotel Quinta Real Monterey (Monterrey)
Diego Rivera # 500 Fraccionamiento Valle Oriente
Monterrey, MEXICO 66260
Tel: 866 621.9288 (US and Canada toll-free)
Tel: 011 52 818.368.1000
Fax: 011 52 818.368.1070
Email: reservaciones@quintareal.com
Web: www.quintareal.com

COASTAL

Westin Resort (Cabo San Lucas)
Carretera Transpeninsular K
San Jose Del Cabo, MEXICO
Tel: 800 754.6835 (US toll-free)
Tel: 011 52 624.142.9000
Fax: 011 52 624.142.9050
Email: reservations.01087@westin.com
Web: www.starwoodhotels.com

Hotel El Tapatio & Resort (Guadalajara)
Blvd. Aeropuerto #4275, Tiaquepaque
C.P. 45599
Guadalajara, Jalisco, MEXICO
Tel: 800 327.1847 (US toll-free)
Tel: 011 52 33.3837.2929
Fax: 011 52 33.3635.6664
Email: customer-service@hotel-tapatio
    .com
Web: www.hotel-tapatio.com

Hotel Villa Ganz (Guadalajara)
Lopez Cotilla #1739, Col. Lafayette 44140
Guadalajara, Jalisco, MEXICO
Tel: 800 813.2333 (US toll-free)
Tel: 011 52 33.3120.1416
Fax: 800 813.2333 (US toll-free)
Email: reservaciones@villaganz.com
Web: www.villaganz.com

■ HOTELS: MODERATE

ALONG THE BORDERS: CALIFORNIA AND ARIZONA

Hotel Emporio (Tijuana)
Blvd. Agua Caliente 11553, Col. Aviación
C.P. 22420
Tijuana, B.C. MEXICO
Tel: 866 936.7674 (US and Canada toll-free)
Tel: 011 52 664.622.6600
Fax: 011 664.622.6602
Email: tijuana.ventas@hotelesemporio.com
Web: www.hotelesemporio.com

Holiday Inn Express (Chula Vista, CA)
4450 Main Street
Chula Vista, CA 91911
Tel: 619 422.2600
Fax: 619 425.4605
Web: www.hiexpress.com

ALONG THE BORDERS: TEXAS AND NEW MEXICO

Camino Real Hotel El Paso (El Paso, TX)
101 S El Paso St
El Paso, TX 79901
Tel: 800 769.4300 (US toll-free)
Tel: 915 534.3000
Fax: 915 534.3090
Email: elpaso@caminoreal.com.mx
Web: www.caminoreal.com

Hilton Garden Inn Monterrey (Monterrey)
Blvd. Antonio L. Rodriguez #1880
Monterrey, Nuevo Leon, MEXICO 64650
Tel: 011 52 8122.8000
Fax: 011 52 8122.8001
Web: www.hiltongardeninn.hilton.com

ALONG THE COAST

Casa De Leyendas (Mazatlan)
Venustiano Carranza 4
Centro Historico
Mazatlan, MEXICO
Tel: 011 52 669.981.6180
Tel: 011 52 602.445.6192
Email: info@CasaDeLeyendas.com
Web: www.casadeleyendas.com

Hotel Emporio (Mazatlan)
Av. Camarón Sábalo #51, Zona Dorada,
C.P. 82110
Mazatlán, Sinaloa, MEXICO
Tel: 866 936.7674 (US and Canada toll-free)
Tel: 011 52 669.983.4822
Fax: 011 52 669.984.4532
Email: reservaciones@hotelesemporio.com
Web: www.hotelesemporio.com

DESTINATION: **SINGAPORE**

■ AT A GLANCE

Singapore City

Language:	English (primary language), Mandarin, Malay, Tamil
Time Zone:	GMT+8
Country Dialing Code:	65
Electricity:	230V, Plug type G
Currency:	Singapore Dollars (SGD)
Visa Required?	Not for stays shorter than 90 days
Required Immunizations:	None
Treatment Specialties:	Cardiovascular, General Surgery, Neurology, Oncology, Orthopedics, Stem Cell Therapy
Leading Hospitals and Clinics:	National Healthcare Group, Parkway Group Healthcare, Raffles Hospital Network, Singapore Health Services (SingHealth)
Standards and Accreditation:	Specialists Accreditation Board, Singapore Ministry of Health, JCI
JCI-Accredited Hospitals:	Alexandra Hospital, Changi General Hospital, Gleneagles Hospital, Institute of Mental Health/Woodbridge Hospital, Johns Hopkins Singapore International Medical Centre, KK Women's and Children's Hospital, Mount Elizabeth Hospital, National Heart Centre of Singapore, National University Hospital, Singapore General Hospital, Tan Tock Seng Hospital

■ TREATMENT BRIEF

Like Malaysia, Singapore is less familiar to US patients as a health travel destination than Thailand and India. However, Singapore has been an international healthcare destination since the 1980s, and more than 374,000 international patients visited Singapore in 2005. The country boasts 11 JCI-accredited hospitals — more than any other nation besides the US — and one-third of all JCI-accredited facilities in Asia. Singapore is also home to Asia's second largest hospital network, Parkway Group Healthcare, with 1,500 beds, 1,400 specialists, and three JCI-accredited treatment centers.

In 2000 the World Health Organization ranked Singapore's healthcare system number one in Asia and sixth in the world. Singapore has one of the lowest infant (1.9/1,000 births) and maternal (0.0 to 1.0/1,000 live or stillbirths) mortality rates in the world. Life expectancy averages 79.3 years; males live an average of 77.4 years and females, 81.3 years.

Singapore doctors are sent on "Health Manpower Development Programmes" to the best medical centers around the world, and they return to serve and improve the quality of services to match international standards.

Having invested a great deal of time, money, and energy in the quality of the healthcare professionals, facilities, and infrastructure through the past decades of economic plenty, Singapore finds itself in the curious position of having insufficient sick people to sustain the quality of health-care services it has developed. Singapore must serve a larger population than its 4.5 million people — hence, the large "insourcing" of patients."

Singapore Medicine Initiative In 2003 the government of Singapore launched the Singapore Medicine Initiative to develop and maintain Singapore as a medical travel destination and to consolidate its considerable medical offerings. The Singapore government supports the healthcare industry — as confirmed by the nation's four major government and private hospital networks.

Research partnerships with US universities, such as Johns Hopkins and Duke Medical Center, along with formal relationships with GlaxoSmithKline and Novartis, underscore Singapore's sustained commitment to cutting-edge healthcare.

Healthcare Specialties Singapore boasts a wider range of healthcare services than most other countries. Special highlights include SingHealth's National Cancer Center Singapore and the Biopolis biotechnology research center.

The National Cancer Center is one of Asia's leading hospitals for oncology diagnosis and treatment. This multidisciplinary research and treatment complex offers specialties in bone, breast, brain, cervical, colon, liver, lymph, lung, ovarian, and prostate cancers.

The new hub of Singapore's health sciences effort is the $300 million Biopolis, a seven-building, two-million-square-foot biotechnology research center that opened in late 2003. Among other projects, Biopolis will house a stem cell bank to parlay some of the world's most liberal laws on the use of human embryonic cells into research and experimentation. Researchers hope that stem cells, the all-purpose building blocks that turn into specific tissue like bone, muscle, or nerves, can be cultivated and used to treat congenital defects, injuries, and a host of other maladies. Dozens of US and European scientists have been lured to Biopolis, which has, in turn, yielded partnerships with prominent universities, research centers, and pharmaceutical and healthcare companies.

Health travelers enjoy the widespread use of English as the preferred business language. Because Singapore is one of Asia's wealthiest nations and has Southeast

Asia's highest standard of living, medical travelers are spared the glaring cultural and economic contrasts often seen in India, Central America, and South America. Most of Singapore is squeaky clean, with some city streets so filled with US retail store-fronts that they feel eerily like home.

Those seeking scenic side trips or exotic vacations should know that Singapore is all urban and suburban, offering few opportunities for rural or beach excursions. Malaysia and Thailand, both excellent medical destinations in their own right, are relatively short hops by air from Singapore.

All these advantages come with a catch. While most treatments are far less costly than in the US, Singapore remains one of Asia's most expensive medical stops, catering largely to patrons from the adjacent countries, the Middle East, Europe, and Africa, seeking higher quality care. However, the Singapore government is seeking to attract one million medical travelers by 2012, and in doing so will likely become more competitively priced.

■ TYPICAL TREATMENTS AND COSTS

Cardiovascular:

Angiography: $2,500-$3,750

Angioplasty: $9,950-$16,400

Bypass + Valve Replacement
  Single Valve: $21,000-$23,500
  Double Valve: $22,500-25,000

Coronary Artery Bypass Graft: $12,050-$20,500

Pacemaker (single-chambered): $550

Pacemaker (double-chambered): $750

Cosmetic:

Botox: $300-$1,000

Breast:
  Augmentation: $5,000-$10,000
  Lift/Reduction: $5,000-$10,000
  Reconstruction: $3,500-$5,000

Calf Augmentation: $3,075

Cheek Implants (each): $200

Ear Reconstruction: $2,500

Eyelid Reconstruction: $2,500

Facelift: $5,000-$10,000
  Mini: $3,000-$7,500

Laser:
  Hair Removal: $450
  Skin Resurfacing: $2,400

Liposuction (stomach, hips, and waist): $3,000-$10,000

Neck Lift: $3,000-$15,000

Nose Reconstruction: $2,000-$5,000

Thermage: $1,000-$5,000

Tummy Tuck: $4,000-$8,000

Dental Care:

Crowns (all porcelain): $275-$325

Extractions:

Surgical (per tooth): $50-$125

Wisdom Teeth (per tooth): $175

Implants: $2,500-$3,200

Inlays and Onlays (per tooth):$425

Veneers (porcelain): $250-$300

General Surgery:

Gall Bladder: $1,950-$3,850

Hernia Repair (one): $1,950-$3,350

Prostate (TURP): $3,550-$6,950

Ophthalmology:

Cataract (per eye): $1,850-$4,000

Glaucoma (per eye): $500-$4,150

LASIK (per eye): $925-$1,800

Orthopedics:

Birmingham Hip Resurfacing: $12,000

Carpal Tunnel: $850-$1,250

Joint Replacement:

Ankle: $4,500-$6,000

Hip: $12,000

Knee: $8,350-$10,900

Shoulder: $5,500-$6,800

Weight Loss:

LAP-BAND System: $8,800

Gastric Bypass: $13,000-$40,000

■ HEALTH TRAVEL AGENTS

Global Choice Healthcare

9200 San Mateo NE

Albuquerque, NM 87114

Tel: 800 392.5189 (US toll-free)

Tel: 505 858.0123

Fax: 505 858.0128

Email: info@gchcare.com

Web: www.gchcare.com

A newcomer to the US health travel planning arena (founded 2006), Global Choice Healthcare currently serves India, Singapore, and Costa Rica. The firm has formed partnerships with leading hospitals in these countries to offer cardiovascular services, cosmetic surgery, dental care, neurosurgery, ophthalmology, and orthopedics. A helpful treatment-pricing calculator is located on the "Procedures" page of the GCH Web site. The site also features a growing list of doctors, along with their treatment specialties, hospital affiliations, credentials, number of surgeries performed, and other useful information.

Global Choice patient services include trip planning, transfer of medical records, and passport/visa assistance. The agency makes all travel and medical arrangements (airfare, hotel, hospital, surgeon/physician contact, and scheduling) and books hotels and tours. An in-country concierge service (for an extra fee) provides airport and medical appointment transfers, cell phones, and a 24-hour emergency contact number. Third-party financing is available, and GCH is currently working with insurance companies to offer creative financing plans for health travelers.

Planet Hospital
23679 Calabasas Road, Suite 150
Calabasas, CA 91302
Tel: 800 243.0172 (US toll-free)
Tel: 818 591.1668
Fax: 818 665.4810
Email: rudy@planethospital.com
Web: www.planethospital.com

Founded by Rudy Rupak in 2002 when his fiancé fell ill in Thailand, Planet Hospital currently serves six countries, including Belgium, Costa Rica, India, Mexico, Singapore, and Thailand, and will soon be offering services to Dubai and Israel. Since opening its doors, Planet Hospital has sent more than 1,000 patients abroad. Specialties include cardiovascular services, cosmetic surgery, dental care, fertility/reproduction, oncology, and ophthalmology in addition to weight management, diabetes management, and sex-change operations.

Planet Hospital's Web site offers a long list of major hospitals in its service area, along with a sampling of its top recommended physicians and their credentials. A robust testimonials page features real clients with real names. At this writing, Planet Hospital is sending 80 patients per month abroad for treatment.

■ HOSPITALS AND CLINICS

Essentially all four healthcare provider groups in Singapore are private limited companies. National Healthcare Group and Singapore Health Services (also known as SingHealth) are public sector services, owned by the government. Private providers include the Parkway Group Healthcare and many other medical centers, such as the Johns Hopkins Singapore International Medical Centre.

Sorting through these four healthcare groups and their 22 hospitals and clinics can be daunting! The following lists the hospitals most frequently used by international patients.

National Healthcare Group
Alexandra Hospital*
Institute of Mental Health / Woodbridge
 Hospital*
National University Hospital*
Tan Tock Seng Hospital*

Parkway Group Healthcare
East Shore Hospitals
Gleneagles Hospital*
Mount Elizabeth Hospital*

Singapore Health Services
Hospitals
Changi General Hospital*
KK Women's and Children's Hospital*
Singapore General Hospital*

National Centres
Cancer
Dental
Heart*
Eye
Neuroscience Institute

Other Medical Groups and Centers
eMenders
Johns Hopkins Singapore International
 Medical Centre*
Mount Alvernia Hospital
Raffles Hospital
Thomson Medical Centre
Surgeons International
The West Clinic
*JCI-accredited hospitals

NATIONAL HEALTHCARE GROUP

National Healthcare Group (NHG) (www
.nhg.com.sg) is a leader in public healthcare in Singapore, recognized at home and
abroad for the quality of its medical expertise and facilities. In 2005, NHG became
Singapore's first healthcare provider to
achieve JCI accreditation.

The hospitals in this group provide a full
range of healthcare services, from health
screening to tertiary specialist services and
medical research. Health travelers use a
one-stop International Patient Liaison Centre (IPLC) that facilitates access to all services in NHG. IPLC acts as a liaison between
NHG and referral sources, patients and
families, and payers outside of Singapore.

As a major healthcare provider in Singapore, NHG provides an integrated network
of nine primary healthcare polyclinics, four
tertiary acute care hospitals, one national
center, three specialty institutes, and five
business divisions.

Alexandra Hospital

International Patient Services (IPS)
Level 3 Administration Block
378 Alexandra Road
SINGAPORE 159964
Tel: 011 65 6472.2000 (general info)
Tel: 011 65 6476.8828 (IPS)
Fax: 011 65 6379.5348
Fax: 011 65 6379.3880 (IPS)
Email: ips@alexhosp.com.sg
Web: www.alexhosp.com.sg

Formerly the British Military Hospital, Alexandra received a total makeover in 2000
under the auspices of the National Healthcare Group. The hospital ranks highest in

the Singapore Ministry of Health's patient
satisfaction survey.

Specialties include cardiology, dentistry,
diabetes diagnosis and treatment, endocrinology, gastroenterology, general surgery,
neurology, ophthalmology, orthopedics,
and neck and head surgery.

Transportation is provided to and from
the airport, and Alexandra has negotiated
discount rates with nearby hotels. IPS can
make restaurant and sightseeing reservations and help with transportation to and
from local destinations. This service may be
helpful, considering that Singapore receives
nearly 10 million international visitors a year.
Alexandra Hospital does not arrange air
transportation or hotel accommodations.

National University Hospital

5 Lower Kent Ridge Road
SINGAPORE 119074
Tel: 011 65 6779.2777 (24-hour helpline)
Fax: 011 65 6777.8065
Email: iplc@nhg.com.sg
Web: www.nuh.com.sg

Singapore's only acute-care tertiary university hospital provides clinical disciplines
including cardiovascular care and surgery,
liver transplants, obstetrics and gynecology, oncology, and pediatrics. Constantly at
the forefront of clinical research, the
928-bed hospital is also the country's first
hospital to have received JCI accreditation.

Tan Tock Seng Hospital

11 Jalan Tan Tock Seng
SINGAPORE 308433
Tel: 011 65 6779.2777 (24-hour helpline)
Fax: 011 65 6777.8065
Email: iplc@nhg.com.sg
Web: www.ttsh.com.sg

TTSH is a 1,400-bed hospital, the second largest in Singapore, with strengths in geriatric medicine, infectious diseases, rehabilitation medicine, respiratory medicine, and rheumatology. The hospital is a major referral center for diagnostic radiology, emergency medicine, gastroenterology, otolaryngology (ears, nose, and throat), and orthopedic surgery.

Johns Hopkins Singapore International Medical Centre

11 Jalan Tan Tock Seng
SINGAPORE 308433
Tel: 011 65 6880.2222
Fax: 011 65 6880.2233
Email: info@imc.jhmi.edu
Web: www.imc.jhmi.edu

Johns Hopkins Singapore (JHS) was established by the US university of the same name in 1998 as its base of medical operations in Southeast Asia. The center concentrates on patient care, education, and research. In 2005 the medical center relocated to Tan Tock Seng Hospital.

The center provides Hopkins-quality oncology services to local and international patients. JHS uses the most up-to-date therapies and new technologies, working in collaboration with researchers at Johns Hopkins University, the National University of Singapore, and National University Hospital.

Research and educational activities are carried out by the Division of Biomedical Sciences, an academic division of the medical school, with a focus on cellular and immunotherapies and a specific interest in stem cell research.

PARKWAY GROUP HEALTHCARE

Parkway Group Healthcare Pte Ltd (www .parkway.com.sg) is a wholly owned subsidiary of Parkway Holdings Limited. Another of Asia's massive private healthcare organizations, Parkway has an extensive network of hospitals and integrated healthcare facilities throughout Singapore.

Eastshore Hospital

321 Joo Chiat Place
SINGAPORE 427990
Tel: 011 65 6344.7588
Fax: 011 65 6345.4966
Email: mrc@parkway.sg
Website: www.eastshore.com.sg

East Shore Hospital is a 123-bed private general acute care hospital. In addition to general medicine, the hospital offers specialties such as pediatrics, radiology and imaging, obstetrics and gynecology, and rehabilitation therapy.

Gleneagles Hospital and Medical Centre

6A Napier Road
SINGAPORE 258500
Tel: 011 65 6473.7222
Fax: 011 65 6475.1832
Email: mrc@parkway.sg
Website: www.gleneagles.com.sg

Established in 1957 and purchased by Parkway in 1987, the JCI-accredited Gleneagles Medical Centre has expanded to a ten-story building with 380 beds. Gleneagles has forged partnerships with Johns Hopkins Hospital and Thames Valley University (UK).

One hundred and fifty specialists address cardiovascular treatment and surgery (including interventional radiology), cosmetic surgery, diagnostic radiology and imaging, fertility, colorectal surgery, hematology, oncology, ophthalmology, orthopedics, respiratory medicine, sleep disorders, liver transplantation, and urology.

Healthcare packages are offered in cardiology (angiogram); ophthalmology (cataract lens implant with Phaco and Visicoat); orthopedics (arthroscopies, total hip and knee replacements, and spinal surgery); and urology (TURP).

Perhaps the best-kept secret at Gleneagles is its **Asian Centre for Liver Diseases and Transplantation**. Established in 1994, the ACLDT was the first private center in Asia dedicated to the treatment of liver disease in adults and children. Areas of expertise range from treatment for patients with chronic liver disease to interventional radiological procedures. ACLDT specializes in chemotherapy, radio frequency ablation (RFA), chemoembolization, endoscopic treatment (for banding of esophageal varices and stenting), liver cancer and cysts, diseases of the biliary tract and pancreatic cancer, and congenital abnormalities in children (including biliary atresia and choledochal cyst). Gleneagles was the first hospital in Southeast Asia to perform a pediatric liver transplant from a living donor.

Mount Elizabeth Hospital and Medical Centre
3 Mount Elizabeth
SINGAPORE 228510
Tel: 011 65 6737.2666
Fax: 011 65 6737.1189
Email: mrc@parkway.sg
Website: www.mountelizabeth.com.sg

Mount Elizabeth Hospital is a 505-bed private tertiary acute care hospital. It performs the largest number of cardiac surgeries and neurosurgeries in the private sector in the region. It is also known for its hematology and stem cell transplant center, positron emission tomography and computed tomography (PET/CT) scans, and robotic surgery.

SINGAPORE HEALTH SERVICES (SINGHEALTH)

Singapore Health Services Pte Ltd (SingHealth—www.singhealth.com.sg) is Singapore's largest group of healthcare institutions, with three hospitals and five national specialty centers offering care in 40 specialties.

Singapore General Hospital, one of the three hospitals under SingHealth, is Asia's largest and the world's second largest hospital to be JCI-accredited.

SingHealth also provides healthcare management consultancy services in the areas of design, planning, facilities management, quality accreditation, operations, manpower planning, and integrated technology. SingHealth has consultancy projects in China, Southeast Asia, India, and the Middle East.

■ HOSPITALS

Changi General Hospital
2 Simei Street 3
SINGAPORE 529889
Tel: 011 65 6260.3725
Tel: 011 65 6788.8833 (after office hours)
Fax: 011 65 6850.2905
Email: international@cgh.com.sg
Web: www.cgh.com.sg

Changi General Hospital (CGH) is a 776-bed hospital, located ten minutes from Changi International Airport. CGH's clinical expertise includes cartilage transplant and arthroscopic surgery, gastroenterology, male impotence, prostate management, sports medicine, and urinary incontinence.

KK Women's and Children's Hospital
100 Bukit Timah Road
SINGAPORE 229899
Tel: 011 65 6293.4044
Fax: 011 65 6293.7933
Email: info@kkh.com.sg
Web: www.kkh.com.sg

KKH is the only integrated women's and children's hospital in Singapore. It boasts JCI accreditation and more then 80 years of experience. The 830-bed hospital offers tertiary services in breast health, obstetrics and gynecology, otolaryngology, pediatrics, and plastic surgery (cosmetic and reconstructive).

Singapore General Hospital
Outram Road
SINGAPORE 169608
Tel: 011 65 6222.3322
Fax: 011 65 6224.9221
Email: ims@sgh.com.sg
Web: www.sgh.com.sg

Singapore General Hospital (SGH) is Singapore's largest acute tertiary hospital and national referral center. It is dedicated to research, providing multidisciplinary medical care. Backed by state-of-the-art facilities, it offers team-based quality patient care and has 29 clinical specialties.

■ NATIONAL CENTERS

National Cancer Center
11 Hospital Drive
SINGAPORE 169610
Tel: 011 65 6236.9433
Fax: 011 65 6536.0611
Email: foreign_patient@nccs.com.sg
Web: www.nccs.com.sg

Part of SingHealth's public hospital network, NCC was reorganized in 2002 into 14 specialist oncology clinics. Those most relevant to health travelers include

- **Colorectal Clinic**, which specializes in colon and rectal cancers, including screening, diagnosis. Treatments include surgery, chemotherapy, and radiation.

- **Gynecology Clinic**, which focuses on treatment of cervical, ovarian, and endometrial cancers and other gynecologic malignancies.

■ **Hematology Clinic**, which treats patients with all blood disorders from non-neoplastic disorders like thalassaemia, thrombocytopenia, and anemia to hematological malignancies such as leukemia, multiple myeloma, lymphoproliferative disorders, and myelodysplastic syndromes.

■ **Head and Neck Clinic**, which provides diagnosis, treatment, and continuing care of cancers of the head and neck, with special expertise in nasopharyngeal carcinoma and in squamous cell carcinomas of the head, neck, pharynx, and larynx.

■ **Hepatobiliary Clinic**, which diagnoses and treats primary liver cancers (especially hepatocellular carcinoma), pancreatic cancers, gall bladder cancers, and cholangiocarcinoma.

■ **Lymphoma Clinic**, which treats primarily non-Hodgkin's and Hodgkin's lymphoma. Treatment modalities include chemotherapy, radiation therapy, biological therapy (such as monoclonal antibody), and autologous and allogenic blood stem cell transplantation.

■ **Musculoskeletal Clinic**, which treats sarcomas of bone and soft tissue; and skin cancers such as melanomas.

■ **Urogenital Clinic**, which evaluates and treats bladder cancers, prostate cancers, renal cell carcinomas, and other urothelial cancers.

■ **Thoracic Clinic**, which focuses on the diagnosis, treatment, and care of patients with lung cancer, in addition to thoracic tumors such as mesothelioma and thymic cancers.

■ **Upper Gastrointestinal Tract Cancer Clinic**, which primarily addresses esophageal and stomach cancers.

■ **Neuro-Oncology Clinic**, which focuses on providing comprehensive care to patients with primary brain tumors.

The NCC International Patient Center assists with medical referrals and appointments, and its concierge service provides currency exchange, private nursing, and business center services. The center can also make hotel recommendations and provide airport transfer service.

National Dental Centre

4, Second Hospital Avenue
SINGAPORE 168938
Tel: 011 65 6324.8910
Fax: 011 65 6324.8810
Email: ndc.enquiries@singhealth.com.sg
Web: www.ndc.com.sg

Established in 1997, NDC is the main referral center for oral healthcare in Singapore. Nearly 166,000 patients visit the center each year for a total of 173,000 dental procedures. NDC has 92 dental operating rooms, 150 doctors, and a staff of 277.

National Heart Centre

Mistri Wing
17 Third Hospital Avenue
SINGAPORE 168752
Tel: 011 65 6236.7438
Fax: 011 65 6323.0663
Email: gps@nhc.com.sg
Web: www.nhc.com.sg

Singapore's 186-bed National Heart Centre (NHC) is the national referral center for cardiovascular disease. Reorganized in 2000 as part of SingHealth's public healthcare cluster, NHC provides preventive, diagnostic, therapeutic, and rehabilitative cardiac services to local and overseas patients.

NHC performs more than 1,700 heart surgeries annually, and the center has performed a total of more than 15,000 surgeries since opening its doors in 2000. NHC performed Singapore's first heart transplant in 1990, and a total of 24 transplants have been performed to date. Survival rates are 98+ percent, on par with US rates.

In 1999 NHC began its lung transplant program, and performed its first lung transplant in 2000. The center deploys a complete range of FDA-approved mechanical-assist devices, which are available for surgical procedures or as a bridge to future heart transplantation.

NHC's Global Patient Services (GPS) team helps arrange hospital admission and provides advice on approximate length of stay, along with preadmission fee estimates. GPS helps foreign patients schedule appointments and provides access to the 32 specialties and sub-specialties across the SingHealth network. A concierge service provides currency exchange, private nursing, and business center services. GPS can also make hotel recommendations and provide airport transfer service.

National Eye Centre

11 Third Hospital Avenue
SINGAPORE 168751
Tel: 011 65 6236.7438
Fax: 011 65 6323.0663
Email: gps@nhc.com.sg
Web: www.snec.com.sg

Since opening its doors in 1990, the National Eye Centre (NEC) has become Singapore's top center for ophthalmic education, research, and treatment. NEC now performs 14,000 major eye surgeries annually, as well as 13,000 laser procedures. It also performs more than 750 complex glaucoma operations annually and has recently become involved in research trials into new glaucoma medications, including the latest prostaglandin analogue group of antiglaucoma medications.

NEC has nine sub-specialties:

- **Cataract and Comprehensive Ophthalmology Services** include cataract and lens implantation surgery for the treatment of secondary, congenital, and endocapsular cataracts; secondary lens implantation; subluxated implants; and treatment of aniridia. The center deploys modern ophthalmologic instrumentation, including ultrasound, applanation, immersion and intraocular lens noncontact biometry, computerized cornea tomography, and contrast sensitivity.

- **Cornea Services** include diagnosis and treatment of pterygium, corneal trauma and infections, inherited corneal disorders, corneal complications arising from other forms of ocular surgery, and ocular surface disorders such as dry eye syndromes, blepharitis, and conjunctival and scleral diseases.

- **Glaucoma Service** manages more than 17,000 glaucoma attendances each year. Its *Glaucoma Diagnostics Center* uses some of the latest equipment and procedures for the early detection of glaucoma, including Humphrey's visual field analyzer, stereoscopic optic disc photography, GDx Nerve Fibre Analyzer Mk III, Heidelberg retinal tomography, optical coherence tomography, and ultrasound biomicroscopy. Its *Laser Centre* has six lasers that cater to patients requiring laser therapy, such as those who have narrow-angle or closed-angle glaucoma.

A resident glaucoma consultant manages and refers cases of congenital and childhood glaucoma. A team of orthoptists and optometrists provides visual rehabilitation services for the child and counseling for the family.

■ **Neuro-Ophthalmology Service** provides evaluation, diagnosis, and treatment of patients with ophthalmic disorders related to the nervous system, such as blurring of vision and double vision. Specialists treat optic nerve disorders from acquired and inherited causes; conditions affecting the visual pathway, such as strokes or brain tumors; eye movement disorders due to cranial nerve palsies, muscle problems, or myopathies; neuromuscular disorders such as myasthenia gravis; jerky eye movement conditions or nystagmus; and diagnostic problems of unexplained visual loss. A full range of electrophysiological testing (multifocal, pattern and full-field ERG, flash pattern and multifocal VEP) allows differentiation between retinal and optic nerve disorders and assists in locating the site of pathology along the visual pathway.

■ **Ocular Inflammation and Immunology Service** provides investigations, diagnosis, and management of a wide range of uveitic and ocular immunological disorders, including HLA-B27 related anterior uveitis; Fuch's heterochromic iridocyclitis; Posner Schlossman syndrome; intermediate uveitis; Behcet's disease; Vogt-Koyanagi-Harada syndrome; ocular infections such as acute and chronic endophthalmitis; toxoplasmosis chorioretinitis; tuberculosis uveitis; and ocular malignancies such as ocular lymphoma.

■ **Oculoplastic and Aesthetic Eye Plastic Service** addresses plastic and reconstructive surgery in disorders of the eyelids, orbit, and lachrymal system, performing more than 700 oculoplastic procedures annually. Services including comprehensive management of thyroid eye disease; cosmetic surgery (brow lifts and midfacelifts); eyelid surgery (disorders such as drooping eyelids and eyelid tumors); and lachrymal surgery (disorders of the tear duct glands).

■ **Pediatric Ophthalmology** diagnoses and treats a variety of childhood eye diseases, including recurrent red, itchy, painful, watery eyes; refractive errors; hyperopia (long-sightedness); myopia (short-sightedness); and astigmatism. Specialists treat children with amblyopia (lazy eyes), children with poor vision from other causes (such as cataracts, glaucoma, optic nerve, retina, or other medical problems), and children and adults with strabismus (squints).

■ The National Eye Centre is particularly proud of its **Refractive Surgery Service**, which has performed more than 32,000 such procedures since 1992. The center treats around 500 cases per month, making it one of the highest-volume practices in the world. Not surprisingly, the NEC uses the most modern equipment, such as wavefront-guided LASIK, LADARVision 4000 laser, and the Zyoptix Z100 laser system (with iris recognition wavefront technology, as well as femtosecond lasers).

■ **Vitreoretinal Service** provides diagnosis and treatment of diseases of the retina, vitreous, and choroids (such as retinal detachment, diabetic retinopathy, age-related macular degeneration, retinal problems related to myopia, retinal vascular occlusion, ocular trauma, and ocular infections).

The service performs more than 500 vitreoretinal surgeries annually, most commonly retinal detachment surgery. The center treats patients with complex diabetic eye disease, and uses vitreoretinal surgical techniques for diabetic vitrectomies.

Finally, the service treats a variety of macular diseases, including age-related macular degeneration (AMD), choroidal neovascularization (CNV), idiopathic polypoidal choroidal vasculopathy (IPCV), and central serous retinopathy (CSR). The service has extensive experience using laser photocoagulation and FDA-approved photodynamic therapy (PDT).

National Neuroscience Institute
11 Jalan Tan Tock Seng
SINGAPORE 308433
Tel: 011 65 6357.7095
Fax: 011 65 6457.7103
Email: nni_secretariat@nni.com.sg
Web: www.nni.com.sg

National Neuroscience Institute (NNI) is the international specialist center for the management and care of neurological diseases. It provides treatment for a broad range of illnesses that affect the brain, spine, nerves, and muscles. The institute also conducts clinical neuroscience research and training.

■ RAFFLES HOSPITAL NETWORK

Raffles Hospital
585 North Bridge Road
SINGAPORE
Tel: 011 65 6311.1666
Fax: 011 65 6311.2333
Email: enquiries@raffleshospital.com
Web: www.raffleshospital.com

Raffles Hospital is the flagship center of Singapore's Raffles Medical Group, Singapore's second largest healthcare network, with 60 clinics throughout the island. Raffles Hospital in downtown Singapore is by far its largest center, with ten super-specialty clinics across 35 disciplines.

Main clinics and super-specialties include

■ **Raffles Aesthetics Centre**, which provides rejuvenation procedures (chemical peel, skin whitening by iontophoresis, Botox treatments, Titan tummy lift); aesthetic laser surgery (tattoo removal, removal of epidermal veins, removal of benign pigmented skin lesions), Cool-Glide laser hair and varicose vein removal; and aesthetic surgery (breast firming and enlargement, double eyelids, eye bag removal, facelift, liposuction, nose reshaping, and tummy tuck).

■ **Raffles Cancer Centre**, which provides cancer screening, early detection, chemotherapy, surgery, hormone therapy, psychological support, and an oncology pharmacy.

■ **Raffles Heart Centre**, which is one of Singapore's largest cardiovascular specialty centers, providing specialist care for screening, diagnosis, and treatment of nearly every heart condition. Major services and surgeries offered include angiogram, angioplasty and stent implantation; cardiac surgery (including coronary artery bypass grafting and other common congenital and valvular heart surgeries); and implantation of pacemakers and automatic defibrillators.

■ **Raffles Orthopedic Centre**, which offers a wide range of surgical sub-specialties, supported by complementary services such as physiotherapy and acupuncture. Specific areas of expertise include surgeries to treat arthritis, correct limb and spinal deformities, replace hips and knees, and remove musculoskeletal tumors. Physicians and surgeons also treat slipped discs, backaches, and related spinal problems, neurological problems of the limbs, and pediatric disorders and diseases.

■ For those interested in Chinese and alternative treatments, Raffles boasts its **Chinese Medicine Center**, one of the few such clinics outside China sponsored by a large hospital. Treatments include acupuncture, acupressure, moxa, and Chinese herbal medicine. There, a team of Chinese medicine specialists focuses on treatment of migraine headaches, stroke recovery, digestive system disorders, musculoskeletal disorders, respiratory conditions, mental health conditions, women's health, skin conditions, and urogenital disorders.

Raffles's International Patients Centre assists with medical referrals and appointments, travel planning, airport transportation, and concierge services (including currency exchange, car rental, booking of manicure and pedicure services, and access to business center).

■ HOTELS: DELUXE

Sheraton Towers Singapore
39 Scotts Road
SINGAPORE 228230
Tel: 011 65 6737.6888
Fax: 011 65 6737.1072
Email: sheraton.towers.singapore@sheraton.com
Web: www.sheraton.com/singaporetowers

Traders Hotel Singapore
1A Cuscaden Road
SINGAPORE 249716
Tel: 011 65 6738.2222
Fax: 011 65 6831.4314
Email: ths@shangri-la.com
Web: www.tradershotels.com

The Elizabeth Hotel
24 Mount Elizabeth
SINGAPORE 228518
Tel: 011 65 6738.1188
Fax: 011 65 6739.8005
Email: reservations@theelizabeth.com.sg
Web: www.theelizabeth.com.sg

**Grand Copthorne Waterfront Hotel
Singapore**
392 Havelock Road
SINGAPORE 169663
Tel: 011 65 6733.0880
Tel: 011 65 6233.1122
Fax: 011 65 6737.8880
Email: frontoffice@grandcopthorne.com.sg
Web: http://www.millenniumhotels.com

Intercontinental Singapore
80 Middle Road
SINGAPORE 188966
Tel: 011 65 6338.7600
Fax: 011 65 6338.7366
Email: singapore@interconti.com
Web: www.ichotelsgroup.com

Conrad Centennial Singapore
Two Temasek Boulevard
SINGAPORE 038982
Tel: 011 65 6334.8888
Fax: 011 65 6333.9166
Email: singaporeinfo@conradhotels.com
Web: www.conradhotels.com

■ HOTELS: MODERATE

Perak Hotel
12 Perak Road
SINGAPORE 208133
Tel: 011 65 6299.7733
Fax: 011 65 6392.0919
Email: reservations@peraklodge.net
Web: www.peraklodge.com

Holiday Inn Singapore Atrium
317 Outram Road
SINGAPORE 169075
Tel: 011 65 6733.0188
Fax: 011 65 6733.0989
Email: hiatrium@hiatrium.com
Web: www.ichotelsgroup.com

DESTINATION: SOUTH AFRICA
(CAPE TOWN AND JOHANNESBURG)

■ **AT A GLANCE**

Cape Town, Johannesburg

Language:	Afrikaans and 12 other languages (English widely spoken)
Time Zone:	GMT +2
Country Dialing Code:	27
Electricity:	230V; Plug type M & C
Currency:	Rand
Visa Required?	No
Required Immunizations:	None
Treatment Specialties:	Addiction Recovery, Cardiovascular, Cosmetic, Dental Care, Ophthalmology, Orthopedics
Leading Hospitals and Clinics:	Bayview Private Hospital, Cape Town Medi-Clinic, Christiaan Barnard Hospital, Kingsbury Hospital, Netcare Olivedale Hospital, Pretoria Eye Clinic, Rosedale Hospital
JCI-Accredited Hospitals:	None
Standards and Accreditations:	South African Medical Association, Health Professions Council of South Africa, The Council for Health Service Accreditation of Southern Africa (a member of the International Society for Quality in Health Care), Association of Plastic and Reconstructive Surgeons of South Africa, International Society of Aesthetic Plastic Surgery

■ TREATMENT BRIEF

Since Dr. Christiaan Barnard performed the world's first heart transplant operation in 1967, South Africa and medicine have been synonymous. Capitalizing on its superb medical reputation as one way of overcoming the stigma of apartheid, South Africa has emerged as a world-class destination for health travelers.

Because of South Africa's long travel times and relatively high treatment costs, most health travelers choose this country for its privacy, its unique sightseeing opportunities, or both. For those who do not wish friends and family to know about their cosmetic and other elective procedures, what better excuse for a month's absence than an African safari? Or, for patients with a more charitable bent, South Africa and its neighboring nations offer vast opportunities for a few weeks' volunteer work. Either option is a convenient way to pass a month or two and then return home rested and healed.

Those sensitive to cultural and language differences may prefer South Africa over some South American, Asian, or European countries because they're more likely to be greeted in English. Cape Town and Johannesburg — South Africa's two main medical cities — are distinctly Anglo-centric within a melting pot of cultures and social classes.

Long known as a center of high-quality, cosmetic surgeries coupled with first-rate surgeons, South Africa has nearly as long a history of first-rate dental care, particularly restorative and cosmetic. More recently, orthopedic surgery — primarily hip and knee work — is attracting European health travelers who are willing to pay higher treatment costs to avoid the cultural rigors of India or Brazil.

South Africa also boasts an enviable stable of well-established health travel agents whose services can be a godsend to any prospective international patient. The newly formed Medical Tourism Association of South Africa helps to maintain quality standards and service and to foster excellent relationships among patients, treatment centers, in-country third-party facilities, and international partners.

A word of caution: If you're thinking "exotic far-flung vacation" when you think South Africa, you're on the right track. Remember, however, that most cosmetic surgeries specifically caution against exposure to the sun after treatment. Since there's no shortage of sun in that part of the world, plan to take your safari, bush trip, or beach getaway *prior* to your procedure.

■ TYPICAL TREATMENTS AND COSTS

Cardiovascular:

Bypass + Valve Replacement (single): $35,000

Cosmetic:

Breast:

  Augmentation: $3,800-$4,500

  Lift/Reduction: $5,500-$6,000

Facelift: $5,700-$6,300

Liposuction (stomach, hips, and waist): $3,900-$4,400

Tummy Tuck: $4,200-$5,000

Dental Care:

Bridges (per tooth): $700-$750

Crowns (all porcelain): $750-$800

Extractions:

    Surgical: $225-$275

    Wisdom Teeth: $375

Implants: $1,800-$2,100

Opthalmology:

LASIK (per eye): $2,200-$2,500

■ HEALTH TRAVEL AGENTS

Surgeon and Safari

158 Mount Street, Bryanston

Johannesburg, SOUTH AFRICA

Tel: 011 27 11.463.3154

Fax 011 27 11.706.5582

Email: info@surgeon-and-safari.co.za

Web: www.surgeon-and-safari.co.za

This is perhaps the best known of all cosmetic surgery travel agencies. Its founder, Lorraine Melvill, opened Surgeon and Safari to UK clients in 2000. Now more then one-third of its patients are from the US. Sometimes jokingly referred to as the 'beauty and the beast" agency, Surgeon and Safari provides A to Z services, including help with medical evaluation and consultations, appointments with surgeons, airport transport, and medical transfers. A Surgeon and Safari representative personally accompanies each patient to all medical appointments and stays with him or her on the day of surgery. Patients can call family and friends back home when surgery has been completed.

One of the principal facilities used by Surgeons and Safari is Cape Town's world-famous Christiaan Barnard Memorial Hospital.

Those planning surgery in Johannesburg may want to look into Surgeon and Safari's own accommodation facility, a small, cozy recovery guesthouse with six rooms for patients and their companions. Available only to S and S patients, the guesthouse provides most hotel amenities, plus round-the-clock recuperation assistance for guests. Prices at Surgeon and Safari's recovery retreat are about half those of a five-star Johannesburg hotel.

In addition to cosmetic and plastic surgery procedures, Surgeon and Safari has recently begun offering dental care, ophthalmology, and orthopedics.

Surgical Attractions

45 Bristol Road

Parkwood, Johannesburg

Gauteng, SOUTH AFRICA

Tel: 011 27 11.880.5122

Fax: 011 27 11.788.9043

Email: info@surgicalattractions.com

Web: www.surgicalattractions.com

Ingrid Lomas established Surgical Attractions in 2002. Based in Johannesburg, this agency serves Cape Town as well. Surgical Attractions offers the full range of services, including pre-op and post-op care, rejuvenation tours, and transportation to and from airports and medical facilities. For those who wish additional travel services, Surgical Attractions can put patients in touch with in-country travel agencies that can assist with international travel, visas, and other nonmedical travel details.

If you want to avoid hotels, Surgical Attractions maintains partnerships in Cape Town and Johannesburg with various guest care lodges, private homes of medical nursing sisters who provide care for recovering patients. These accommodations provide medical assistance 24/7, companionship for patients traveling alone, and three home-cooked meals per day.

■ HOSPITALS AND CLINICS

While no South African hospitals currently carry JCI accreditation, several are in progress. The country has long enjoyed a reliable medical infrastructure in compliance with the accreditation standards of international associations and of a host of in-country accreditation agencies. The standards apply to general practice as well as to cosmetic and dental surgery.

Regarding cosmetic surgery in South Africa, few dedicated clinics exist. Rather, plastic surgery (including cosmetic and reconstructive) is more likely to be performed by a well-regarded specialist in an excellent private hospital. Patients interested in traveling to South Africa for cosmetic surgery should consult the services of a health travel agent who specializes in that arena.

Bay View Private Hospital
P.O. Box 287
Mossel Bay, SOUTH AFRICA 6500
Tel: 011 27 44.691.3718
Fax: 011 27 44.691.3717
Email: bayview@pixie.co.za
Web: www.bayviewprivatehospital.com

One of South Africa's finest hospitals occupies one of the world's most beautiful settings for a treatment center. Set along the Garden Route, a three-hour eastward coastal drive (or 40-minute flight) from Cape Town, the facilities overlook the Indian Ocean, where porpoises can be seen frolicking outside patients' rooms.

Established in 1995, Bay View now has 106 beds. The hospital prides itself on the high-profile care administered in the center's geographical remoteness. Twenty-three physicians and surgeons and a staff of 300 have seen thousands of international patients over the past decade. Bay View performs more than 200 cardiac surgeries and 1,800 orthopedic surgeries annually.

Bay View is best known for its **Cardiac Cath Lab**, founded in 1999 by Christiaan Barnard. At Bay View the full gamut of heart diagnostics and surgeries is performed at less than half the cost of comparable treatments in the US.

In addition to the full range of orthopedics surgeries, Bay View's **Orthopedics Clinic** also offers the Birmingham hip resurfacing procedure. This popular alternative to traditional hip replacement, only recently authorized in the United States, costs about $10,000 at Bay View. Patients specifically seeking this procedure may consider South Africa a more convenient destination than India or Southeast Asian countries.

Other specialties include surgery, urology, gastroenterology, general and endoscopic surgery, neurology and neurosurgery, and ophthalmology.

While the hospital's international clientele hails mostly from the UK and Germany, Bay View's International Services Director can help US patients with bookings, hotels, and transportation. Bay View pays for the 40-minute flight from Cape Town to the clinic.

Cape Town Medi-Clinic

P O Box 12199, Mill Street 8010
21 Hof Street, Oranjezicht 8001
Cape Town, SOUTH AFRICA
Tel: 011 27 21.464.5500
Email: hospmngrcapet@mediclinic.co.za
Web: www.capetownmc.co.za

Located in the quiet Cape Town suburb of
Oranjezicht, the 150-bed Cape Town Medi-
Clinic is one of 40 private hospitals that
form the Medi-Clinic Group, one of South
Africa's largest private hospital networks.

Five operating theaters carry out
general and super-specialties, including
cardiothoracic surgery, clinical sexology,
dentistry, dermatology, general surgery,
neurology and neurosurgery, orthopedics,
pediatric surgery, plastic and reconstructive
surgery, spinal surgery, and urology.

Carter Gordon Clinic

13 Anthony Street
Plettenberg Bay
Western Cape, SOUTH AFRICA 6600
Tel: 011 27 82.491.5761
Fax: 011 27 44.534.8277
Email: info@my-rehab.co.za
Web: www.my-rehab.co.za

Many individuals grappling with addiction and emotional dependency require
extended clinical, supervised help. Some
are advised to undergo the more rigorous
programs (à la Hazelton or Betty Ford) in a
professional setting far away from home,
family, friends, and work.

Just opened by two addiction and
recovery specialists, the 14-bed Carter
Gordon Clinic is patterned after the "Minne-
sota Model," combining a longer-term stay
with the Alcoholics Anonymous 12-step

program. All types of substance addiction
and addictive behaviors are addressed,
including alcoholism and addiction to nar-
cotics, sex, and gambling. Rigorous group
and individual counseling make up a good
part of the day, with morning walks on the
beach and evening tours at game parks and
nearby marvels. More than half of Carter
Gordon's clients arrive from the UK, Hol-
land, and Germany.

The clinic is an unforgettably beautiful five-hour drive east from Cape Town to
upscale and reposed Plettenberg Bay, the
jewel of South Africa's famed Garden Route.
Clients can arrange to be met by a driver at
Cape Town International Airport.

Typical recovery programs at Carter
Gordon last six weeks, where a patient is
brought through the first five steps of the
AA 12-Step program. For those in need of a
clinically monitored regimen, the $10,500
fee (inclusive of lodging, meals, and activities) is a bargain compared to similar programs in the US.

Christiaan Barnard Memorial Hospital

181 Longmarket Street
Cape Town 8010, SOUTH AFRICA
Tel: 011 27 21.480.6111
Fax: 011 27 21 422.0488
Email: cttxp@cape.netcare.co.za (general
info)
Web: www.netcare.co.za (general info)

Named after heart transplant pioneer, Dr.
Christiaan Barnard, Memorial Hospital is
most noted for cardiac and kidney transplant surgeries, although it provides a
variety of medical services with top-flight
surgeons specializing in cardiac surgery,
urology, orthopedics, and dental care. The

hospital treats many heads of states, partly because of its reputation for confidentiality.

Health travel agency Surgeon and Safari recommends its patients to this facility.

Kingsbury Hospital
Wilderness Road
Claremont, SOUTH AFRICA 7700
Tel: 011 27 21.670.4000
Fax: 011 27 21.683.5138
Email: janet.young@lifehealthcare.co.za
Web: www.lifehealthcare.co.za

Kingsbury Hospital, located near Cape Town, is part of another large, quality-care hospital network, with 62 facilities throughout South Africa. One hundred thirty-four beds and six theaters support the usual gamut of medical disciplines, including treatment of breast diseases, colorectal surgery, dentistry, dermatology, gastroenterology, general surgery, neurology and neurosurgery, ophthalmology, orthopedics, plastic and reconstructive surgery, urology, and vascular surgery.

Kingsbury boasts two super-specialties:

■ **Repair of Abdominal Aortic Aneurysm:** Most often diagnosed in men over 60, an abdominal aortic aneurysm is a dilation of the body's largest artery, which lies in the abdominal cavity. If an undetected aneurysm enlarges, its sudden rupture is usually fatal. Kingsbury has invested in sophisticated ultrasound detection and diagnosis, as well as in a revolutionary technique for treatment that involves inserting stent grafts through the groin into the affected artery — without having to open up the abdomen.

■ **Obesity Surgery:** Recognizing the epidemic rise of obesity worldwide (and its associated maladies of heart attack, stroke, high blood pressure, cancer, depression, arthritis, and sleep disorders), Kingsbury's *Chrysalis Clinic* takes a holistic approach to obesity and weight loss. A team of specialists carefully examines a patient's history and health status, then works with the patient to consider all options.

Non-surgical options are considered first, involving a combination of dietetic treatment, exercise, pharmacological treatment, and psychotherapy. Patients are assessed by an endocrinologist/physician, a dietician, a surgeon, a biokineticist, and a psychiatrist or psychologist from the Chrysalis Clinic team. A program is then developed around the findings, which may include surgical interventions.

Netcare Olivedale Hospital
Pres Fouche/Windsor Way
Olivedale
Johannesburg, SOUTH AFRICA
Tel: 011 27 11.777.2000
Fax: 011 27 11.462.8382
Email: marketing@olivedale.netcare.co.za
Web: www.olivedaleclinic.co.za

Olivedale is owned and managed by the Netcare Group. Since 1996, Netcare has grown to include 62 hospitals owned and managed by the group. At total of 7,200 beds, 319 operating theaters, and 128 specialty medical units are supported by 2,500 medical specialists.

Olivedale's 263 beds and 13 operating theaters make it one of the largest in the network. Specialties include cardiology and cardiothoracic surgeries, diabetes diagnosis and treatment, general surgery, neurology, nuclear medicine, oncology, ophthalmology, orthopedics, and urology.

Pretoria Eye Institute

630 Schoeman Street,
Arcadia
Pretoria, SOUTH AFRICA
Tel: 011 27 12.343.5873
Fax: 011 27 12.344.4541
Email: info@eyeinstitute.co.za
Web: www.eyeinstitute.co.za

Opened in 1991 as a private hospital, the Pretoria Eye Institute has grown into Africa's largest, with a staff of 150. Its 40-bed facility treats 6,000 patients per month, and more than 7,200 surgeries are performed annually in six operating theaters. PEI's 20-chair day facility is manned by a separate ophthalmic staff.

Surgeries performed by 18 ophthalmologists are offered for cataract retinal detachments, diabetic retinopathy, glaucoma, refractive/LASIK, lens implantation, and macular degeneration. The Institute is situated close to several embassies in Pretoria, and some of the savvier diplomatic travelers schedule eye exams, LASIK treatments, and other procedures while there. PEI also serves a large crowd from the UK, taking advantage of the considerable cost savings.

Rosedale Day Clinic
Rosedale Dental Clinic

Arcadia Avenue
Uitenhage, SOUTH AFRICA
Tel: 011 27 41.988.2222 (Day clinic)
Tel: 011 27 41.988.4935 (Dental clinic)

Located in Uitenhage, near Port Elizabeth and part of the Nelson Mandela Metropole, Rosedale is known for its discretion and skill in cosmetic and dental cosmetic surgeries.

■ RECOVERY ACCOMMODATIONS

At this writing, independent recovery retreats have not appeared on the scene in South Africa. Because of the large number of medical travelers visiting South Africa, most deluxe hotels are responsive to the care and dietary needs of traveling patients. If you desire specialized medical care, ask your health travel agent to recommend accommodations.

■ HOTELS: DELUXE

Mount Nelson Hotel

76 Orange Street
Cape Town, SOUTH AFRICA 8001
Tel: 011 27 21.483.1000
Tel: 800 237.1236 (US and Canada toll-free)
Fax: 011 27 21.483.1001
Email: reservations@mountnelson.co.za
Web: www.mountnelson.co.za

The Table Bay Hotel

Victoria and Alfred Waterfront
Cape Town, SOUTH AFRICA
Tel: 011 27 21.701.1202
Fax: 011 27 21.406.5686
Email: tablebay@accommodationsouth
africa.co.za
Web: www.accommodationasouthafrica
.co.za

The Westcliff
67 Jan Smuts Avenue
Westcliff
Johannesburg, SOUTH AFRICA
Tel: 011 27 11.481.6000
Tel: 800 237.1236 (US toll-free)
Fax: 011 27 11.481.6010
Email: reservations@westcliff.co.za
Web: www.westcliff.co.za

Park Hyatt Johannesburg
191 Oxford Road, Rosebank
Johannesburg, SOUTH AFRICA
Tel: 011 27 11.280.1234
Fax: 011 27 11.280.1238
Email: garry.friend@hyattintl.com
Web: www.johannesburg.park.hyatt.com

Hilton Sandton Johannesburg
138 Rivonia Road
Sandton, SOUTH AFRICA
Tel: 011 27 11.322.1888
Tel: 800 664.6835 (US toll-free)
Fax: 011 27 11.322.1818
Email: reservations.sandton@hilton.com
Web: www.hilton.com

Melrose Place
12a North Street/30 Victoria Ave.
Melrose, Johannesburg, SOUTH AFRICA
Tel: 011 27 11.442.5231
Cell: 011 083.457.4021
Fax: 011 27 11.880.2371
Web: www.melroseplace.co.za

■ HOTELS: MODERATE

Highlands Country House Hotel
36 Tennant Road
Kenilworth, 7708
Cape Town, SOUTH AFRICA
Tel: 011 27 21.797.8810
Fax: 011 27 21.761.0017
Email: info@highlands.co.za
Web: www.highlands.co.za

DESTINATION: **THAILAND**

■ AT A GLANCE

Bangkok and Phuket

Language:	Thai (English widely spoken in business and medical circles)
Time Zone:	GMT +7
Country Dialing Code:	66
Electricity:	220V, Plug types A, B, C
Currency:	Thai Baht
Visa Required?	Yes
Required Immunizations:	None
Treatment Specialties:	Cardiovascular, Cosmetic, Dental Care, Gender Reassignment, Neurology, Oncology, Ophthalmology, Orthopedics, Weight Loss
Leading Hospitals and Clinics:	Bangkok Hospital Group Medical Center, Bumrungrad International Hospital, Samitivej Hospital, Bangkok Dental Group, Bangkok International Dental Center, Bangkok Hospital Phuket, Phuket International Hospital
JCI-Accredited Hospitals:	Bumrungrad Hospital, Samitivej Hospital
Standards and Accreditation:	Institute of Hospital Quality Improvement and Accreditation, Society of Plastic and Reconstructive Surgeons of Thailand, Thai Association of Orthodontists, and JCI

■ TREATMENT BRIEF

Although it now shares the spotlight with India, Singapore, and Malaysia, the Kingdom of Thailand is the rightful wellspring of contemporary medical travel. Ten years ago, with the crash of the Thai Bhat, busi-ness and governmental leaders capitalized on Thailand's excellent medical infrastructure to attract international patients from nearby countries with less robust health-care choices. Patients from Japan, Vietnam, Korea, and China were rapidly followed by European clients. Now thousands of Americans and Canadians head to Bangkok or Phuket, mostly to save on elective surgeries that more than compensate for the uncomfortably long flight.

Thailand's huge medical calling card is Bangkok's venerated, JCI-accredited Bumrungrad Hospital, covering a one-million-square-foot complex in downtown Bangkok. More than 900 full-time and consulting physicians representing every imaginable specialty and subspecialty practice there.

Bumrungrad has set the pace for both quality and quantity of contemporary international healthcare throughout Asia and the world. Yet, not surprisingly, Bumrungrad's aggressive marketing and sheer size have spawned recent complaints of excessive red tape and impersonal care, which the hospital is taking pains to address.

Bumrungrad's large presence is not without its competition, and the equally impressive Dusit Medical Group owns and operates a network of 17 hospitals throughout Thailand, including Bangkok International Hospital, Bangkok Phuket Hospital, Bangkok General Hospital, and Samitivej Hospital.

Although not Thailand's native tongue, English is widely spoken in Thai cities and resort centers, and English is taught as a second language in Thai schools. While extremes of wealth and poverty can be readily witnessed, health travelers may feel more comfortable in Thai culture than in India or Africa.

SEX AND THE CITY . . . THAI-STYLE

No discussion of healthcare in Thailand would be complete without at least a men-tion of sex change treatments (or "genital reassignment surgery" (GSA), in the medical vernacular). Difficult to obtain in the US without a good deal of red tape, sex reassignment treatment options are probably more available in Bangkok than anywhere else on the planet.

Women can choose from a reproductive smorgasbord ranging from vaginoplasty (a rejuvenative tightening of the vagina) to full female-to-male gender reassignment; men are offered single or full orchiectomies (testicle removal), penile-width enhancement, penile lengthening, and full male-to-female gender reassignment.

Partially because of Bangkok's well-publicized sex industry, hundreds of sex change clinics have seized on Thailand's recent successes in medical travel, and many prey on the vulnerable. Thus, as with any other medical procedure, patients should conduct careful investigations, including thorough reference checks and redoubled research on clinic accreditation and physician experience.

■ TYPICAL TREATMENTS AND COSTS

Cardiovascular:

Angioplasty: $13,000

Coronary Artery Bypass Graft: $11,000-$12,000

Valve Replacement:
Single: $10,000
Double: $13,000

Cosmetic:

Breast
   Augmentation: $2,700-$3,300
   Lift/Reduction: $2,700-$3,300
Facelift: $2,800-$4,000
Liposuction (stomach, hips, and waist):
   $1,400-$2,200
Tummy Tuck: $2,900-$3,500

Dental Care:

Cleaning: $25
Crowns (all porcelain): $275
Dentures (upper and lower): $900
Extractions (surgical, each tooth): $125
Implants: $1,500-$1,750
Inlays and Onlays: $400
Root Canals (each): $125
   With Cap: $200-$350
Veneers (porcelain): $250

Gender Reassignment:

Colon Cut Vaginoplasty: $4,000
Orchiectomy (testis removal): $2,000
Penile Skin Inversion Plus Skin Graft: $7,000
Scrotal Skin Graft Vaginoplasty: $5,000

General Surgery:

Gall Bladder Removal: $3,800-$4,500
Prostate Surgery (TURP): $5,600

Ophthalmology:

Glaucoma (per eye): $975
LASIK (per eye): $875-$1,100

Orthopedics:

Replacement:
   Total Hip: $12,000
   Total Knee: $10,000
Spinal Fusion: $7,000

Weight Loss:

LAP-BAND® System: $8,800

■ HEALTH TRAVEL AGENTS

Cosmetic Surgery Travel LLC
20701 North Scottsdale Road
Suite 107-478
Scottsdale, Arizona 85255
Tel: 610 688.3550
Fax: 440 699.2401
Email: julie@cosmeticsurgerytravel.com
Web: www.cosmeticsurgerytravel.com

The "beauty" part of Cosmetic Surgery Travel is apparently only skin deep, as the agency also handles patients seeking a wide variety of non-cosmetic treatments, including bariatric surgery, dentistry, eye surgery, adult stem cell surgery, cardiac, neurological, cancer and orthopedic procedures.

Julie Munro, founder and Chief Medical Concierge of Cosmetic Surgery Travel has lived in Thailand and regularly travels between the US and Thailand. Munro and a team of American, Australian, Canadian, and European expatriate women provide "medical concierge" services to patients seeking treatment in Bangkok.

Patients using Cosmetic Surgery travel are assigned an English-speaking Certified Medical Concierge, which acts as the patient's contact with the surgeon, hospital staff, hotel, transportation, and even family back home.

The oldest medical travel agency serving Thailand, the company has booked more than US$2 million in surgery for medical travelers since 2003. Now expanding to include Singapore medical providers, the company's mission is to provide the safest medical journey for every international patient.

International Medical Resources
West Coast Office
885 Scott Blvd, Suite 4
Santa Clara, CA 95050

East Coast Office
8250 Branch Road
Annandale, VA 22003
Tel: 800 436.0154 (US toll-free)
Fax: 408 842.1656
Email: info@medinfoonline.com
Web: www.medinfoonline.com

This US-based agent sends patients mostly to Bangkok's "other" medical tourist center, Bangkok International Hospital (BIH). IMR's Founder James Perry asserts that his clients receive treatment quality equal to Bumrungrad's in friendlier, less bureaucratic surroundings.

Unlike staff members in most other health travel firms, Perry and his team boast medical backgrounds. Perry, a licensed medical practitioner, was a PA (physician's assistant) for 25 years. While US liability concerns preclude IMR from offering specific medical advice, Perry asserts his medical expertise gives his agency an advantage in arranging for the best physicians and hospitals.

"In specializing in Thailand and Bangkok International Hospital, we're not trying to be everything to everyone," he says. "We offer patients who have chosen Thailand for their healthcare an excellent alternative to the more impersonal hospital settings."

MedRetreat
1121 Annapolis Road, PMB 160
Odenton, MD 21113
Tel: 877.876.3373 (US toll-free)
Fax: 847 .680.0484
Email: customerservice@medretreat.com
Web: www.medtreatreat.com

Established in 2003, MedRetreat is one of the more established US-based health travel planning agencies, serving primarily Asia, and Central and South America. Founder Patrick Marsek reports that MedRetreat has sent more than 500 patients abroad over the past two years.

For an upfront fee of $195 (which is deducted from any medical trip booked through MedRetreat), members receive a comprehensive treatment quote (including pricing, hospital information, physicians' biographies, recommended physicians, and lodging estimates), a 15-minute consultation with a physician by telephone, scheduling of air travel, hotel booking, scheduling of medical procedure, forwarding of medical records, and in-country medical consultation.

Patients who wish to forego the $195 membership fee can receive MedRetreat's services gratis on a first-come, first-serve basis.

■ HOSPITALS AND CLINICS

BANGKOK

Home to six million, Bangkok is Thailand's capital city, administrative center, and the economic lifeblood of the kingdom. Bangkok is a large, bustling city of extremes — endless traffic jams, glittering golden temples, huge and sprawling shopping complexes, and of course, its thriving and nefarious sex industry.

Despite its highly visible extremes, Bangkok is embedded in tradition, and international travelers are always struck by the overwhelming politeness of the Thai people. Customs and ritual are taken seriously both in the cities and in the countryside, and learning some cultural do's and don'ts will be broadly appreciated by your newfound friends and associates.

Bangkok Hospital Group Medical Center

2 Soi Soonvijai 7, New Petchburi Rd
Bangkok, THAILAND
Tel: 011 66 2.310.3101
Fax: 011 66 2.310.3367
Email: medinfo@bgh.co.th
Web: www.bangkokinternationalhospital
.com

Owned by the mammoth Dusit Group, Southeast Asia's largest network of private hospitals, the Bangkok Hospital Group Medical Center (BMC for short) has now grown to 15 hospitals located throughout Bangkok and Thailand. Of these centers, the best known to health travelers are Bangkok International Hospital (BIH) and Samitivej, including its new Children's Hospital. More than 600 doctors and surgeons and 2200 staffers work at these centers, with most of the effort focused upon three large specialty areas: heart, neurology and oncology.

BMC's main centers include the following:

■ Bangkok International Hospital (BIH)

was the first Thai medical center to serve international patients. Its International Medical Center (IMC) improved and expanded its services in 2002, particularly for international patients, and now the IMC serves more than 100,000 patients annually from 60 countries. Sixteen specialized centers, ranging from orthopedics to neurology to cardiology, have brought together internationally trained physicians and state-of-the-art medical technology to attract visitors from all parts of the world.

IMC's impressive rooms rival the best hospitals in the US. They include a guest sofa bed for a companion, personal telephone for international calls, microwave oven, refrigerator, personal safe, free Internet access, free English language newspaper, and an inpatient library.

IMC's team of 60 specialists helps overseas visitors overcome cultural and language barriers, in addition to providing the usual amenities, including visa assistance, liaison services with embassies, airport pickup, around the clock contact for medical assessments, advice on treatment options and doctors' appointments, arrangements for special diets, arranging shopping and sightseeing tours, liaison with embassies and international organizations, and insurance claims liaison assistance.

BIH's International Medical Center refers international clients to two health travel agents: International Medical

Resources and Cosmetic Surgery Travel (see "Health Travel Agents" above). These agencies can also direct patients to the best specialty centers and departments for cardiology, orthopedics, oncology, neurology, and more.

■ **Bangkok Heart Hospital (BHH)** is Thailand's first and only dedicated private heart hospital. It is equipped with the most advanced technology and staffed by dedicated personnel who deal with nearly every heart condition, including diagnostics, interventional cardiology, cardiac surgery, and rehabilitation. BHH boasts Thailand's only DaVinci robotic system, which is used in the newer minimally invasive surgeries. Procedures include cardiac magnetic resonance imaging (MRI), computed tomography (CT) angiogram, adult stem cell therapies, radiofrequency ablation, pacemaker, and an all-artery cardiac bypass surgery.

■ **Wattanasoth Cancer Hospital (WH)** is the only dedicated private cancer hospital in Thailand. The center is equipped with state-of-the-art technologies, including positive emission tomography (PET) and CT scan for fast and accurate diagnosis, NOVALIS for intensity modulated radiosurgery and radiotherapy, and Gamma Knife for radiosurgery of the brain.

■ At the **Bangkok Neuroscience Center**, 12 neurologists and 14 neurosurgeons treat a host of diseases and traumas, including headaches; dizziness and vertigo; stroke and its aftermath; seizures; Parkinson's and related diseases; Alzheimer's; brain and spinal cord injury; tumors of the brain and spinal cord; muscle and nerve diseases; paresthesia of limbs, trunk, or face;

developmental disorders; and genetic anomalies.

The center's test and instrumentation inventory includes CT, MRI, cerebral angiogram, electroencephalography (EEG), EEG monitoring, brain stem auditory evoked response, somatosensory evoked response, neurosonology carotid ultrasound and transcranial Doppler, and spinal cord stimulation drug infusion system.

Super-specialties within the center include clinics to treat stroke and cardiovascular disorders, pain, headache, epilepsy, movement disorders, neuromuscular diseases, and neurogenetics.

Neurosurgeons specialize in head trauma and spinal cord injuries, tumor and skull-base surgery, cerebral hemorrhage, aneurysms and spinal surgery, Parkinson's disease, movement disorders and epilepsy.

The BIH Neuroscience Center is the first and only hospital in Thailand to acquire and deploy the highly-touted Leskell Gamma Knife, a new radiosurgical device that enables doctors to treat deep-seated brain lesions without the risks of open-skull surgery. Hundreds of precisely targeted beams of cobalt gamma radiation painlessly "cut" through brain tumors, blood vessel malformations, and other brain abnormalities, allowing neurosurgeons to correct disorders not currently treatable using established procedures. With Gamma Knife treatment, patients experience less discomfort and greatly shortened recovery periods. There are only 180 Gamma Knives in use worldwide as of this writing.

Bangkok Nursing Home (BNH) Hospital

9/1 Convent Road
Silom, Bangrak
Bangkok, THAILAND 10500
Tel: 011 66 2.686.2700
Fax: 011 66 2.632.0577
Email: info@bnhhospital.com
Web: www.bnhhospital.com

Don't be fooled by the name — BNH is not a nursing home in the American sense of the word. BNH is a modern, full-service 225-bed hospital that meets international standards. Founded in the 19th century, BNH is one of Thailand's oldest healthcare facilities. More than 50,000 international patients visit BNH annually from 70 different countries, making it Bangkok's third largest international hospital.

The hospital has nearly 200 physicians from every medical service area. Specialties include a spine center, gastroenterology and liver clinic, and women's health clinic. The Preecha Aesthetic Institute (see below) is housed within BNH.

Bumrungrad International Hospital

33 Sukhumvit 3 (Soi Nana Nua)
Wattana
Bangkok, THAILAND 10110
Tel: 011 66 2.667.1000
Fax: 011 66 2.667.2525
Email: info@bumrungrad.com
Web: www.bumrungrad.com

Established in 1980, Bumrungrad is Asia's monolithic, monster hospital, the largest in Southeast Asia, serving more than one million patients per year, including 150,000 international visitors (20,000 from the US). Its 554-bed facility provides a full range of tertiary healthcare services, including 19 operating rooms equipped for most general surgery and surgical specialties, some minimally invasive, including cardiothoracic, orthopedics, urological, ophthalmological, laser, transplant, and otolaryngology (ear, nose, and throat) surgeries.

At this writing, Bumrungrad is one of Thailand's two JCI-accredited hospitals; it was the first Asian hospital to receive JCI accreditation (2002). Of its 900 physicians, surgeons, and consultants, some 200 are US board-certified.

Bumrungrad's clinics include endocrinology (diabetes and metabolism), nephrology (kidneys), neurology (nervous system), and nutrition. Bumrungrad's renowned heart center offers pacemaker implantation, invasive and noninvasive procedures for congenital heart disease, valvoplasty (balloon valve treatment) and valve replacement, and coronary artery bypass graft (CABG).

Directed by a US-trained medical director, Bumrungrad International sponsors an active continuing medical education program for its physicians, who also actively participate in clinical research through the *Bumrungrad International Clinical Research Center*.

Bumrungrad's impressive claims to fame are also its shortcomings. It can sometimes resemble the worst of American hospitals — impersonal service, unresponsive personnel, oceans of red tape, rushed consultations, and poor post-operative care.

For patients who wish to recover near the hospital and under the hospital's auspices, Bumrungrad offers two locations, Bumrungrad Residences and Bumrungrad Suites. For rates and further information, inquire at Bumrungrad International Services.

Preecha Aesthetic Institute

7th Floor, BNH Hospital
9/1 Convent Rd.
Silom, Bangruk
Bangkok, THAILAND 10500
Tel: 011 66 2.632.2540
Fax: 011 66 2.632.2542
Email: consult@pai.co.th
Web: www.pai.co.th

The Preecha Institute is located on the seventh floor of the 100-year old BNH Hospital, one of Bangkok's best established. Preecha is fully supported by more than 20 medical specialty centers, with the hospital's 200+ physicians close at hand.

Preecha Institute was founded by Dr. Preecha Tiewtranon, often called simply Dr. Preecha. With 33 years of practice, Dr. Preecha has personally performed more than 30,000 cosmetic and plastic surgeries. He reigns as Bangkok's undisputed leader in gender reassignment. His techniques have become standard practice throughout the world, and he trained most of Thailand's qualified sex reassignment surgeons. From 1980 to 2005, Dr. Preecha has personally performed more than 3,500 sex reassignment and facial feminization surgeries.

Preecha's patients can take advantage of BNH's private luxury rooms, which include private bathroom, electric bed, cable/satellite television, refrigerator, remote control light systems, individual safe lock, telephone, air-conditioning, and high speed Internet service. Upon arrival, patients are also given a mobile phone, with all of Preecha's surgeon and staff contacts preprogrammed for easy in-country calling.

PAI's services include facial contouring, eye therapies, rhinoplasty, cheekbone contouring, hair transplant and laser hair removal, breast surgery, body contouring, jaw contouring, labiaplasty, vaginoplasty and various surgeries of the ear, lips, and chin.

Samitivej Hospitals

133 Sukhumvit 49, Klongtan Nua
Vadhana
Bangkok, THAILAND 10110
Tel: 011 66 2.711.8000
Fax: 011 66 2.391.1290
Email: info@samitivej.co.th
Web: www.samitivej.co.th

Founded in 1979 and a part of the giant privately owned Dusit Group, Samitivej is one of Thailand's leading private hospital groups. Two large centers, **Samitivej Sukhumvit Hospital** (downtown) and **Samitivej Srinakarin** (on the east side of town), together offer a full array of patient services and specialty centers.

Samitivej Sukhumvit currently has 270 beds, 87 examination suites, 1,200 caregivers, 400 specialists, and a full-service International Patient Center. Sukhumvit is one of the few Thai hospitals to have received the Prime Minister's Award for Most Recognized Service (2004). It is accredited by Thailand's Hospital Accreditation Board. Americans will feel at home, with a 7-Eleven, Starbucks, and ATMs on the ground level of the hospital.

Specialty centers include

- **Eye Clinic,** which specializes in general ophthalmology; retinal and vitreous conditions; glaucoma; pediatric ophthalmology and strabismus; and oculoplastic reconstruction and ocular oncology.

- **Hemodialysis Department** for patients with acute or chronic renal (kidney) failure. The hemodialysis center deploys artificial kidney machines. It has been certified by the Royal College of Physicians of Thailand. Known throughout Thailand for its success rates in kidney transplants, the Hemodialysis Department receives its kidneys from the Thai Red Cross's Organ Donation Center.

■ **Liver and Digestive Institute,** where a team of gastroenterologists treats the full gamut of liver and digestive abnormalities, including cirrhosis, fatty liver disease, pancreatitis, gall bladder infection, and bile duct infection. Specialty surgeries include liver, bile ducts, gall bladder, esophagus, stomach, small and large intestine, and liver transplantation.

■ **Samitivej Srinakarin** is Samitivej's newest addition in Bangkok. It has 17 stories and 400 beds, located on Bangkok's east side, a few minutes from the newly opened Suvarnabhumi International Airport. The hospital's 21 acres of landscaped gardens and fountains foster an environment of tranquility not commonly found on the grounds of US hospitals. Specialty centers include both *Srinakarin's Cancer Center* and *Sukhumvit's Oncology Clinic*, which focus on prevention; screening, diagnosis, and treatment of out-service patients. A full team of multilingual medical oncologists, radiation oncologists, physicists, technicians, oncology nurses, and intravenous nurses render Bangkok's best in cancer treatment.

Seven dental units, three X-ray operating suites, a panoramic X-ray machine, a laser system, and an intraoral camera make *Srinakarin's Dental Center* a state-of-the-art, one-stop shop, with no need for multiple trips to outside labs. The full range of dental services and oral surgeries is offered, including orthodontics, root canals, full and partial dentures, crowns and bridges, implants, extractions, bone graft surgery, and treatment of gum diseases.

■ The **Samitivej Srinakarin Children's Hospital** opened its doors in July 2003; it is now Thailand's first and only dedicated private hospital for children. The center offers a mind-boggling array of pediatric specialties and sub-specialties, ranging from pediatric snoring to bone marrow transplant.

Specialty centers include

■ **Allergy Clinic,** which diagnoses and treats asthma, hay fever, atopic dermatitis, food allergy, drug allergy, and chronic sinusitis.

■ **Growth, Endocrine, and Diabetes Center for Children,** which diagnoses and treats growth hormone deficiency, thyroid disease and abnormalities, precocious and delayed puberty, ambiguous genitalia (including micropenis or undescended testis), adrenal gland disease or disorder, obesity, juvenile diabetes, and other endocrine system disorders.

■ **Pediatric Hearing Center,** which provides complete hearing evaluations and diagnostics, sales of analog and digital hearing aids (much less expensive in Thailand than in the US), and cochlear implants.

■ **Pediatric Cardiology Clinic,** which offers diagnosis and treatment for congenital heart diseases, abnormal heart rhythm, heart muscle inflammation, pericardial diseases, valve diseases, aortic aneurysm, rheumatic diseases, and Kawasaki disease.

■ **Pediatric Nephrology Clinic,** which provides early detection of kidney disease and abnormalities, as well as treatment for childhood nephrotic syndrome.

■ **Pediatric Orthopedic Clinic,** which focuses on early detection and treatment of bone and joint diseases in children; sports injuries; brachial plexus palsy and arm and shoulder paralysis due to difficult deliveries; pediatric spinal disorders (e.g. congenital scoliosis); congenital hip dislocation; and cerebral palsy.

■ **Infectious Disease Clinic,** which focuses on rare, complicated, or drug-resistant infectious diseases; also diagnosis and treatment for all infectious diseases, including bloodstream infections (septicemia), meningitis, pneumonia, and pediatric HIV.

Samitivej Srinakarin is one of the first Thai hospitals to have received Hospital Accreditation from the Institute of Hospital Quality Improvement Accreditation (2003).

Both hospitals have applied for JCI accreditation. They expect to become fully JCI-accredited by the end of 2007.

Bangkok Dental Group
Siam Square Street 2
Unit 236/3 to 236/4 (Level 2 to 4)
Pratuwan
Bangkok, THAILAND 10330
Tel: 011 66 2.658.4774
Fax: 011 66 2.248.6196
Email: contact@bangkokdental.com
Web: www.bangkokdental.com

Bangkok Dental Home
1701/12 Phaholyothin Road
Jatujuk
Bangkok, THAILAND 10900
Tel: 011 66 2.930.1144
Fax: 011 66 2.930.1814
Email: contact@bangkokdental.com
Web: www.bangkokdental.com

Bangkok International Dental Center
157 Ratchadapesik Rd.
Din Daeng District
Bangkok, THAILAND 10400
Tel: 011 66 2.658.4774
Fax: 011 66 2.248.6196
Email: contact@bangkokdentalcenter.com
Web: www.thailanddental.com
Web: www.bangkokdentalcenter.com

Bangkok is peppered with dental clinics. You can probably find three of them for every temple in the town! A few cater specifically to international tourists, and the Bangkok Dental Group is one of the most enduring and expansive of them. The group's three locations around Bangkok have treated more than 1,500 foreign visitors since opening their doors in 2003. Together, the centers employ 45 full-time dental specialists and surgeons, with a staff of nearly 90 practicing in 20 treatment rooms. Most dentists have been trained and certified overseas, and a large and comforting number received their degrees in the United States. All practitioners' credentials are posted on the BDG Web site, grouped by area of expertise.

Specialties include aesthetic and cosmetic dentistry; crowns (porcelain and zirconium); root canals; periodontics (gum disease); orthodontics (including braces, retainers and invisible braces); implantology; and prosthodontics (including full and partial dentures).

PHUKET

Once a brisk trading port, the island of Phuket (pronounced approximately poo GET) is now a leading tourist center nestled within a cluster of 40 islands in the Andaman Sea. Known as the "Pearl of the Andaman," Phuket's culturally mixed and multinational setting has fostered a major center of medical travel, with the emphasis on travel.

Thus, where a health traveler to Thailand might favor Bangkok for more invasive treatment such as orthopedic or cardiovascular surgery, those seeking less physically taxing procedures (such as cosmetic surgery, dental care, and opthalmological treatments) might well be tempted to head to the resort beaches of this beautiful island.

Although smaller, the hospitals are as good and the treatment specialties nearly as robust. If you're willing to stay a little farther from the epicenter of Thailand's healthcare, Phuket's beaches, five-star resorts, and relaxed surroundings are alluring.

Phuket's medical infrastructure has largely recovered from the devastating effects of the Indian Ocean tsunami of 2004.

Bangkok Hospital Phuket
2/1 Hongyok Utis Rd.
Muang District
Phuket, THAILAND 83000
Tel: 011 66 76. 254.425
Fax: 011 66 76. 254.597
Email: info@phukethospital.com
Web: www.phukethospital.com

A sister hospital to Bangkok International Hospital (see above), Bangkok Hospital Phuket belongs to the Bangkok Hospital Group, a network of 15 private hospitals that form the largest healthcare provider in Southeast Asia. Forty-two full time specialists, 50 consulting physicians, and 96 nurses make this 155-bed center Phuket's largest and most prestigious medical facility.

As with its sister hospital in Bangkok, PIH opened its own International Medical Center in 2005, catering exclusively to medical travelers. Specialties include closed- and open-heart surgery, keyhole surgery, and hip and knee replacement. Its **Aesthetic Centre** provides a full range of plastic surgeries (cosmetic and reconstructive). The hospital also boasts a full-service dental clinic.

As with all hospitals within the group, Bangkok Hospital Phuket is accredited through Thailand's Institute of Hospital Quality Improvement and Accreditation. The hospital, which was in the midst of the 2004 tsunami, is now housed in a new building. For further information, see www.phuketaesthetic.com.

Phuket International Hospital

44 Chalermprakiat Ror 9 Road

Phuket, THAILAND 83000

Tel: 011 66 76.249.400

Fax: 011 66 76.210.936

Email: info@phuket-international-hospital
.com

Web: www.phuket-international-hospital
.com

Founded in 1982, Phuket International Hospital was the first private hospital to open its doors on Phuket. The center's 100-bed complex is set on beautifully landscaped grounds, resembling a hotel more than a brass-and-glass modern medical institution. PIH centers specialize in allergy, cardiology, dentistry, ophthalmology, hair restoration, neurosurgery, orthopedics, and cosmetic surgery.

PIH aggressively promotes its medical checkup packages tailored for Western patients. A variety of tests and exam packages are offered at prices well below fees encountered in the US.

For those interested in alternative therapies, the **Traditional Health Center** at PIH offers an array of traditional Chinese herbal medicine, including acupuncture, massage, and cupping (the use of suction cups in place of needles at acupuncture points).

Inpatient room rates are attractive (deluxe private rooms for less than $60 per day), and the rooms include bathroom, bedside sofa, separate lounge area, and refrigerator.

■ HOTELS: DELUXE:

BANGKOK

The Emerald Hotel

99/1 Ratchadapisek Road

Din Daeng,

Bangkok, THAILAND 10400

Tel: 011 66 2.276.4567

Fax: 011 66 2.276.4555

E-mail: info@emeraldhotel.com

Web: www.emeraldhotel.com

Imperial Queen's Park Hotel

199 Sukhumvit Soi 22

Bangkok, THAILAND 10110

Tel: 011 66 2.261.9000

Fax: 011 66 2.261.9530

Email: reservation@imperialhotels.com

Web: www.imperialhotels.com

InterContinental Bangkok (near
Bumrumgrad)

973 Ploenchit Road

Patumwan

Bangkok, THAILAND 10330

Tel: 011 66 2.656.0444

Tel: 800 900.6429 (US toll-free)

Fax: 011 66 2.656.0555

Email: bangkok@interconti.com

Web: www.ichotelsgroup.com

Novotel Suvarnabhumi (at the aiport and
near Samitivej Srinakarin Hospital)

999 Suvarnabhumi Airport Hotel

Moo 1 Nongprue Bang Phli Samutprakarn

Bangkok, THAILAND 10540

Tel: 011 66 2.131.1111

Fax: 011 66 2.131.1188

E-mail: res@novotelsuvarnabhumi.com

Web: www.novotelsuvarnabhumi.com

PHUKET

Le Meridien Phuket Beach Resort
29 Soi Karon Nui, Tambon Karon
Amphur Muang
Phuket, THAILAND 83100
Tel: 011 66 76 370.100
Tel: 800 315.2621 (US toll-free)
Fax: 011 66 76 340.479
Email: reservations.phuketbeach@
    lemeridien.com
Web: www.starwoodhotels.com

■ HOTELS: MODERATE

BANGKOK

Amari Atrium Hotel (near Bangkok International Hospital)
1880 New Petchburi Road
Bangkok, THAILAND 10310
Tel: 011 66 2.718.2000
Fax: 011 66 2.718.2002
Email: reservations@atrium.amari.com
Web: www.amari.com

Siam Beverly Hotel
188 Ratchadapisek Rd.
Huaykwang
Bangkok, THAILAND 10320
Tel: 011 66 2.275.4397
Fax: 011 66 2.275.4049
Email: info@siambeverly.com
Web: www.siambeverly.com

Swissôtel Le Concorde (near Bangkok
Dental Center and Preecha Clinic)
204 Ratchadapisek Road
Huay Kwang
Bangkok, THAILAND 10320
Tel: 011 66 2.694.2222
Fax: 011 66 2.694.2223
Email: Bangkok-leconcorde@swissotel.com
Web: www.swissotel.com/index.shtml

PHUKET

Holiday Inn Resort Phuket
52 Thaweewong Road
Patong Beach
Phuket, THAILAND 83150
Tel: 011 66 76 340.608
Tel: 800 315.2621 (US toll-free)
Fax: 011 66 76 340.435
Email: reservations@holidayinn.com
Web: www.holidayinn.com

DESTINATION: UAE: DUBAI

■ AT A GLANCE

Dubai

Language:	Arabic, Persian, (English widely spoken)
Time Zone:	GMT +4
Country Dialing Code:	971
Electricity:	240V, Plug type G
Currency:	UAE Dirham
Visa Required?	Yes
Required Immunizations:	None
Treatment Specialties:	Cardiovascular, Dermatology, Oncology, Orthopedic
Leading Hospitals and Clinics:	American Hospital Dubai, Tawam Hospital
JCI Accredited Hospitals:	American Hospital Dubai, Tawam Hospital
Standards and Accreditation:	College of American Pathologists (CAP), German-Arab Medical Society, International Pan Arab Critical Care Medicine Society IPACCMS), Society of International Radiology.

■ TREATMENT BRIEF

Slightly smaller than the state of Maine, the United Arab Emirates (UAE) is a federation of seven "emirates" or states. Bordered by Oman and Saudi Arabia, the UAE was once considered a desert wasteland. Now, however, it is an international blend of Eastern values and Western technologies—without the Western crime rates. The kingdom of Dubai, the second-largest emirate, is situated on the Persian Gulf—one of the Middle East's most popular beach resorts.

While many Americans shy away from traveling to an Arab country for healthcare, much less a vacation, the UAE is surprisingly safe and welcoming. On the healthcare front, Dubai already claims two JCI-accredited hospitals (the American Hospital and Tawam) and a number of specialty clinics. That's apparently only the beginning. With the help of Harvard Medical International (HMI), a subsidiary of Harvard Medical School, the UAE is targeted to open Dubai Healthcare City before 2010. This 435-acre, 4.1-million-square-foot, state-of-the-art international mecca for healthcare will cater to medical travelers from all over the globe, and promises to keep treatment costs competitive throughout Asia.

For the past five years, Arab nationals have traveled to Thailand, Singapore, India, and other Asian hospitals for healthcare. After a purse tally, the Dubai government decided it was time to reclaim its regional base of patients. More than $100 million has been raised to realize this vision, which will include facilities for medical care and wellness, research, and education. The Harvard Medical School Dubai Center, a postgraduate and continuing education facility, will ensure that local medical school graduates, including females, are trained in specialty fields.

Planned operating facilities include American, Belgium, and German medical centers; a cosmetic surgery center; laser eye care; a German heart center; and a nutrition center. While Harvard will not provide direct care, the organization will be setting the standards and supervising quality control. More information on the Dubai Healthcare City can be found at www.dhcc.ae.

If you're interested in learning more about healthcare in the Middle East, you may want to familiarize yourself with ArabMedicare Medical Tourism Center of North Carolina. Although not a health travel agent, the clearinghouse has been promoting hospitals and clinics in the Middle East

since 1999. For more information, go to www.arabmedicare.com.

Note: Unfortunately, politics remains an issue in UAE, and travelers with an Israeli passport or with Israeli stamps in their passports will be denied entry into the country.

■ TYPICAL TREATMENTS AND COSTS

Healthcare in Dubai is more expensive than in some other countries, although still a bargain compared to US prices.

Doctor Visits:
Initial visits: $125
Follow-up visits: $90

Cardiovascular:
Angiogram: $4,000-$5,000
Coronary Artery Bypass Graft: $32,500-$35,500
Bypass + Valve Replacement (single): $44,000
Bypass + Valve Replacement (double): $50,000
Pacemaker (single-chambered): $4,300
Pacemaker (double-chambered): $10,350

Dental:
Crowns (porcelain): $500
Implants: $1,800
Inlays and Onlays: $300
Extractions (surgical): $175
Extractions (wisdom teeth): $225
Veneers (porcelain): $500

General Surgery:

Orthopedic:

Total Hip Replacement: $40,000

Total Knee Replacement: $35,000

Ankle Joint Replacement: $38,000

Total Shoulder Replacement: $42,000

■ HEALTH TRAVEL AGENTS

Planet Hospital

23679 Calabasas Rd #150

Calabasas, CA 91302

Tel: 800 243.0172 (US toll-free)

Tel: 818 591.6681

Fax: 818 665.3810

Email: info@planethospital.com

Web: www.planethospital.com

For more information on Planet Hospital, see Singapore.

■ HOSPITALS AND CLINICS

American Hospital Dubai

19th Street, Old Metha Area

P.O. Box 5566

Dubai, UNITED ARAB EMIRATES

Tel: 011 971 4.336.7777

Fax: 011 971 4.336.5176

Email: info@ahdubai.com

Web: www.ahdubai.com

Opened in 1996, the American Hospital Dubai (AHD) is an acute care hospital devoted to providing American standards of healthcare in the Middle East. The hospital was the first Middle East facility to be certified by JCI and CAP; in 2006 was awarded its third JCI accreditation.

American Hospital is located in the Bur Dubai district, which is central to the city center and the beaches. AHD currently has 143 beds and is expanding to 350 by 2009. The 60 full-time hospital physicians are US board-certified or are equivalent physician specialists. By the end of the expansion, the hospital will have 110 physicians.

American Hospital is a multicultural organization, with the staff representing 35 nationalities. English is the platform language spoken, although other common languages include Arabic, French, and German.

AHD offers general surgery, including laparoscopic and neuralgic, in addition to gastrointestinal endoscopies.

Centers of Excellence include the following:

- ■ **Cancer Care Unit** offers quiet, relaxing suites and state-of-the-art treatment.

- ■ **Diabetes Center** treats all diabetic needs including diagnosis, medical care and supervision, information and education, and family support. The dialysis unit has private rooms, and separate clinics treat all ages: children, adolescents, adults, and the elderly.

- ■ **Endocrinology and Digestive Disease Center** offers diagnosis and management of digestive and liver diseases. Services include upper and lower gastrointestinal (GI) endoscopy and enteroscopy (lower intestine).

- ■ **Heart Center** comprises two areas of treatment: interventional cardiology and surgery. The Heart Center frequently performs angiograms and angioplasties. The center specializes in minimally invasive cardiac surgery and beating-heart bypass surgery, both relatively new techniques in the cardiology field. In addition, the center is committed to introducing advanced techniques, such as endoscopic and robotic procedures, as they become available.

- **Total Joint Replacement Center** is the first of its kind in the Middle East. The center's director has performed more than 2,000 joint replacements, and more than 600 joint replacements have been performed at AHD. Although knee joint replacement is a specialty, the center offers an extensive range of full or partial artificial joints using minimally invasive surgical intervention techniques.

- AHD's **International Patient Center** offers the usual amenities, including assistance with appointments and consultation, interpreters for non-Arabic – speaking patients, Internet connections in rooms, fax, photocopy and courier, and laundry service. Arrangements can be made for ambulance pickup (with a mobile intensive care unit and trained paramedics) at the airport, which is less than a 15-minute ride away from AHD. Once a health traveler checks in, an international patient coordinator assists in making appointments and coordinating referrals to the outpatient clinic, laboratory and pathology, medical imaging, or inpatient surgical procedures.

Tawam Hospital
P.O. Box 15258
Al Ain, UNITED ARAB EMIRATES
Tel: 011 971 3.767.7444
Fax: 011 971 3.767.7634
Email: info@tawam-hosp.gov.ae
Web: www.tawam-hosp.gov.ae

Tawam Hospital is located 100 miles from the cities of Abu Dhabi and Dubai. The 477-bed center meets the standards of European and North American hospitals, and nursing care meets or exceeds international standards. The hospital's nursing team comprises a culturally diverse staff of 900 representing 33 different nationalities.

Tawam is a full-service hospital with several specialties (excluding cardiovascular surgery).

- **Department of Oncology** is the oncology referral center for the UAE and other Gulf States. Established in 2004, the 46-bed department includes hematology, radiology, and palliative care. Nearly half of the rooms are high efficiency particulate air (HEPA) filtered. Diagnostic workup is provided for both benign and malignant disorders, including all types of solid tumors and hematological disorders. The medical staff comprises more than a dozen oncology specialists.

- **Dental Centre** is a freestanding dental hospital 15 minutes away from the main hospital. The center is distinguished as one of the first dental facilities in the Gulf region to provide a complete implant dentistry service, specializing in one- and two-stage dental implant replacements. Two clinics treat oral and facial surgery. The center employs a total of 120 people including 16 general dentists and 14 consultants or specialists, representing every clinical specialty. The majority of dentists have Western qualifications or experience. Some have held appointments at American, Canadian, or European universities.

■ **Department of Surgery** is the latest medical department at Tawam. It covers all sub-specialties except for cardiovascular surgery. The department has six fully equipped operating rooms, and more than 4,000 inpatient and outpatient surgeries are performed each year. Most common surgical procedures include orthoscopic surgery for knee and hip replacements; ear, nose, and throat (ENT) surgery using endoscopes; prostatic surgeries; neurosurgery; and reconstructive surgeries, especially to treat burn cases.

■ **Clinical Nutrition Department** has a unique service to manage inherited metabolic diseases such as disorders of amino acid metabolism and fatty acid oxidation.

Skin Laser Dubai
Dr. Mahaveer Mehta Medical Clinic
Al Ghurair City, 641-B, Office Tower 4
P.O. Box 14477
Dubai, UNITED ARAB EMIRATES
Tel: 011 971 4.228.2444
Fax: 011 971 4.767.77634
Email: drmmehta@emirates.net.ae
Web: www.skinlaserdubai.com

Founded in 1990, the Mehta Medical Clinic employs seven full-time staff members who speak English, Arabic, and Hindi-Urdu. Each year, approximately 5,000 patients from more than 100 countries, including the United States and Europe, visit the clinic.

The Mehta clinic was one of the first centers in the Middle East and Asia to offer laser technology for skin treatments. The center now treats cellulite, psoriasis, vitiligo, pigmented lesions (including tattoo removals), unwanted hair, and spider veins with various lasers. In addition, the center offers skin filler injections including Botox, Restylane, and Perlane. Dr. Mehta has performed more than 5,000 laser hair reductions and 5,000 laser skin surgeries

■ **RECOVERY ACCOMMODATIONS**

Although recovery accommodations are not available in Dubai, the area has a number of deluxe and moderately priced hotels.

■ **HOTELS: DELUXE**

The deluxe hotels in Dubai can be expensive, so make sure to include lodging in your budget plan. Note that the Movenpick Hotel is directly across the street from the American Hospital Dubai.

JW Marriott Hotel Dubai
Abu Baker Al Siddique Road
Dubai, UNITED ARAB EMIRATES 16590
Tel: 1 800 228.9290 (US toll-free)
Tel: 011 971 4.262.4444
Fax: 011 971 4.262.6264
Email: marriott@emirates.net.ae
Web: www.marriott.com

Movenpick Hotel
19th Street, Old Metha Area
PO Box 32733
Dubai, UNITED ARAB EMIRATES
Tel: 011 971 4.336.6000
Fax: 011 971 4.336.6626
Email: hotel.burdubai@moevenpick-hotels
.com
Web: www.moevenpick-hotels.com/
hotels/dubai

Renaissance Dubai Hotel
Salah Al Din Road, Deira
PO Box 8668
Dubai, UNITED ARAB EMIRATES
Tel: 1 800 HOTELS.1 (US toll-free)
Tel: 011 971 4.262.5555
Fax: 011 971 4.269.7358
Email: rendubai@emirates.net.ae
Web: www.renaissancehotels.com

Sheraton Dubai Creek Hotel & Towers
Baniyas Street/Creek Road
PO Box 4250
Dubai, UNITED ARAB EMIRATES
Tel: 1 800 325.3535 (US toll-free)
Tel: 011 971 4.228.1111
Fax: 011 971 4.221.3468
Email: dubai.creek@sheraton.com
Web: www.starwoodhotels.com/sheraton

■ HOTELS: MODERATE

Al Khalidia Hotel Apartments
Al Maktoum Street
PO Box 63890
Dubai, UNITED ARAB EMIRATES
Tel: 011 971 4.228.2280
Fax: 011 971 4.221.1222
Email: khappt@emirates.net.ae
Web: www.khalidiahotelapartments.ae

Avari Hotel
Deira
PO Box 50400
Dubai, UNITED ARAB EMIRATES
Tel: 011 971 4.295.6666
Fax: 011 971 4.295.9459
Email: info@avari-dubai.co.ae
Web: www.avari.com/avaridubai.htm

Ramada Hotel Dubai
Al Mankhool Street, Bur Dubai
PO Box 7979
Dubai, UNITED ARAB EMIRATES
Tel: 011 971 4.351.9999
Fax: 011 971 4.352.1033
Email: rhdxb@emirates.net.ae
Web: www.ramadadubai.com

PART THREE

Resources
and References

ADDITIONAL RESOURCES

World, Country and City Information

The World Factbook Cataloged by country, *The* World *Factbook* — compiled by the Central Intelligence Agency — is an excellent source of general, up-to-date information about the geography, economy, and history of countries around the world. Go to www.cia.gov. In the left column, find "Library and Reference," then click on "The World Factbook." Your tax dollars at work

Lonely Planet This feisty travel book publisher has compiled useful online snippets (more as teases to get you to buy their books), along with useful links. Once you've narrowed your destination preference(s), go to www.lonelyplanet .com and search by country for background, fast facts, transport, events, and more.

World Travel Guide The Web site www. worldtravelguide.net is sponsored by the publishers of the *Columbus World Travel Guide*. This heavily sponsored site offers good information on countries and major metropolitan areas throughout the world. Once you've settled on a destination, go to the Web site's "Choose Guide" search to find information on airports, tours, attractions, cruises, and more. Not all cities featured in this book are currently listed.

World Atlas

Google Earth If you've not downloaded Google Earth, go there and do so. It's truly one of the wonders of the online world. After you download it, you can zoom to your home's rooftop or "fly" to any continent, country, or city on the planet just by typing in the appropriate keywords. Legends include city names, roads, terrain, populated places, borders, 3-D buildings, and more. Go to http:// earth.google.com/ and follow the download instructions.

Encarta Microsoft's free Encarta Atlas is easy to use, and it allows you to quickly click your way around the planet, then obtain information on your country of interest. Go to www.encarta.com and click on the "World Atlas" tab.

Passports and Visas

Travisa Dozens of online visa agencies offer similar services. We've found Travisa to be reliable and accessible by telephone. The agency offers good customer service and follow-up. Travisa's Web site, www .travisa.com, also carries information links to immunization requirements, travel warnings, current weather, and more.

Currency Converter

xe.com To learn quickly how much your dollar is worth in a given country, go to the www.xe.com homepage and click on "Quick Currency Converter."

International Hospital Accreditation

Joint Commission International Mentioned frequently throughout this book, the Joint Commission International (JCI) remains the only game in town for international hospital accreditation. For a current list of accredited hospitals by country, go to http://www.joint

commissioninternational.com/10241.
Then search by region.

Medical Dictionary

Merriam-Webster's Medical Dictionary
If a multisyllabic medical term stumps
you, don't run out and purchase an
unabridged brick of a medical dictionary.
Several free online medical glossaries
provide more than you probably want to
know on most health topics. *Merriam-
Webster's Medical Dictionary* is provided
on a number of sites, including MedlinePlus (http://medlineplus.gov) and
InteliHealth (www.intelihealth.com). The
simplest access is through http://
dictionary.reference.com. Just type in
a medical word or phrase and voila! For
a richer exploration of a given medical
term, sources such as MedicineNet
(www.medicinenet.com) offer articles,
services, and a thicket of sponsored links.

Medical Information

MedlinePlus is another great example of
your tax dollars at work. This federally
sponsored medical site brings together a
wealth of information from sources such
as the National Library of Medicine (the
world's largest medical library), the National Institutes of Health, *Merriam-
Webster's Medical Dictionary*, and the
United States Pharmacopeia. Go to www
.medlineplus.gov and, on the left column,
click the various choices. The online tour
www.nlm.nih.gov/medlineplus/tour/
medlineplustour.html helps you navigate
this massive site.

Medical Travel Resources

Medical Nomad Newly introduced to
the Web, www.medicalnomad.com was
established in 2004 by a group of medical professionals, technology geeks, and
consultants who have brought together an
impressive body of information, including specific data on treatments, clinics,
physicians, accreditation, and other topics
of interest to the health traveler. Medical Nomad's extensive database allows
readers to search by procedure, provider,
and destination, with clinic and country
summaries, as well as lay summaries of
common treatments.

Medical Tourism Insight is a monthly,
online newsletter written for the medical
travel industry as well as employers, benefits managers, government officials, and
prospective patients. Coverage includes
objective and timely information on overseas medical care and related issues, such
as health insurance and employee health
benefits. The Web site is www
.medicaltourisminsight.com.

Beauty from Afar If you're seeking more
specialized information on cosmetic or
aesthetic surgery or dental care, author
and medical traveler Jeff Schult has
gathered information on the main destinations, leading clinics and facilities,
and third-party agents. Published in July
2006, this 224-page paperback is written
in an anecdotal style, providing numerous first-hand accounts that give prospective patients a thorough perspective on
the health travel experience.

Web Search Resources

The Google Guide While most of us
don't care to become wild-eyed experts

on the nuances of search engines, a little additional knowledge can greatly enhance your success in efficiently narrowing your health travel choices. Consultant and Internet search guru Nancy Blachman (co-author of the book *How to do Everything with Google*) has posted a useful online tutorial entitled "The Google Guide." Go to www.googleguide.com, click on "Novice," and you'll find a wealth of information on conducting Internet searches that will greatly improve your online health travel quests. Most of this information applies to other search engines as well, including Yahoo, MSN, and AOL.

Forums and Feedback

Health Traveler Learn what other health travelers are saying and recommending, then share your experiences and suggestions with others at www.patientsbeyond borders.com. The author and editors of *Patients Beyond Borders* invite you to join a community of patients who can help broaden one another's horizons and get up-to-the minute news about a wide variety of health travel topics. You can sign in, go to the "Revisions and Additions" page, and post messages (anonymously if you prefer; your privacy is protected).

MEDICAL GLOSSARY

General Terms

Many medical terms are used in this book, far more than we can define in these pages. The following is a list of the most commonly used terms, arranged by areas of study. For further information, consult a medical dictionary or your physician.

Addiction. Occurs when a person has no control over the use of a substance such as drugs or alcohol. Also includes addictions to food, gambling, and sex. Physical addiction is when a person's body becomes dependent on a particular substance. Psychological addiction occurs when a person's will is overcome by a desire or craving.

Anesthesia. Loss of physical sensation produced by sedation. Anesthesia may be given as (1) general, which affects the entire body and is accompanied by loss of consciousness; (2) regional, affecting a specific region of the body; or (3) local, which affects a limited region of the body (usually superficial).

Computed Tomography (CT). Sometimes known as CAT scan, or computer assisted tomography. A noninvasive diagnostic tool that uses x-rays to provide cross-sectional images of the body. Used to detect cancer, study heart function, and provide images of body organs. May be used in conjunction with MRI or PET scans.

Magnetic Resonance Imaging (MRI). A noninvasive diagnostic tool that produces clear images of the human body without the use of x-rays. MRI, which uses a large magnet, radio waves, and a computer, is used to diagnose spine and joint problems, heart disease, and cancer.

Otolaryngology. A branch of medicine that studies and treats ear, nose, and throat disorders.

Positron Emission Tomography (PET). Known as PET imaging or PET scan. A noninvasive diagnostic tool that takes images of the human body by detecting positrons or tiny particles from radioactive material. Used to detect cancer and study heart function, May also help diagnose Alzheimer's. May be used in conjunction with the CT scan.

Wellness. An area of preventative medicine that promotes health and well-being through various means such as diet, exercise, yoga, Tai Chi, and social connections.

Cardiovascular

Angiogram (angiography). An x-ray technique to measure blood flow and blood pressure in the coronary arteries. Dye is injected into the arteries during a cardiac catheterization.

Angioplasty. Procedure performed to help open narrowing(s) in the coronary arteries, which supply the heart with blood. This procedure requires a cardiac catheterization, during which a small balloon is passed into the artery and blown up to expand the narrowing.

Annuloplasty. A variety of techniques used to repair a valve or support a valve after repair.

Aorta. The largest artery in the body and the initial vessel to supply blood to the abdominal cavity.

Aortic Aneurysm. An enlargement or dilation of the aorta, the largest artery of the body, which exits the heart.

Aortic Valve. One of four valves in the heart. The aortic valve controls the outflow of blood from the left ventricle to the aorta.

Cardiac Catheterization. A procedure that uses a fine tube or catheter, which is threaded from the groin into the heart. Used with angiography, it is now a primary tool for visualizing the heart and blood vessels and then diagnosing or treating heart disease.

Cardiovascular. Pertaining to the heart and blood vessels that compose the circulatory system.

Coronary Artery Bypass Graft (CABG) (open-heart surgery). Surgical procedure to create bypasses around obstructions in the coronary arteries, most often using arteries or veins from other parts of the body.

Electrophysiological Study (EPS). A test that uses cardiac catheterization to study abnormal heartbeats.

Minimally Invasive Heart Surgery. Describes a variety of approaches to reduce the trauma of surgery and to speed recovery. These approaches include "keyhole" surgery (small incisions rather than a large incision down the chest) and beating-heart surgery, which does not use a heart-lung bypass machine.

Mitral Valve. One of four heart valves. The mitral valve controls blood flow between the chambers of the left side of the heart, the atrium (top) and ventricle (bottom).

Pacemaker. Small battery-powered device implanted permanently into the body to monitor electrical impulses and deliver electrical stimuli to make the heart beat in a normal rhythm. Can have one or two chambers.

Radionuclide Imaging. A diagnostic study that uses a harmless radioactive substance injected in the bloodstream to take pictures and show information about blood flow through the coronary arteries.

Stent. A coiled wire, sometimes medicated, that may be inserted into a narrowed coronary artery after angioplasty. The stent is used to keep the vessel open.

Valve Replacement. Heart valves, particularly the aortic or mitral valve, may need to be repaired or replaced if they are damaged or malfunctioning.

Cosmetic (Plastic Surgery)

Botox. A non-surgical, physician-administered treatment to temporarily reduce moderate to severe wrinkles, especially frown lines between the brows of the face.

Breast Augmentation (augmentation mammoplasty). Surgical procedure to enhance the size of the breasts by using inflatable implants, usually filled with saline or silicone.

Breast Lift (mastopexy). Surgical procedure to raise and reshape sagging breasts by removing excess skin and repositioning remaining tissue and nipples.

Chemical Peel (phenol and trichloroacetic acid [TCA]). Procedure to remove wrinkles, blemishes, or unevenly pigmented or sun-damaged facial skin. A chemical solution is used to peel away the skin's top layers.

Dermabrasion. Mechanical scraping of the top layers of the skin using a high-speed rotary wheel. Softens surface irregularities caused by acne, scars, or wrinkles (especially around the mouth).

Ear Reconstruction (otoplasty). Surgical procedure to set prominent ears back closer to the head or to reduce the size of large ears.

Eyelid Surgery (blepharoplasty). Surgical procedure to correct drooping upper eyelids and puffy bags below the eyes by removing excess fat, skin, and muscle.

Facelift (rhytidectomy). Surgical procedure to improve sagging facial skin, jowls, and loose neck skin by removing excess fat, tightening muscles, and redraping skin.

Forehead Lift (brow lift). Surgical procedure to minimize forehead creases, drooping eyebrows, hooding over eyes, furrowed forehead, and frown lines by removing excess tissue, altering muscles, and tightening forehead skin.

Hair Restoration. Surgical procedure to fill in balding areas with a patient's own hair. Various techniques are used including punch grafts or plugs, strip grafts, and scalp reduction.

Implants (breast, facial). Small sacks, usually filled with saline or silicone, that are inserted under the skin to reshape the breast, chin, cheekbones, or jaw line.

Laser Resurfacing. Lasers are used to treat a variety of skin conditions including birthmarks, growths, uneven pigmentation, damaged skin, fine wrinkles, and other cosmetic complaints. A variety of lasers work by producing an intense beam of bright light that can cut, seal, or vaporize skin tissue and blood vessels and remove hair.

Liposuction (suction-assisted lipectomy). Procedure to improve body shape by removing exercise-resistant fat deposits with a tube and vacuum device.

Nose Reconstruction (rhinoplasty). Surgical procedure to reshape nose by reducing or increasing the size, removing a hump, changing the shape of tip or bridge, narrowing the span of nostrils, or changing the angle between nose and upper lip.

Plastic Surgery. Plastic surgery encompasses two fields: (1) reconstructive surgery, which is the reconstruction of facial and body parts disfigured by birth disorders, trauma, burns, or disease, and (2) cosmetic or aesthetic surgery, which is the enhancement of appearance by reshaping normal structures.

Thermage Lifting. Known as a nonsurgical facelift, the procedure is performed using an advanced radio frequency energy called ThermaCool TC to tighten and lift the skin.

Tummy Tuck (abdominoplasty). Major surgical procedure to remove abdominal fat and extra skin present in obesity or after pregnancies. A mini-tummy tuck may be performed in smaller affected areas.

Dental Care

Crown. A cap, often made of porcelain, used to restore a tooth to its original shape.

Extraction. The process of removing a tooth or tooth parts.

General Dentist. Primary care provider for patients of all ages. Provides diagnosis, treatment, and management of services to meet oral health needs.

Implant. Permanent tooth replacement often made of porcelain, that looks and functions like a natural tooth. The replacement is cemented onto a metal post that is implanted into the jawbone.

Inlay and Onlay. Rather than using a filling or a crown, the dentist may choose an inlay or onlay made of porcelain, gold, composite, or a ceramic resin. An inlay is similar to a filling because it lies inside the cusp tips of the tooth. An onlay is a more extensive reconstruction that may cover one or more cusps of the tooth. Inlays and onlays are custom-made to fit the prepared cavity.

Porcelain. Material that is tooth-colored and used for fillings or veneer. It is now a preferred material because of its strength and color.

Restorative Dentistry. Process of restoring missing, damaged, or diseased teeth. Performed by a general dentist.

Root Canal (endodontic therapy). Removal of a diseased portion of the pulp cavity inside the root of a tooth. The pulp contains nerves, blood vessels, and tissue.

Surgical Extraction. A more involved procedure to remove an imbedded tooth or tooth parts.

Temporomandibular Joint (TMJ) Disorder. Problems relating to the joint between the base of the skull and the lower jaw. Causes locking of the jaw, frequent headaches and muscle aches, and painful clicking of the jaw.

Veneer. A layer of tooth-colored material made from composite, porcelain, ceramic, or acrylic resin. It is attached to the surface of the tooth, often by dental cement or resin.

Wisdom Teeth. The last or third set of molars, which usually appear between the ages of 17 and 24. They may require extraction if they are adversely affecting other teeth.

Fertility/Reproductive Health

Assisted Hatching (AH). Procedure in which artificial weakness is created in the shell surrounding the embryo. Performed in embryos selected for transfer.

Assisted Reproductive Technology (ART). General term for treatments used to assist conception and ensure healthy pregnancy.

Blastocyst Culture. Development of an embryo that was fertilized five to seven days prior. Considered a best-quality embryo for transfer.

Gamete Donation. Egg or sperm donation to be used for reproduction.

Hormonal Therapy. Using the results of hormone blood tests, doctors prescribe a treatment regime to ensure that the woman has correct hormones to induce fertilization or to prepare the lining of the uterus to receive an embryo.

Intracytoplasmic Sperm Injection (ICSI). A form of in vitro fertilization. Egg is fertilized outside the body by injecting the sperm directly into it.

Intrauterine Insemination (IUI). Introduction of prepared sperm (either male partner's or donor's) into the uterus to improve chances of pregnancy. Success rate is 10–15 percent per cycle.

In Vitro Fertilization (IVF). Popularly known as the "test-tube baby" technique. Eggs are fertilized outside the body, then embryos are introduced into the uterus.

Gender Reassignment

Orchiectomy. Also known as gonadectomy; removal of testicles to eliminate the sources of androgen (male hormone) production.

Vaginoplasty. Medical procedure to restructure or create a vagina, often using an autologous (donor and recipient same person) graft such as the colon (colon cut vaginoplasty), scrotum (scrotal skin graft), or penis (penile skin inversion technique).

General Surgery

Gall Bladder Removal (cholecystecomy). The gall bladder, which stores bile, sometimes becomes obstructed or damaged and needs to be removed.

Transurethral resection of the prostate (TURP). The prostate, a small gland found in males below the bladder, makes some of the semen used to carry sperm. It may become enlarged in older men, preventing the bladder from emptying completely. A partial or total resection (TURP) allows the bladder to function fully.

Ophthalmology (Eye)

Cataracts. Cloudiness of the lens in the eye, which affects vision. Cataracts, which often occur in older people, can be corrected with surgery to replace the damaged lens with an artificial plastic lens, known as an intraocular lens (IOL).

LASIK (laser assisted *in situ* keratomileusis). A laser procedure to reduce dependency on eyeglasses or contact lenses by permanently changing the shape of the cornea, the clear covering of the front of the eye.

Glaucoma. A group of eye diseases that occur gradually and damage the optic nerve, leading to vision loss. Treatment (eye drops, medications, laser treatment, and surgery) is aimed at reducing intraocular pressure by improving aqueous (fluids inside eye) outflow, or reducing aqueous production, or both.

Orthopedics (Bones and Muscles)

Birmingham Hip Resurfacing. Surgical procedure that replaces worn ball-and-socket surfaces in the hip joint with smooth, durable high carbide cobalt chrome. Considered a bone-conserving alternative to total hip replacement surgery, especially in younger people. Approved by the US Food and Drug Administration in May 2006.

Joint Replacement Surgery. Surgically removing all or parts of a damaged joint and replacing it with a new joint, called a prosthesis. Shoulder, hip, knee, and ankle are the most commonly replaced joints.

Prosthesis. An artificial limb or organ made of plastic, metal, or some other material.

Weight Loss

Bariatric Surgery. General term for surgical weight-loss procedures.

Gastric Bypass. A direct surgical connection that hooks part of the intestine to the stomach pouch, thereby bypassing part of the small intestine and creating malabsorption.

LAP-BAND System. An adjustable gastric silicone band inserted laproscopically around the upper part of the stomach, thereby reducing the food acceptance area of the stomach.

Lymphatic Drainage. A delicate massage said to stimulate the lymphatic circulation to help eliminate waste and boost the immune system. Often given in conjunction with weight-loss surgery.

Vertical Banded Gastroplasty (VBG). Surgically reducing the size of the stomach pouch with bands and staples to combat obesity.

GENERAL INDEX

The *Patients Beyond Borders* General Index includes general references and terms found in Chapters One through Eight. For specific treatment information, please see the Treatment Index on page 322.

TREATMENT INDEX

The *Patients Beyond Borders* Treatment Index includes information on the most common procedures found the Medical Glossary on page 312. For general information on health travel planning, see the General Index on page 317.

ABOUT THE AUTHOR

Josef Woodman has spent more than three years researching contemporary medical tourism, interviewing patients, practitioners, administrators, government officials and specialists in the field, while conducting an extensive analysis of safety records, accreditations, success rates and consumer trends. With significant resources and contacts from his pioneering background in health technology on the Web, Woodman has compiled a wealth of information for the American public about important healthcare choices.

ISBN-13: 978-0-9791079-0-0
ISBN-10: 0-9791079-0-3